HELPING CHILDREN OVERCOME LEARNING DIFFICULTIES

Helping Children Overcome Learning Difficulties

THIRD EDITION

Jerome Rosner

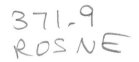

371.9
ROSNE

First published in the United States of America in
1993 by Walker Publishing Company, Inc.

Library of Congress Cataloging-in-Publication Data
Rosner, Jerome.
    Helping children overcome learning difficulties / Jerome Rosner.—3rd ed.
        p.   cm.
    Includes bibliographical references and index.
    ISBN 1-4392-3180-X
    1. Learning disabled children—Education.   I. Title.
LC4704.R67   1993
371.9—dc20   92-38190
                                        CIP

Printed in the United States of America

20 19 18 17

CONTENTS

ACKNOWLEDGMENTS

IT IS IMPOSSIBLE to recognize all those who helped me write this book. There are simply too many names to list: teachers, parents, children, and colleagues who have influenced my thinking. Therefore, I will limit my thanks to those few I know best and who influenced me the most profoundly: my children, Carolyn (and her son, Zef), Joyce, Matthew, and Michael, and my wife and colleague, Joy.

PREFACE

DURING THE MID-1970s, I wrote a book about how to help children with enigmatic learning problems. It told what I had learned about such children up to that point in my life—as a practicing optometrist since 1944, as a researcher in various public school systems and the University of Pittsburgh's Learning Research and Development Center since 1965, as a cofounder of a private school for children with dyslexia (Pace School) in 1968, and as a developer of tests and remedial programs since 1973. The book was (and, in fact, the second edition continues to be) well received and judged to be useful by many teachers and parents (I get letters from readers once in a while; I like that).

In the mid-1970s I decided to become an educator in my own profession: optometry. I left Pittsburgh and joined the faculty at the University of Houston, specializing in teaching pediatric optometry courses and supervising students in the children's unit of the clinic.

At first, I did very little research in the dyslexia–learning disability field, but eventually I was drawn to the topic once again because there was a void. Even though, by that time, plenty of people were able to identify these children, and there were lots of compensatory instructional programs being published, and there were a number of perceptual development treatment centers being opened, there remained a persistent problem: no one was weaving these three areas into something cohesive that parents and teachers could use.

Each group "did their thing" and left it at that. The school diagnosticians told teachers about children's strengths and weaknesses but never really got around to telling them enough about how to help such children. The schoolteachers—depending on their knowledge, skills, motivation, and administrative support—tried different instructional approaches that sometimes seemed to reflect what the diagnosticians reported and sometimes did not. And the perceptual skills developmental experts, working in the private sector, saw only a small fraction of these children and—depending on their respective skills, knowledge, motivation, and integrity—engaged the youngsters in activities that ranged in relative value from worthless to helpful.

Some children, but by no means all, showed improvement in their classrooms, ostensibly because of their teachers' efforts; a few even showed improvement in the classroom perhaps because of what they had done in their perceptual skills treatment programs. But there was no way of making generalizations, of extrapolating basic principles that could be applied generally. These situations were too loaded with confounding factors that ruled out valid assessment.

So, here we are in the 1990s and there still are no integrative approaches, no sequence of decision-making steps that would help the average teacher or parent map out an organized treatment plan for these children, a plan that provided a road map along which progress could be monitored and, in turn, guidance about how to teach the child.

That is why I wrote the third edition of this book—that, and the fact that during the 1980s my wife and colleague, Joy, not only bore our two sons (at my age—imagine!) but also took the time to work with me on a sequence of research projects that enabled us to discover (and report in our professional journals) close links between farsightedness and delayed visual perceptual skills development, and more recently (with the support of a research grant from the Bausch & Lomb Company) close links between farsightedness and school achievement.

At first, I was not sure whether this book would be just an updated printing or whether I should make it a major revision, a new edition. I ultimately decided upon the latter. True, this edition contains information first presented in the original publication. If something in that first edition was really worthwhile and needed repeating here, I did so. (For example, I included in this volume the information about how and why to administer the Test of Visual Analysis Skills [TVAS] and the Test of Auditory Analysis Skills [TAAS]. Both tests remain unchanged. They have been adopted by enough researchers and clinicians to justify their continued use in their original form.) However, much of the information in the third edition is new, and all of it is organized into a usable action plan—a road map that does what I think needs to be done.

The action plan offers a way of monitoring a child's location in his educational journey; it identifies how to determine if he can do what he should be able to do, given his age and grade level, and thereby gives the child's parents and teachers information about what to do next.

Over the almost fifty years that I have been working with children, I have come to believe, on the basis of real evidence—case records and research data—that a learning disability (or dyslexia or attention deficit disorder or whatever other label is attached to it) need not be a permanent condition. True, the problem is real, it is insidious, *but it can be overcome,* and, even more important, it can be prevented if detected early enough in the child's school (or, more accurately, preschool) life.

INTRODUCTION

THIS BOOK IS ABOUT the many children—20 percent by some estimates—who have school learning problems for which there is no apparent explanation; children whose learning difficulties cannot be attributed to a low IQ, or to a physical, emotional, or neuromotor problem; children who try hard to meet school expectations, at least during the early grades, but do not succeed.

They are often described in medical-sounding terms as having a *learning disability* (LD), an *attention deficit disorder* (ADD), *attention deficit and hyperactive disorder* (ADHD), or *dyslexia,* or something else along that line. The implication: despite at least average intelligence (as documented by their IQ scores), their brains do not function normally (sometimes the eyes are blamed; sometime the ears). This prevents them from being able to learn as much and as fast as they should. And because no one knows how to cure them, it is assumed that although they may be identified and placed in special school programs, these youngsters really do have abnormal brains and are destined to live with the problem for the rest of their lives.

The effects of all this are confusion, frustration, and despair. Parents are upset because they want to help but do not know how. Teachers are upset because they are expected to be able to help but are uncertain about how; in fact, given the unusual nature of the problem, they are not sure that anything they do can help. And the children are upset because they are not able to satisfy their parents' and teachers' expectations; they think of themselves as failures.

GOALS OF THIS BOOK

One of the two main goals of this book is to dispel the notion that these children have a permanent condition that will forever prevent them from achieving their learning potential and are therefore destined to a lifetime of the emotional pain that accompanies failure. This is not so.

True, they do have a fundamental problem, *but it is not in their general learning abilities; it is specific to mastering the coding and decoding systems of the classroom during the years when this is supposed to happen:* to acquiring basic fluency in reading, writing, spelling, and arithmetic while in the primary grades. It is very obvious that their subsequent chronic school learning difficulties stem from this poor beginning.

Can they learn these coding and decoding systems during those first few school years? Yes. There are no quick fixes, no magic cures, but neither is there any doubt that the vast majority of these children can make satisfactory progress in school if they are identified during the early years and treated and taught properly. We must think of them not as having long-term learning problems but rather as having *specific instructional needs* that, once defined and met, will not impede their ability to make satisfactory progress in school.

What about those children who do not master these coding and decoding systems during the primary grades? Are their fates sealed? No. They too can get back on track, but it will be more difficult; they will have gotten behind in school; it will take time and effort; they and those who teach them will have to work harder. *But it can be done. A learning disability need not be forever!*

This brings us to the second goal of this book: to shift at least some of the responsibility for succeeding in school from the children to ourselves—their parents, their teachers, and their doctors. What should we do? We should make sure that all children are "ready" when they enter school; specifically, that they have *developed* the basic analytic aptitudes and *learned* the basic information assumed (and required) by standard school instructional programs, and, with those children who do enter school "unready," to teach them in a way that enables them to progress despite their deficiencies.

In the pages that follow, I will explain why and how to identify a child's analytic aptitude and knowledge deficits, how to determine his* unique instructional needs (the earlier the better), and how to treat and teach him effectively on the basis of those needs.

To achieve these two major goals, I established the following set of subordinate objectives:

• Describe *learning disability, dyslexia, attention deficit disorder,* and the other conditions like these in behavioral rather than medical terms; state what children† who bear these labels are not able to do that

---

*I know that many readers are justifiably sensitive to gender designations. However, with apologies and for the sake of simplicity, I will consistently refer to the child as *he* and to the teacher as *she.*

†I recognize that these labels are also applied to adults, but, except for those adults whose learning problems stem from brain injuries or other circumstances suffered after having gotten off to a good start in school, all of them first manifested their difficulties

gets in the way of their classroom performance, and explain why these behaviors are so influential.

• Define how children with learning disabilities are identified; explain the tests that are used and identify who should do the testing.

• Identify and describe the tests that should be administered once a child has been identified as a candidate for the learning disability designation, and explain what these follow-up tests test, who should administer them, and why that information is important.

• Explain how to interpret these follow-up test results in terms of what they reveal about the child in his present state and about how to help him.

• Describe, in a practical, easy-to-follow way, how to institute that help by exercising one (or two, or all three) of three options.

1. *Retain.* Keep the child at his present academic level for a while longer. Give him time to develop better analytic aptitudes and learn more information (and better language skills) before moving on to a more demanding instructional level.

2. *Remediate.* Change the child; help him overcome the basic aptitude and knowledge deficits that are impeding his progress in the standard school program.

3. *Accommodate.* Modify the instructional conditions (make them nonstandard) in ways that enable the child to progress satisfactorily despite his deficits.

• Emphasize the importance of early (preschool) assessment and identification, and describe the signs and symptoms that signal "trouble ahead" for the preschool child.

• Communicate clearly and concisely, avoiding technical jargon and complicated explanations. In other words, make the information immediately useful to teachers, to health care professionals—school nurses, physicians, optometrists, psychologists, speech/language specialists, occupational and physical therapists—and, most of all, to those persons who have the greatest long-term influence on the lives of these youngsters—their parents.

FORMAT

The following *Action Plan* serves two purposes: it maps out the steps to take in order to help the child who has a learning disability (or dyslexia or ADD) and it provides the structure upon which the contents of this book is organized. Each of the steps in the Action Plan is keyed to the

---

during their early school years. Just about every adult with an inexplicable learning problem was once a child with an inexplicable learning problem. Hence the focus on children.

chapter where you will find the information you need to understand and carry out the recommended actions.

ACTION PLAN

• Child is having unexpected difficulty in school. (He seems bright enough, but his school work is not satisfactory.) His teacher thinks he may have a *learning disability* (LD), an *attention deficit disorder* (ADD), or *dyslexia*. What do these terms mean? *(See chapter 1.)*

• Obtain and compare child's IQ to his achievement test scores. If they are not compatible—if IQ is average or above and achievement scores are significantly below what IQ predicts—suspect a learning disability (LD). *(See chapter 2.)*

• Rule out (or identify and treat) physical, emotional, and neuromotor conditions that might be contributing directly to child's problem. If the learning problem persists (once this has been done), child qualifies for a special education designation. *(See chapter 3.)*

• Assess child's visual and auditory analysis skills and compare these to what is expected for his age or grade. *(See chapter 4.)*

• Assess child's expressive and receptive language abilities and compare these to what is expected for his age or grade. *(See chapter 5.)*

• Relate test results (visual and auditory analysis skills and expressive and receptive language abilities) to the child's school difficulties. Examine the links between his language skills, his perceptual skills, and his reading, spelling, writing, and arithmetic abilities. *(See chapter 6.)*

· Enough testing; time to do something helpful.

Options

1. *Delay.* Arrange for the child to have more time to develop better perceptual skills and learn better language abilities before moving him into a more demanding instructional environment. If he is not yet in kindergarten, put off the entering date; if he is in kindergarten or beyond, ask that he be retained in that grade for an additional year.

2. *Remediate.* Engage child in activities that are designed to improve his perceptual skills and/or language abilities; eliminate or significantly reduce the deficit(s).

3. *Compensate.* Change the child's instructional environment (teacher, program and/or physical conditions of classroom) in ways that accommodate his deficits.

Make your treatment decision on the basis of

1. The possible/probable cause of the child's perceptual skills and/or language deficit(s) (whether it is simply a normal variation in development or from some traumatic event or other physiological problem).

2. The child's age and the extent of his educational deficit (how far behind he is in school).

3. The available emotional/physical resources (the time and energy available to work on remediation). *(See chapter 7.)*

↓

· If decision is to improve child's visual and/or auditory perceptual skills, design and implement a remedial program. *(See chapter 8.)*

↓

· If decision is to improve child's language abilities, design and implement a remedial program. *(See chapter 9.)*

↓

· If evidence indicates a need for special (compensatory) classroom conditions, investigate the feasibility of changing one or more of the following:

teacher

instructional program

other classroom factors

(See chapters 10 and 11.)

↓

· Monitor child's progress. If treatment plan was chosen and implemented appropriately, some initial improvement should be evident within a month or two. *(See chapters 8 through 12.)*

1
LEARNING DISABILITY, DYSLEXIA, ATTENTION DEFICIT DISORDER, AND OTHER SUCH CONDITIONS

WHAT THE DIFFERENT LABELS MEAN

IF YOU WERE TO VISIT a first grade classroom in a *standard* school in a typical middle-class neighborhood in this country, you would discover a remarkable situation. Approximately five of the twenty-five children in that classroom are not progressing at a satisfactory rate, even though they are "normal": adequately intelligent, adequately motivated, and free of other encumbering handicaps. (The *standard classroom* will be discussed later in this chapter. For now, it is sufficient to define the term *standard* as "circumstances wherein children are expected to progress at a predictable rate with little need for special attention from the teacher.")

Depending upon where they live, and a variety of other factors, the enigmatic learning problems these children display will earn them different labels, the most common being learning disability (LD), dyslexia, and attention deficit disorder (ADD).

Learning Disability

We start with learning disability because it is generic (it does not pertain to a specific school subject) and because it is used more often than the others. It describes a child who, for no apparent reason, experiences difficulty in one or more of the basic school subjects (reading, writing, spelling, arithmetic). The child's school difficulties usually come as a surprise to his parents and the others who knew him before he entered kindergarten, and remember him as a bright, eager-to-learn youngster who seemed to absorb and express information with little effort. And describe is all that the label does. It offers us no information that can be translated into helpful actions.

Four or five decades ago, this same child would have been labeled something different: emotionally disturbed, probably, or as having a mental block. Later, in the sixties and seventies—when it became evident

1

that very few of these children had significant emotional problems until after they had experienced the upsets of school failure—he would have been called minimally brain damaged, or neurologically handicapped, or educationally maladjusted—the list goes on. As far back as 1966, the United States Department of Health, Education, and Welfare listed over twenty such labels, all equally objectionable to parents and none useful when it came to determining ways to help the children.

Most of those labels have gone out of use, only to be replaced by others that, though less offensive, are not much more helpful. As we just observed, the term *learning disability,* like the others that follow, is only a descriptor. It is not really any better for providing guidance toward treatment, but at least it sounds less malignant than some of the others, and, as we will see shortly, that is important.

Dyslexia

Dyslexia, which the dictionary defines as a "disturbance of the ability to read," is a type of learning disability, just as *dyscalculia* (a term rarely used in schools, meaning a disturbance in the ability to calculate) is another type of learning disability; as is *dysgraphia* (a disturbance in the ability to write). Years ago, persons were called dyslexic only if they had once been able to read and then lost that ability following brain injury from trauma or a sustained high fever or something else that affected the central nervous system. But this is no longer the case.

Today, to most people who use the term (and that includes teachers), dyslexia does nothing more than describe a difficulty in learning to read that cannot be attributed to impaired general intelligence, a physical handicap, or an emotional disorder.

The loss of a previously established ability to read is no longer part of the definition. If one has inexplicable difficulty learning to read, he is a candidate for the label "dyslexic." The connotation of a medical cause persists, but solely by implication rather than documentation. This stems from the fact that so many of these children also have very poor handwriting and exhibit other puzzling and related traits, such as a tendency to print and read certain letters and words backward (*b* and *d,* for example, and such words as *was* and *saw*).

Attention Deficit Disorder

Attention deficit disorder (ADD) is similar to learning disability in that it does not refer to a specific school learning activity in which the child is having trouble. It also differs from *learning disability* in that it refers to, or rather, describes some of the child's general classroom behaviors. It indicates that in addition to not making satisfactory progress, he does not pay adequate attention to instruction and is too easily distracted.

Attention Deficit and Hyperactive Disorder

Attention deficit and hyperactive disorder (ADHD) describes the child who, in addition to having a short attention span (ADD), is also "hyperactive": he squirms and fidgets excessively, touches things that he should not touch, and moves about more than he should. (Before the label ADHD was introduced, these children were often described as displaying the so-called Strauss syndrome of being hyperactive and distractible because of inferred or apparent brain damage.)

Some might disagree with calling ADHD merely a descriptor of a child's behavior, and offer as evidence the fact that there is a medical treatment for the condition: Ritalin is the treatment drug used most often. I agree that Ritalin does indeed appear to quiet down some children, but there is no evidence that it has a positive effect on a child's classroom performance. In fact, taking the argument a bit farther, many parents who give their youngsters Ritalin refrain from using it during school holiday periods, and, interestingly, a good number observe that their children are not very hyperactive during those times. On the strength of these observations, I believe that although Ritalin may reduce hyperactivity in some children, a number of those children would probably not have been hyperactive in the first place if they were in school situations that were less frustrating and that came closer to meeting their instructional needs.

Other Labels

There are other labels—and the list gets longer every year—but thus far none offers very much of practical value. Although each label seems to imply a different underlying cause, there are very few differences between the children who bear these labels. They are all children whose unsatisfactory progress in a standard instructional environment cannot be explained in any reasonable way. None of the labels is diagnostic; none leads to a specific and/or different treatment the way a medical diagnosis of high blood pressure or diabetes does. They are *descriptors of behaviors* rather than identifiers of different conditions. And by and large, they all describe the same phenomenon: a child who should not be having the trouble he is having in school. That is why I will use only one label in this book: the generic label learning disability (LD) as defined earlier. Be assured that the information presented here applies as well to those children who bear the other labels.

WHY SO MANY LABELS?

Labels serve different purposes under different conditions. Sometimes they reflect a practical, economic problem: insurance companies may refuse to pay for the testing and treatment of a condition under one label but will pay for it if it is called something else. Sometimes it is because the state law that governs the distribution of educational funds allocates more money for one condition than for another. Sometimes it is because the supporters of a new label argue convincingly (through written and spoken media) that the old label is inadequately precise. Sometimes it is simply because the new label sounds more scientific, more "correct"; sometimes it is because it is less stigmatic, more socially acceptable. (It is not that long ago that the mentally retarded children we now call *exceptional* were classified as either idiots or imbeciles or morons. Replacing these labels did nothing educationally for the children who bore them, but they were certainly less objectionable to their parents.)

THE RISK INHERENT IN LABELS

Should parents be apprehensive about having their children labeled? Probably. We would all agree that describing a child as learning disabled is better (and more accurate) than calling him brain injured, neurologically handicapped, or dumb.

But, on the minus side, like *dumb,* the term *learning disability* suggests that the fault lies with the child, not the school; that it is *his* failure, *he is different* in a vague, unfortunate way; therefore he (and his parents) should recognize that it is his problem; they should be thankful for any special help the school provides.

This is neither accurate nor to the child's advantage. Once a label is applied, it is difficult to shed, and it may in some subtle, unintentional way cause his teachers to scale down their expectations—and their efforts—for improving his classroom performance. The phenomenon of the self-fulfilling prophecy has been well documented in many classrooms.

Granted, these labels also provide some benefits. By mandate of law, they designate the child as handicapped. Hence, they earn him the right to receive whatever special help the law requires and his school district provides. But surely, other, more correct labels—labels that identify the child's unique instructional needs rather than his performance inadequacies—would better serve that purpose.

After all, when confronted with a physically handicapped child who cannot climb stairs, society does not simply label him and leave it to his parents and others to invent a proper vehicle or design navigable ramps.

Society recognizes the child's special needs and provides them, and if what is available is insufficient, society accepts the responsibility for trying to develop something better. There is no reason why the same principles cannot apply to the children we are discussing in this book.

I therefore suggest that parents remain apprehensive about the labels in use today, and stay on the lookout for a new label—one that places the burden on the school rather than on the child—a label that identifies the child as having unique but not unreasonable instructional needs, as requiring something different than what standard instructional conditions provide but not something that is beyond the fundamental responsibilities and capabilities of competent educators.

STANDARD INSTRUCTIONAL CONDITIONS

I have emphasized the phrase *standard instructional conditions* since the beginning of this book. Why? Because it identifies the kind of conditions that all ostensibly normal children have to contend with until they are labeled something that earns them nonstandard treatment. If we fail to keep this in mind, we will not be able to plan effectively for the child who has been identified as having a learning disability.

Standard instructional conditions refers to the kinds of circumstances most children encounter from the time they begin formal schooling: a public school classroom wherein a teacher of average* knowledge, skills, energy, and motivation, spends about 150 to 175 hours during a school year trying to teach a prescribed set of facts and skills about reading, spelling, arithmetic, or any other subject that is taught daily to a group of twenty-five to thirty children who are at different levels of school achievement, using materials and lessons that were designed to be effective with average children. These conditions do not meet the special needs of the children who are the subject of this book.

Normal primary grade children are expected to make satisfactory progress under these conditions, and most (about 80 percent) do. They "pass" and the school takes the credit. Those who do not make satisfactory progress "fail" and bear the blame. Clearly, there is something wrong with such a system. Referring back to our illustration involving the handicapped child who could not climb stairs, it is akin to failing the physically handicapped child and then justifying the action by pointing out that the vast majority of the children are able to move about the building in its existing (standard) state.

---

*The word *average*, in this context, does not mean inadequate or mediocre. It literally means average—about midway between the extremes.

2
IDENTIFYING THE PROBLEM

P R O F E S S I O N A L S   F R O M   M A N Y different clinical disciplines believe that they can diagnose a learning disability by giving *their* tests; by examining for a number of conditions and behaviors that have been linked with (but not shown to be the cause of) enigmatic learning disorders. This leads to lots of testing.

I question the value of extensive (and expensive) testing in most of these cases. Tests do not cure; they are merely tools that help you gather information in organized ways. Once a learning disability has been identified, tests that do not provide additional information about how to treat the problem are not very useful even though they purportedly assess some related condition. After all, how many different kinds of thermometers do you need to measure air temperature?

I believe that although a variety of professionals can correctly *suspect* a learning disability on the basis of related behaviors (see list on pp. 15–17), it is a school-based problem and the actual responsibility for documenting it (and coordinating its treatment) falls within the scope of school personnel. The people who should make the initial identification are the child's classroom teacher in collaboration with a school diagnostician.

Two types of tests—IQ and school achievement—are sufficient for that initial identification. If a child's IQ is average or above and his school achievement in one or more pivotal school subjects (such as reading and/ or arithmetic) is significantly below average—or, said differently, below what his IQ predicts—then he is identified as probably deserving of special help in school.

True, other factors, such as physical, emotional, and certain (neuro-motor) functional problems, will have to be ruled out (see chapter 3) in order to meet the technical definition of LD, and other tests will have to be given in order to design an appropriate instructional program, but there is really no need for additional psychoeducational testing in order to identify a learning disability.

ACHIEVEMENT TESTS

Achievement tests are designed to measure how much a child has learned in a given subject area. There are achievement tests for reading, arithmetic, spelling, science, social studies, and practically every other subject in the school curriculum; and often, each of these tests is organized into subsections, each designed to investigate different aspects of the overall ability.

Most achievement tests are designed for group administration and employ a multiple-choice format, with the answers recorded on specially designed sheets that can be scanned and scored by a computer. The child's performance (test score) is compared to "norms" that were acquired when the same test was standardized, that is, given to a large number of children who were representative of a range of socioeconomic and racial backgrounds, and who lived in a number of different locales (i.e., rural, suburban, inner-city).

Test results are usually reported in terms of *grade equivalent,* although they may also be stated in *percentiles* and *stanines.* There is no need to discuss the last two beyond a brief description (see below), but a few words of explanation about grade equivalent might be worthwhile.

Grade Equivalent

Grade equivalent is expressed as a number in which a decimal point is embedded. The number to the left of the decimal point indicates the grade level; the number to the right of the decimal indicates the school month within that school year. For example, if the child's reading achievement is reported to be at the grade equivalent (GE) of 3.4, it means that he responded to the test the way the average youngster who is in the fourth month of the third grade is likely to respond.

Achievement tests are designed to yield a so-called normal distribution of scores. For example, the test for second graders is designed so that when it is administered to enough second grade children (who are representative of the different socioeconomic, racial, and geographical circumstances previously mentioned) during a specific month in the year, about two-thirds of them will achieve a score that falls within a reasonably limited range above or below the average score expected from children at that point in the second grade—what the statisticians describe as being within one standard deviation above or below the mean. The other third will be split; about half of them will obtain significantly better than average scores and the remaining one-sixth will do just the opposite.

The children in this last group and those in the lower end of the middle group who have average or above-average IQs are likely candidates for the LD label.

Stanines and Percentiles

Grade equivalent designations translate directly into percentiles and stanines. Attainment of the expected score for a given grade level is representative of the fifth stanine and the fiftieth percentile. Performance that exceeds the expected level in grade equivalent will obviously also earn a designation higher than the fiftieth percentile and higher than the fifth stanine, with the ninth stanine being the highest category. Performance that falls short of the expected level in grade equivalent will, in turn, earn a designation lower than the fiftieth percentile and lower than the fifth stanine, with the first stanine being the lowest category.

Reading Achievement Tests

There are a number of reading achievement tests on the market, but they are much more alike than different. At the primary grade level, reading achievement is typically measured on the basis of four sets of abilities: (1) the child's knowledge of the printed letters, (2) his word attack (or word recognition) skills, the ability to translate printed words into their oral forms on the basis of a familiarity with key letter-sound relationships, (3) his vocabulary, knowledge of the meanings of different words; and (4) comprehension, the ability to extract and retain information from printed material. Some children show mixed strengths and weaknesses in these four abilities; some do not.

For example, a child may score high in word recognition skills and significantly low on comprehension—that is, he may be able to read the words fluently yet not be able to retain and interpret very much of what he read (or, for that matter, what was read to him). Or, as is more often the case, the reverse may be true: he may be able to understand and remember information read to him, but not be able to translate the print into language on his own.

We will come back to these individual strengths and weaknesses later, when we discuss the basic learning aptitudes we call *perceptual* (or *analysis*) *skills,* and again when we examine ways to help children who have reading problems. (See chapters 6 and 11.) For now it is enough that we recognize that there are different reading subskills, and that each has its own list of prerequisite abilities.

Arithmetic Achievement Tests

Arithmetic achievement is usually measured on the basis of at least two sets of abilities: the child's ability to calculate, and his understanding of the mathematical concepts that underlie those calculations. As in reading, a child may score well in one but not in the other; he may be able to execute mathematical calculations reasonably well, yet have a very poor grasp of the underlying concepts, or vice versa. We will come back to this topic later on. It is sufficient for now simply to recognize that a child's overall ability in arithmetic (as assessed by a standardized achievement test) may be attributable to a weakness in only one area of measurement.

Spelling Achievement Tests

Spelling achievement tests follow the same principles on which reading and arithmetic achievement tests are based. Depending on the test, children may be asked to spell from dictation or simply identify misspelled words in a text. In all instances, the test is intended to reflect the child's ability to spell accurately in comparison to what is typical of children at his grade level.

The Validity of Achievement Tests

Are school achievement tests valid? Do they really provide an accurate measure of a child's learning? In general, the answer is a qualified yes, but we must also recognize that they could yield wrong information under certain circumstances.

First of all, for the most part they are timed tests, and some children respond very poorly to real or implied demands for speed. This is particularly true of those children whose confidence has been undermined and who have begun to question their ability to make satisfactory progress in school.

In addition, achievement tests depend upon accurate sampling, on the assumption that if a certain percentage of the apples in a barrel is ripe, then it is reasonable to conclude that all of the apples in the barrel are ripe. Achievement tests cannot and do not attempt to measure *everything* the child should have learned by this point in his school program but rather depend upon representative test items. It is conceivable that the child might have small gaps in his knowledge—gaps that, by coincidence, are reflected by just that information that the test designers selected as representative of school achievement.

There are lots of other possibilities of this sort (including the obvious fact that the youngster may simply be having a "bad day" on the day he takes his achievement tests), and they all have the potential to result in underestimating a child's accomplishments.

There are also some more general possibilities. For example, although all standard reading instruction programs used in this country are similar in that they strive to teach children how to read and comprehend text in which the words and information become more demanding with each grade level, they often differ in how beginning reading is taught.

Some reading programs introduce sight words early on—words that do not sound precisely the way they are spelled (e.g., the words *the, said, some, saw*)—and expect the children to be able to read a substantial number of these by the end of first grade. Some reading programs place more emphasis on phonics, on using only regularly spelled words at the outset, words that sound just the way they are spelled (e.g., *mat, cat, top, stop*), and delay introducing all but a few of the more irregularly spelled (sight) words until certain basic reading abilities are established. Obviously, if the reading achievement test administered at the end of first grade is one that uses lots of sight words, then children who have been in a phonics-emphasizing program may be misjudged; many of them, even though they can read what they have been taught to read, will not be able to read the sight words presented in the test.

These differences in instructional approach disappear by fourth grade. By then, children are expected to have acquired basic reading abilities regardless of how they were taught. What remains for them to learn from this point on is a more extensive vocabulary and greater fluency, which, in combination, enable the reader to gain information from text. Schoolteachers often express it this way: during the first three years of school, children learn to read; from fourth grade on, they read to learn. Hence, reading achievement tests are less prone to misjudge a child from fourth grade on, although it is always a possibility.

INTELLIGENCE QUOTIENT

Any discussion about intelligence quotient (IQ) should begin with a statement about what it is not. It is *not* an indicator of one's brain power or learning potential, nor was it ever designed to provide that kind of information. So far, no one has been able to figure out how to measure an individual's brain power and learning potential.

The primary purpose of an IQ test is to give educators a reasonably accurate way of predicting how well a youngster will progress in a *standard instructional setting.* Most respected IQ tests do that fairly well, but they are not foolproof; they all do what they are supposed to do, on average, but they are often wrong with individual children.

This bring us to another question: just what do the numbers tell us? IQ is best thought of as representative of the score one earned on an IQ test as compared to the score expected from someone his age. Obviously, then, if we are to understand IQ, we must know something about IQ tests.

The General Design of IQ Tests

There are quite a few IQ tests on the market, but they do not differ all that much. In essence, most respected IQ tests in use today consist of a series of questions and some puzzlelike problems that require spatial reasoning, and provide a method for converting the individual's score in these activities to a so-called *mental age,* which is a comparison between the performance of the person who took the test and the average age of the people in the norming sample who earned a similar score. (As with achievement tests, the norming sample is usually made up of people from different socioeconomic, racial, and geographic backgrounds.) The IQ is then determined by dividing mental age by chronological age, and multiplying this by 100.

For example, if someone's score on the test indicates a mental age of 120 months (that is, he scored precisely what the average 10-year-old does), and he is, in fact, 120 months old, then his IQ is 100 (120 ÷ 120 × 100 = 100). In effect, he is exactly the same age, cognitively and chronologically. On the other hand, if his mental age (as determined by the IQ test) is 180 months (15 years) and his chronological age is 120 months, then his IQ is 150, far above the average.

The Wechsler Intelligence Scale for Children (WISC-III)

The revised (i.e., updated from an earlier version) Wechsler Intelligence Scale for Children is the test of preference in most U.S. schools. It is designed to be administered individually to children who are between six and sixteen years of age. (The WISC bypasses specifically determining the child's mental age but, for all practical purposes, calculates IQ just about the same way as described.)

The WISC is unique in that it consists of two sets of subtests, each set focusing on a different kind of general ability. One set is known as *Verbal* tests; the other, *Performance* tests.

WISC Verbal Tests

Information. The child is asked questions that attempt to measure his store of factual knowledge. For example, "Who was the first president of the United States?" (Note: this question and the examples given for the other subtests described below are not really from the test; I fabricated them to illustrate the type of questions used in the different subtests.)

Similarities. The child is asked to explain how two different objects are the same and/or different. For example, "In what way are milk and orange juice alike?" "In what way are they different?"

Arithmetic. The child is asked to solve mental arithmetic problems that range from simply counting a limited number of objects to solving word problems that require an understanding of fractions. This is a timed test.

Vocabulary. The child is asked to define certain words. For example, "What does spoon mean?" Or, at a higher level, "What does cacophony mean?"

Comprehension. The child is asked to respond to questions that are designed to assess his understanding of established social rules. For example, "What is the thing to do if you see your younger brother hit a smaller child?"

Digit Span. The child is asked to repeat numeral sequences forward as well as backward; the sequences range from two numerals to as many as seven.

WISC Performance Tests

Picture Completion. The child is shown drawings of various common objects from which something has been omitted, and asked to identify what is missing. For example, a wheel from an automobile. This is a timed test.

Picture Arrangement. The child is shown a series of picture cards that are out of order and asked to arrange them in an order that tells a sensible story. For example: three picture cards, the first showing a boy whose stomach is obviously distended and aching, sitting at a table on which there is an empty plate; the second, a picture of the same boy eating food from the plate; the third, the same boy, but with a much flatter stomach, sitting at the table on which there is a plate full of food. This is a timed test.

Block Design. The child is shown drawings of block arrangements (the faces of the blocks are painted different colors) and asked to reproduce the drawings with real blocks—wooden cubes—painted the same way. This is a timed test.

Object Assembly. The child is asked to assemble jigsaw puzzles that consist of anywhere from five to twelve pieces that when assembled comprise a line drawing of a person, an animal, or an object. This is a timed test.

Coding. This subtest has two levels of difficulty. For children age eight and older, the child is shown a key in which the numerals one through nine are contained in individual squares and a simple geometric design appears in a square beneath each of the numerals. For example, in the square under the numeral one, there is a circle, in the square under the numeral two, there is a dot, and so on.

The examiner explains the key to the child, then shows him a long sequence of squares, each containing a numeral, randomly organized, and asks him to draw the correct geometric design in the blank square under each of the numerals, completing as many as he can within the time limit of the test.

For children younger than eight, the test is much the same but, instead of numerals, the key consists of five geometric designs (e.g., circle, star, square), each of which contains a unique shape, such as a vertical line, two horizontal lines, a circle, and so on. The child's task, once the key has been explained, is to draw the appropriate shape inside a randomly organized sequence of the geometric designs, completing as many as possible within the time limit of the test.

Mazes. The child is shown line mazes of increasing complexity and asked to trace the path from the central starting point to a designated exit within a fixed period of time. This is a timed test.

What the WISC Scores Tell You

After administering all the subtests, the child's raw scores (the number of items responded to correctly in each of the subtests) are converted into scaled scores. This conversion reflects the child's chronological age. If two children, one age seven, the other age nine, get the same number of items correct in a given subtest, the younger of the two earns a higher scaled score because, being seven years old, he is not expected to do as well as the nine-year-old. A subtest scaled score of ten indicates that the child performed as expected for his age; a scaled score higher than ten indicates that the child performed better than expected for his age; a scaled score lower than ten, vice versa.

The scaled scores from the Verbal and the Performance subtests are then summed and converted into a Verbal Scale IQ and a Performance Scale IQ. These two are then summed and averaged, and the outcome is identified as a Full Scale IQ.

The Unique Contribution of the WISC

On the basis of the Verbal, Performance, and Full Scale IQ scores, we are able to make some observations about the child's store of knowledge about the world in which he lives—information he has *learned,* that he has acquired since birth through experiences, and that reflects his culture (this is derived from the Verbal IQ)—and the child's capacity to solve problems that require spatial reasoning, an ability that does not depend so much upon formal or informal instruction but that *develops naturally,* on a predictable schedule, in all normal, healthy children, regardless of race or geographical setting, as long as they receive adequate nurturing and sensory stimulation (this from the Performance IQ).

Consider the following example: three children, all in the third grade, all with Full Scale IQs of 100—average for their age. Yet they perform differently in school, and some of those differences become a bit more understandable when we look at their Performance and Verbal IQs.

Child A has a Verbal IQ of 100 and a Performance IQ of 100; hence, his Full Scale IQ is 100. He is progressing satisfactorily in school—not exceptionally good, not very bad.

Child B's Full Scale IQ is also 100, but it is derived from a Verbal IQ of 120 and a Performance IQ of 80. (This is not a farfetched example; there are many such children.) Child *B* knows more than most children his age about the world in which he lives, but in contrast he is much less adept than most children his age in approaching tasks that involve analytical spatial reasoning. He is likely to be loquacious, able to read well (probably better than Child *A*, although with not as much comprehension as his teacher would like; we will see why later, when we discuss just what is involved in learning to read), spell adequately (though hardly as well as he reads), but have significantly more difficulty than Child *A* with math concepts and with completing paper and pencil activities neatly and on time.

Child C also has a Full Scale IQ of 100, but his score derives from a Verbal IQ of 80 and a Performance IQ of 120. (This, too, is not that unusual.) He knows much less than most children his age about the world in which he lives but is much more capable than most children his age in accomplishing tasks that require analytical spatial reasoning. He is likely to have considerably more difficulty with basic reading (especially word recognition skills) and spelling that does Child *A*, yet is probably doing better than Child *A* in arithmetic.

Interesting and revealing! Three children with the same Full Scale IQ score—average in all three cases—but markedly different subtest scores. These differences are reflected on their report cards, and, more important, these differences can help us plan more effectively for how to help them overcome their learning problems.

Stanford-Binet IQ Test (Revised)

The Stanford-Binet IQ test was the first well-constructed IQ test to be used in the United States, having been exported from France during the early part of this century. All other IQ tests of any worth derive from it and are validated against it. It was replaced in popularity by the WISC, because of the latter's design that made it possible to define a child's performance in more detail than the single number would allow. (The questions in the WISC do not differ very much from the Stanford-Binet.) Recently, a revised version of the Stanford-Binet has been published (version 4). Its design addresses the shortcomings of the earlier versions; it, like the WISC, supplies subtest scores that give one insight into different aspects of the developed abilities and the acquired knowledge that comprise IQ.

OTHER SIGNS OF A LEARNING DISABILITY

In addition to a mismatch between what a child should be and is able to do in school, there are other signs that should arouse suspicion, and they are important because many of them can be spotted during the child's preschool years.

The list changes as age increases. Many of the behaviors described in this section will show up during the first decade of life, then tend to disappear during adolescence, even though the learning problem persists. (Two cautions: [1] a child may display one or more of these signs, yet not have a learning disability; and [2] do not think of these characteristics [except for the first three on the list, which might be implicated by inference] as the cause of a learning disability; they are merely accompanying signs, the way a high fever is an accompanying sign of infection. Treating them may be worthwhile if the child has not yet started having trouble in school. Treating them in a child who is already well behind in school may be worthwhile for its own sake, but it is not likely to eliminate the child's school problems.)

Generally, most learning disabled children display one or more (but not all) of the following characteristics:

• *A history of significant, albeit brief, trauma at birth or during the first year of life that does not seem to have permanent effects.* For example, thirty seconds or so of oxygen deprivation as part of a complicated birth, a premature delivery, a very high fever during the first year of life that lasted for a day or two, seizures, or some other event that does not appear to damage the child permanently but might be associated with a subsequent delay in some aspect of cognitive development.

• *A history of chronic middle ear infections during the first three or four years of life.* These are often severe enough to require the insertion of drainage tubes but do not permanently impair hearing.

• *Farsightedness (hyperopia).* Not of sufficient magnitude to impair eyesight and therefore often goes undetected until well beyond age five. The farsighted child may also manifest constant or intermittent strabismus (crossed eye); that is, his eyes may appear to be out of alignment some of the time or all of the time. (See pp. 19–21 for more discussion about farsightedness.)

• *Delayed language development.* A slow start in beginning to speak, and in learning new words and the grammatical rules for their use (e.g., correct tenses, use of the plural forms).

• *Speech articulation problems.* Children's spoken communication, if not precise, should at least be understandable by their parents by the time they are two years old and understandable by other adults by the time they are three.

• *Delayed development of consistent hand preference.* Most children are securely right-handed or left-handed by the time they reach their fourth birthday. Many of the children who were still switching hands for eating, printing, brushing their teeth, and so on when they entered kindergarten end up being called learning disabled. Do not think of them as ambidextrous. On the contrary, it is more accurate to call them *nondextrous;* they lack adequate manipulative ability with either hand, and because they switch hands they delay the establishment of the consistent motor patterns that support reliable recall of the ambiguous letters of the lowercase manuscript alphabet.

• *Delayed gross and fine-motor development.* The average four-year-old, for example, can balance and hop on either foot; the average five-year-old can skip. A number of children with learning disabilities were not able to perform these and other related behaviors at the expected ages.

• *Sloppy paperwork.* Improper spacing, resulting in "messy-looking" work. Their printing may border on being illegible, and may or may not be related to a general deficiency in fine-motor skills.

• *Disorganized approach to tasks that involve a sequence of actions.* Child does not recognize that many tasks cannot be accomplished satisfactorily unless they are broken down into a series of steps, and that step one must be dealt with first, then step two, and so on.

• *Poor memory.* Particularly when it comes to remembering spoken directions that comprise more than one or two steps.

• *Avoidance of activities that involve sustained visual and/or auditory attention.* For example, working through puzzles, coloring, cutting, pasting, listening to stories and songs.

• *Confusion in identifying and/or printing certain letters and numerals.* This is most often evidenced by reversals of lowercase *b* and *d*, but it may also occur with other letters and numerals.

• *Confusion in reading certain words that, when read in reverse direction, also spell out meaningful words.* (*On* and *no,* for example.)

• *Losing place frequently when reading or copying printed materials.*

• *Failing to complete written work because time runs out.*

• *Poor classification skills.* Child does not readily recognize that things (objects, people, events, spoken words, etc.) may be categorized on the basis of certain attributes, such as color, size, beginning letter or sound (e.g., *cat, cookie, coat*), function (e.g., things to eat, to wear, to play with), taste (e.g., food that is sweet or sour; that is eaten hot, cold, raw, cooked), and so on.

• *Poor association skills.* Child does not recognize that there are cogent similarities and differences in certain units of information (certain spelling patterns and number facts), which, if noted, facilitate learning new information. For example, the child fails to see how being able to read the words *bit* and *bat* can help him learn to read *fit* and *fat*, and *bin* and *ban*, and *bitter* and *batch*, and so on. Hence, each new word is something to be learned separately, from "scratch."

3
PHYSICAL, EMOTIONAL, AND NEUROMOTOR FACTORS

As NOTED in chapter 2, a child cannot be said to have a learning disability until it has been established that his school difficulties are not due to generally reduced cognitive abilities—that is, a low IQ—and do not stem from a physical, emotional, or neuromotor problem. We have already discussed how cognitive abilities are measured. Our next step is to identify the physical, emotional, and neuromotor deficits that have to be considered, and how to rule them out as contributing factors.

PHYSICAL FACTORS

It is self-evident that a child who is chronically undernourished, seriously ill, in pain, or cannot see or hear well enough is likely to have difficulty making satisfactory progress in a standard classroom. Hence, every child who encounters some difficulty in school should be thoroughly examined by his pediatrician and his eye doctor; the former to assess general health and hearing, the latter to evaluate vision. (As a matter of fact, this statement holds true for *all* children, not just those who show signs of a learning disability. All children should have routine health assessments from birth on; routine, thorough eye examinations should begin by the age of six months.* There is no good reason for delaying health assessment until after a problem becomes manifest if it could have been detected and treated earlier.)

If a pertinent problem is noted in the child's physical status, then, indeed, take action to eliminate the problem. A key word in the above sentence is *pertinent*. Many of us have physical deficits of one sort or another. Some of us are overweight; some, underweight. Some of us need glasses to see clearly; some need a hearing aid. Some of us would probably benefit from vitamin supplements; some not at all. If one (or

---

*This is not a misprint. A child's first thorough eye examination—to be conducted by an eye doctor—should occur at *six months*.

more) of these problems is found in a child, then by all means see to it that the problem is dealt with by the appropriate professional, but do not assume that once the physical problem is addressed the child's learning problems will disappear. This will not happen unless (1) the physical problem really is the *cause* of the learning problem and (2) the child has not fallen too far behind in school. We will put off for a while discussing the latter (see chapter 7), but the former is worth a few words here.

It is a bit like owning an automobile that lacks a motor and a steering wheel and has a big dent in its front right fender. Mending the fender and ignoring the other two defects will not help much. The car will look better, but it will remain inoperative. Replacing the steering wheel and ignoring the missing motor and the dented fender is not the solution either, but at least it is a step in the right direction. Replacing the steering wheel and the motor solves a great deal, so long as everything else in the car works. The dented fender is a problem, but not a *pertinent* one.

The point of all this: do what should be done about the child's physical status, but do not put all your eggs (hopes) into that basket unless you have real reason for doing so.

Vision Assessment: Screening or Full Examination?

Why is it acceptable for the pediatrician (or school nurse) to assess hearing but not vision? Stated simply, this is because hearing problems are revealed by a reduced ability to hear certain sounds and screening tests are pretty good for detecting this. The same cannot be said about the vision screening tests because some vision problems do not cause reduced visual acuity and therefore will not be detected with an eye chart.

Although vision screening tests, administered in school or at the pediatrician's office, are likely to identify nearsighted children and astigmatic children—because their eyesight is affected—such tests often overlook farsightedness (*hyperopia*). Recently reported information shows that hyperopic children should not be overlooked. Specifically, it has been found that children who are only moderately farsighted are at risk for experiencing learning problems in school. (See the list of signs on pp. 15–17.) They should wear glasses, if only for near work.

True, moderately farsighted children usually see quite well, both at distance and near; that is, they have 20/20 acuity. That is why they rarely fail school vision screenings and pediatricians' eye chart tests, and why glasses have been thought to be unnecessary—something like fixing the dented fender in the automobile that lacks a motor. However, we now know that they should be wearing glasses for near work—not to improve their eyesight but rather to enable them to see clearly without eyestrain.

The Special Nature of Farsightedness

A fuller explanation is probably in order. Normal eyes have two sets of muscles: one set—the extraocular muscles that are attached to the outside of the eye—controls where the eyes "aim," be it up, down, to the right or left, to something up close or far away. The other set—the *accommodation* muscles—controls the eye's focusing power, making whatever internal optical adjustments are necessary for seeing clearly at different distances. The extraocular muscles—the first set—are important because they enable us to look around accurately and rapidly, locate what we are looking for, and coordinate the two eyes so that we see singly and appreciate depth. The focusing or accommodation muscles—the second set—are important because they enable us to activate the extra optical power we need to see an object/print clearly even when it is positioned near our eyes—for example, within arm's reach. (Those of us who are beyond the age of forty-five understand the benefit of active focusing muscles because ours have probably matured to the point where they do not function as well as they once did. This is normal, and reading glasses are usually the answer.) We will discuss the aiming muscles later, when we come to the topic of neuromotor functional skills. Focusing muscles are best discussed here.

Normal, properly working eyes see clearly at distance simply because their basic optical elements and size put into focus anything located as far away as twenty feet and beyond. No extra focusing power is needed. Farsighted eyes, however, are "weak" eyes; their basic optical elements and/or size are such that the eyes are underpowered for distance vision, and even more so at near. But farsighted eyes—if they belong to someone young—are capable of clear sight, despite being underpowered, because they have a great deal of extra power on call from their focusing muscles.

As such, the farsighted child sees clearly at distance and near by exercising extra focusing power—more than he would have to were he not farsighted. This is why most of them pass pediatricians' and school vision screening tests. The advantage of this: they see clearly without glasses. The disadvantage: they fatigue faster from sustained eye work than they would if they were not farsighted.

The implication of all this: farsightedness is comparable to carrying an extra weight on your back. Most of us could get through our normal workday even if we were required to wear a twenty-pound backpack. But we would be more fatigued than if we had not been required to carry the pack. Glasses on the moderately farsighted child is analogous to casting off the twenty-pound pack. (Obviously, children who are very farsighted should also wear glasses, but this usually does not require special discussion because those children usually do not see so clearly and they often have a crossed eye; they fail pediatricians' and school vision screening tests.)

Farsightedness has also been linked to delayed development of visual perceptual (analysis) skills. This will be discussed later, as we examine the assessment of visual perceptual skills and their importance to classroom learning (see chapter 6). For now, it is sufficient to cite the relationship and point out that farsightedness should not be ignored simply because it may not have a detrimental effect on eyesight. (I have not devoted any attention to nearsightedness [myopia] or to astigmatism because, as previously stated, children with these conditions rarely escape detection. Their poor eyesight is usually noticed by a parent, a pediatrician, or a school nurse; once detected, they obtain glasses that enable them to see clearly; in addition, myopic and astigmatic children do not earn the designation of learning disabled nearly as often as do farsighted children. In fact, myopic children tend to do better than most in the classroom.)

EMOTIONAL FACTORS

The emotional factors of concern in this context are the child's motivation, his personality, his desire to comply and please. Clearly, the child whose home life is disturbed, the anxiety-ridden child, the abused child, the child who sees no reason why he should care about making satisfactory progress in school, may very well display school learning problems despite an adequate IQ.

It is foolish to take a casual attitude about the impact of a child's emotional status on his classroom performance. But on the other hand, it is reasonable to believe that most elementary school age children enjoy a healthy emotional state; very few are psychopathic or pathologically neurotic. Elementary school children, by and large, want to meet the goals that are placed before them. Very few youngsters that age are lazy. Most, having failed once, are very willing to try again, and try hard. In my judgment, emotional problems are rarely the cause of a learning disability.

It is true, of course, that chronic school failure during the beginning years, if ignored, will inevitably lead to continued failure and ultimately generate frustration, anger, and a variety of other undesirable emotions in a child. But these are not primary causes of learning problems; they are outcomes. However, once established, they must be addressed if the child is to be helped.

Therefore, as a rule of thumb, I usually suggest that it is safe to downplay emotional factors in learning disabled children who have not yet reached fourth grade. (*Do not interpret the word* downplay *to mean ignore*. Certainly, the child should be praised for his efforts and successes and motivated in the other appropriate ways.) In contrast, I suggest that with learning disabled children in fourth grade and above, great concern should be devoted to the emotional conditions relevant to school learning, but not at the expense of ignoring the need for effective instruction. It would be a mistake to do otherwise.

NEUROMOTOR FACTORS

In a simplistic sense, the term *neuromotor factors* pertains to the child's ability to use his neuromuscular systems (vision, speech, hands) *efficiently*. For example, there are children who see clearly, who do not need glasses, and whose eyes coordinate precisely but not efficiently. Such children reflect their problem in how long they can sustain a visual task without experiencing discomfort, headaches, and other eyestrain symptoms. In the same vein, there are children who can speak plainly but not efficiently; they have to work harder than usual at exercising the refined vocomotor coordinations that articulate speech requires. Or there are children who can manipulate a pencil adequately but not with the degree of facility that some of their classroom paper and pencil tasks might require. Such children often show signs that are linked with learning disabilities.

Because neuromotor skills refer to eyes, speech production, and digital manipulation, there is no single profession best trained to carry out assessment and make treatment recommendations. On the positive side, however, there is very little evidence to support the argument that faulty neuromotor process skills are a prevalent cause of a learning disability.

Take, for example, the executing of efficient, precise eye movements. For decades there has been the recurrent theme that poor reading stems from inefficient, inaccurate control of eye movements—that poor readers *are* poor readers because their eye-aiming muscles are not as adept as they should be in moving the eyes across and down the printed page. Indeed, a number of tests have been devised and a number of eye movement execise programs have been put into use.

Unfortunately, none of these exercise programs seems to have had significant impact on solving the LD problem. (More about this in chapter 8.) There is no doubt that children with reading problems demonstrate erratic eye movements when they read, but the evidence does not indicate that the faulty eye movements are the cause of the inadequate reading. In fact, it appears to be the opposite: poor reading ability produces faulty eye movements. Improving a child's eye movement skills and expecting to obtain improvement in reading simply does not pay off. Improving a child's reading ability through effective instruction will improve his eye movements, if that is your goal.

Having said all this, I urge parents not to ignore the child's neuro-motor process skills: visual, speech, digital. They are important. But just as important: discuss thoroughly with the professional making the assess-ment and treatment recommendations, the directness of the cause-and-effect connection between the skill under discussion and the child's classroom performance inadequacies. Do not make your judgments solely on the basis of correlational reasoning.

4
VISUAL AND AUDITORY PERCEPTUAL (ANALYSIS) SKILLS

SPECULATIONS ABOUT THE CAUSE OF A LEARNING DISABILITY

WE HAVE REPEATEDLY DESCRIBED the child with a learning disability as someone whose learning problem is not caused by a physical or emotional handicap, or by a cognitive deficit of the type that is revealed by IQ tests. In short, it is a learning problem that cannot be explained—a *mystery*. But that cannot be literally correct. There *must* be a reasonable explanation.

Consider: what possible reason could there be for an obviously bright preschooler to encounter severe difficulties when he enters formal schooling? Is there something that different about the learning that is expected to occur in the primary grades and the learning that occurs during the preschool years? Or is it that the youngster was never as good a learner as he seemed to be? Or is it that he experienced some trauma just as he started school, and this provoked the problem?

Suppose we begin with the last proposal: could the child have experienced some physical or emotional trauma just as he started school that was severe enough to reduce markedly his ability to learn, yet subtle enough to be unobserved by his parents? Obviously, that is a possibility, but it is hardly sensible to suggest that this type of trauma is experienced each year by about twenty percent of the children entering school.

What about the notion that the youngster was never really as good a learner as he appeared to be, and that this was finally revealed when he started school? Possible? Yes. Probable? Not really. The fact that the children we are talking about have at least average IQs negates that argument. True, IQ scores are not infallible predictors of school performance, but surely it is not rational to suggest that they are that far off the mark with so many children. If that were the case, the IQ test would have been abandoned a long time ago.

Well then, what about the remaining proposition: Is the kind of learning that is expected to occur in school that different from the kind of learning that the child did during his preschool years?

Think about it. A child's preschool years are devoted to learning about the world in which he lives: gathering information about people, places, things—what they look like, what they are called, what they are made of, how they work, and so on. He does all this learning through direct experiences—formal and informal instruction of one sort or another—by looking, listening, touching, smelling, tasting, and reacting emotionally.

He enters school knowing a great deal, and is confronted with a new challenge. He now has to do more than acquire information; *he now has to learn how to code and decode information symbolically, representing oral and spatial language with letters and with numerals;* in other words, he has to learn how to read, write, spell, and do arithmetic.

This is the child's main obligation while he is in the primary (first three) grades. He is expected to learn to do these things fluently and efficiently, to the point where he can do them almost without conscious effort (automatically) thereby freeing his mind to think about the meaning of the information represented by the symbols rather than about how to carry out the underlying coding and decoding processes. And finally, he has to learn to do all this under standard instructional conditions.

Although most children succeed in accomplishing these goals within the allotted time, a substantial number—about 20 percent—do not; and, in many instances, the difficulty that this latter group experiences comes as a complete surprise to their parents who know their children to be bright and eager learners, and never expected to have them labeled anything that reflected school failure. So it appears that if we are to unravel this puzzle, we will have to identify what is different about those apparently bright children who run into difficulty during the primary grades and those who do not.

A Feasible Explanation

Not enough is known about individual differences in the development of complex cognitive functions to identify a specific, underlying cause for this difference between children. However, empirical (clinical) evidence strongly supports the conclusion that whatever the underlying cause turns out to be (there is probably more than one), *the most common, directly related problem these children display is a delay in the development of certain basic analysis (perceptual) skills and/or basic language abilities.* *

*I am not arguing that all—or even most—children who bear the LD label also display perceptual and/or language skills deficits. I *am* arguing that most children who display deficits in one or both of these skills *during their preschool and primary grade years* will ultimately bear the LD label (or one of the other labels that identifies learning problems that cannot be attributed to substandard cognitive ability).

I am proposing that most learning disabled children started school with poor visual and/or auditory perceptual (analysis) and/or language skills and, because of this, failed to make satisfactory progress. Over time, their skills development is likely to catch up, but

The former are learning aptitudes that all humans normally develop on a predictable schedule during the first decade of life; aptitudes that enable us to recognize order in our sensory environment, to induce systems (organization) in what we see and hear (and in what we smell, touch, and taste). The latter are a combination of development (the ability to understand/produce language) and experience (learning a specific language).

Add to this the fact that the instructional programs used in most of our public schools' primary grades are designed for children who have appropriately developed visual and auditory analysis skills and language abilities. Indeed, the programs are designed in ways that make these basic abilities a prerequisite to understanding that reading, writing, spelling, and arithmetic *make sense*, that they are based on systems—"rules" that may be applied logically—rather than being dependent upon the child's ability to memorize vast amounts of unrelated information. (This is explained in greater detail on pp. 125–44.)

Then, consider also the fact that in our society a child's readiness for school is more often determined by his chronological age than by an assessment of his developmental status. In most states, children enter first grade in the September following their sixth birthday; once a child is six years old, he is expected to have developed the basic, prerequisite analysis and language skills, to be "ready" to learn appropriately from the standard school programs. Obviously, this is not always the case, and it certainly is not true with respect to the children who are the subject of this book.

The result: inadequate school progress (that often could have been prevented if certain precautions had been taken) and, in time, a label that designates the child as having an abnormal brain, which causes an intractable learning problem that will require special help from here on out.

In brief, then, the best explanation for the type of learning problems we are discussing is that these children are confronted with the task of learning to read, write, spell, and do arithmetic under standard school conditions *before they have developed the basic (visual and auditory) analysis and language skills that would enable them to recognize that these coding processes are based on systems and therefore need not be memorized.*

Why they have not yet developed these analysis and language skills is yet another question. It is a safe bet that most of them are simply manifesting a normal variation—they are developing these skills, but not at a rate assumed by standard school programs. In addition, there

---

their educational deficits persist. That is why the prevalence of basic aptitude deficits is so much lower in older (high school) children. They outgrow the original problem, but continue to manifest its effects.

probably are a number of children whose developmental delays are due to some undetected central nervous system deficit; a slight injury to the brain at (or before) birth, perhaps, or something of that nature. Both groups present a similar clinical picture, but their educational management might have to differ. We will discuss this shortly. (See chapter 7.)

PERCEPTUAL SKILLS

The phrase *perceptual skills deficits* implies that children with these problems literally see and hear (perceive) differently than other children. That is not so, but it is easy to see why the confusion exists. (See p. 31 for a way you can prove this to yourself.)

Perception is a very complex act that goes far beyond what one sees, hears, smells, tastes, and touches. It involves interpretation; it reflects past experiences and emotions as well as sensory information. Thus we accept the fact that two individuals may see or hear the same thing yet *perceive* them differently.

The perceptual skills discussed in this book are not as complex as all that. It would probably be better, and certainly more accurate, to call them *analysis skills*—the capacity to look at and/or listen to patterns of sensations (meaningful information) analytically, specifically to identify concrete (sensory), structural components and the way those components interrelate.*

VISUAL ANALYSIS SKILLS

Visual analysis skills develop on a fairly predictable schedule, independent of specific experiences. This is a characteristic of our species; it is part of our genetic makeup. We are *systems-inducing organisms*—we are naturally inclined to seek order in our environment, to identify ways to organize information in accord with one or more of its key features.

Our ability to do this is revealed, at least in part, in our visual analysis skills development. If the child lives in an environment that provides spatially organized stimuli, if the child is not deprived of the experiences of exploring these stimuli—touching them, moving them about, taking them apart and putting them back together, and looking at them as he

*From this point on, therefore, I will use the two phrases—*perceptual skills* and *analysis skills*—interchangeably. Another semantic adjustment is probably called for at this point: the abilities referred to here as visual analysis skills are more accurately defined as *spatial analysis skills*. Although most of our examples derive from visible stimuli, there is plenty of evidence to show that blind people also develop the capacity to recognize that the environment can be organized according to its key spatial features.

does these things—and if the child has never had the misfortune of experiencing central nervous system damage (e.g., prolonged high fever, significant deprivation of oxygen), then his visual analysis skills will develop on a reasonably predictable schedule.*

Visual analysis skills begin developing at birth, with the initial stages triggered by the reflexes that the environment normally elicits from the child. Certainly, these skills are crude at the onset, becoming more and more refined as time goes by and development unfolds.

The child learns to recognize certain visual patterns very early in life: his parents' and siblings' faces, the family pet, certain foods, and so on. This is evidence of developing visual analysis skills—of attentiveness to certain identifying concrete visual characteristics—but hardly sufficient for school demands.

By the time he is three years old, the average child will be able to discriminate accurately between a circle, a square, a plus sign, and a triangle; a red block and a green one. He will be able to identify matching pairs of shapes, point to a given shape on oral request, even name some of them correctly; again, evidence of further visual perceptual skills (and language) development, but not yet to the level required by school. The normal, average three-year-old who can do all these things will not yet be able to copy geometric designs more complicated than a single line, oriented vertically, horizontally, or as a circle.

Why is that? Certainly not because he cannot see other designs accurately or clearly; his behaviors refute that argument. Neither should it be attributed to his fine-motor development. True, that may be a factor, but it is rarely the cause of inadequate copying skills.

Then why? Simply stated, it is because seeing is not analogous to carrying out the analysis process that is required for copying something. All of us can recognize ourselves in the mirror. Very few of us can produce a true-to-life self-portrait. Why? Because producing an accurate self-portrait requires far more than seeing clearly; it requires identifying the key details that make up the face, and mapping out the precise spatial relationships among those details. Few people ever acquire the ability to produce an accurate self-portrait. However, most of us—certainly those who fall within the category of "normal"—acquire the ability to reproduce other, less complex designs as we grow and develop.

A number of school-readiness tests reflect this phenomenon by including an assessment of the child's ability to copy geometric designs of varying complexity. Natural development of visual analysis skills continues until around the child's eleventh birthday. Just as natural

---

*There is one important exception to this, mentioned earlier (in chapter 3): namely, significant farsightedness that is ignored, and lenses are not prescribed (and worn) until after age four. There is strong evidence that such children almost always display a delay in visual perceptual skills development.

physical growth stops in all of us at some generally predictable age, so, too, does this naturally developed ability to view concrete information analytically.

True, most individuals continue to acquire even more precise visual analysis skills during their adolescence and adulthood, but these are not the consequence of natural development. They are the product of education, of informal and formal experiences that expand their knowledge about a specific domain. The professional photographer, for example (or the professional "anything," be she cook or surgeon), sees things that those of us who do not share her vocation miss. Are her basic visual perceptual skills better than ours? Probably not. What is better is her knowledge of photography (or cooking or surgery or whatever area she has become familiar with). This translates to her knowing far more than we do about what to look for under certain circumstances.

In other words, the *inclination to look for pertinent details*—details that facilitate the organization of information—is developed naturally; the *knowledge about what to look for* in complex environments is learned through experience.

TESTING VISUAL ANALYSIS SKILLS

There are a number of standardized visual analysis skills tests on the market. We will take an in-depth look at only one: the *Test of Visual Analysis Skills* (TVAS). This test is especially useful in that it provides information not only about the adequacy of a child's visual analysis skills—something all accepted visual perceptual skills tests do—but also about what to do if his skills are deficient and how to design an effective program of remediation. Before we get to the TVAS, however, it would be instructive to discuss visual analysis skills testing in general, and to identify characteristics that all well-accepted tests display.

Most tests of visual analysis skills—and there are many, for example, the *Gesell Copy Form Test*, the *Developmental Test of Visual Motor Integration* (VMI), the *Bender-Gestalt Visual Motor Test,* the *Rutgers Drawing Test*, the *Slosson Drawing Coordination Test*—involve copying geometric designs. Each test has its unique features, some good, some not so good. They differ in the designs they use (although some designs reappear in many tests) and how the child's drawings are scored.

Following are three designs that are often used in these tests: a triangle, an asterisk, and a diamond. As you see, they vary in complexity. The easiest one—the triangle—comprises a few lines with uncomplicated interrelationships; the most difficult one—the diamond—has more lines and more complex interrelationships.

Examples of Different Copying Responses

The figure below shows also how four different children of different ages are likely to respond to these three designs. Jane is the youngest; she was about fifty-four months old when she took the test. Joan is next youngest; she was sixty-three months old. Mike was a bit older at test-taking time, age seventy months; and Matt was the oldest of the bunch, age eighty months. Clearly, they were at different levels of visual analysis skills development, not because of a physical, emotional, or neuromotor deficit but rather simply because their developmental levels are in accord with their chronological ages.

Matt's drawings are obviously the best, but then, he is the oldest.

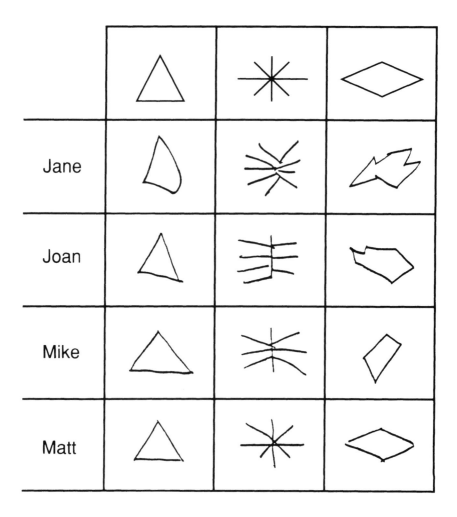

Mike's are next best and, not coincidentally, he is the next oldest. Then, in order of competency, come Joan and, finally, Jane. Jane's drawings are worse than the others but again, not because of a visual perceptual skills deficit but because she is the youngest. Her visual analysis skills are simply not as well developed.

Could these four children have been the same age—seventy-two months, say? Of course. But then our interpretations of their drawings would be different. Jane's drawings and Joan's drawings would be judged as inadequate; Mike, on the other hand, would be seen as developing as expected, while Matt would be judged as precocious.

How to Rule Out Faulty Perception

I stated earlier in this section that children who draw distorted designs do not really see them that way, but it helps for you to have some proof that this is really true.

Assuming that you have available some design-copying responses, select one that is noticeably worse than the model. Place beside it a second drawing that is very much like the model, and ask the child "Which of these two drawings [point to the one that looks like the model and then to the inaccurate one that he drew], looks like this?" (Point to the model.)

By age four, virtually every normal child will select the correct drawing, even though he produced the other one, and for good reason. He recognizes that his drawing is "wrong" but he does not know how to do it correctly.

How to Rule Out a Fine-Motor Skills Problem

Many children with visual perceptual skills deficits also have poor penmanship. Hence, it is logical to conclude that their faulty drawings are caused by deficient motor skills. In fact, that is rarely the case, but it is important to be able to make the distinction.

To do this, first identify one of the child's inaccurately executed drawings. Then show him how to copy that drawing one step (line) at a time. Select the line you want to start with. Draw it on the blank paper. Then ask the child to "make a line like this," and show him where to draw it. Then select a second line—one that relates in some way to the first line, a line that intersects the first one, say, or runs parallel to it.

Continue in this way, working through the pattern, step by step, line by line, having the child draw what you draw, pointing out to him details that he should be paying attention to as he does this.

Chances are he will execute a pretty good copy, one that is far better than his first effort. Why is that? It is because you relieved him of the burden of analyzing the pattern into its separate parts and mapping out their spatial interrelationships. You did this for him. All he had to do was exercise the proper fine-motor skills—draw the lines in their correct positions, one step at a time.

Another, even simpler way: analyze a pattern that the child had difficulty copying, figuring out the different orientations of the lines. Then, draw dots (or *x*'s) on your paper in positions that represent those orientations and have the child simply draw a line from one dot (or *x*) to the other. If he can draw lines in all of the orientations, then you will have to admit that his fine-motor skills are not all that bad.

Drawbacks of Most Copying Tests

Earlier in this section, I named a number of standardized copying tests but pointed out that although all of them are useful in *identifying* the child with deficient visual analysis skills, only one provides information about *how to help him overcome the deficit*. We should therefore now look at the test that provides this kind of information.

THE TEST OF VISUAL ANALYSIS SKILLS

The TVAS, in addition to identifying children with deficient visual analysis skills, provides information about how to remediate the deficient skills by defining what the children have to learn. We can help the child by teaching him to "pass the test."

That is the unique feature of the TVAS. All the other tests become invalid if you teach the child to pass them. For example, if you set about teaching a seven-year-old child who cannot copy a diamond how to do it, you will probably succeed. He is likely to learn how to copy a diamond. But you certainly cannot conclude from that accomplishment that he has also learned the underlying processes needed to copy all shapes of that complexity. Just because a child learns to copy a diamond, and copying a diamond is something expected of seven-year-olds, does not indicate that he has acquired the visual analysis skills of the average seven-year-old.

The opposite is true of the TVAS. As you teach the child to copy patterns like those used in the test, you will be teaching him underlying processes—visual analysis skills. And he will illustrate his gains in the TVAS and all of the other copying tests.

Instructions for administering the TVAS and interpreting the scores are given below. Instructions for using this information in a remediation program are in chapter 8.

Administering the Test

All you need are the test patterns (see pp. 34–38), a sheet of clear acetate, a felt-tip (washable) pen or a crayon, and a tissue. In order to administer the test, redraw the patterns on two-inch squares (see p. 171).

The Test Items

The TVAS consists of eighteen items—geometric designs that are positioned on dot matrices ("maps"). The child's task in the first nine items is to copy the designs onto a matching map. In items ten through eighteen: to copy the designs onto maps in which some (and ultimately, all) of the dots have been removed.

As such, the items differ (and become more difficult) on the basis of the complexity of the design, the number of dots in the map on which the design has been positioned, and the number of dots on the map where the child is to copy the design. The importance of these three pieces of information will become apparent when we discuss remediation in chapter 8.

Start with item one on page 34. It presents two five-dot maps, with a rather simple design plotted on one of the maps. The child's job is to copy that design onto the other five-dot map.

Place a sheet of clear acetate over the five-dot map on which the child is to draw. Seat the child at a suitably sized table, give him the felt-tip pen (or crayon) and ask him to "Make your map [point to the map on which he is to draw] look like this one." (Point to the map on which the design is printed.)

When he is done, check his work. (Do not coach him; if he makes an error, leave it be.) Did he draw the correct number of lines? Are the lines positioned on the correct dots? (His lines need not be precise as though drawn with a ruler, nor need they intersect each of the dots. It is sufficient that his drawing shows that he has identified the correct number of lines and that he knows which dots those lines interconnect. Lines that fail to touch a designated dot but come close enough to indicate that the child intended to draw the line through it, are sufficient. Examples of "pass" and "fail" items are shown in the diagrams on page 39.)

Make a note of whether his copy was correct or incorrect, erase his drawing from the acetate sheet, and position it for use with item two. Be noncommittal with the child about his performance. Say things such as "okay" rather than "right" or "wrong."

Score his performance on item two as either correct or incorrect, and, *unless both items one and two were done incorrectly,* go on to item three.

Notice that item three uses nine-dot maps. The procedure remains

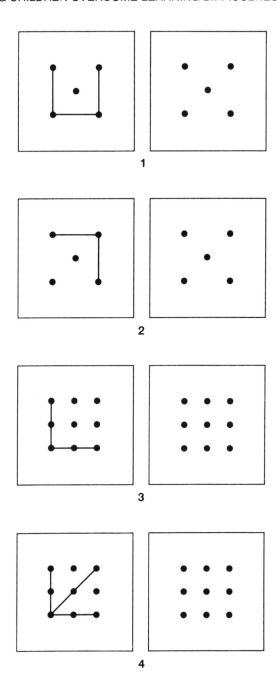

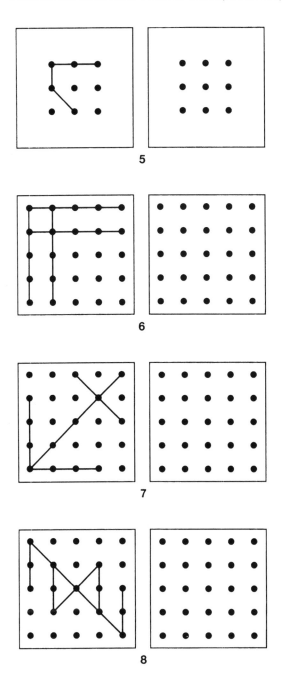

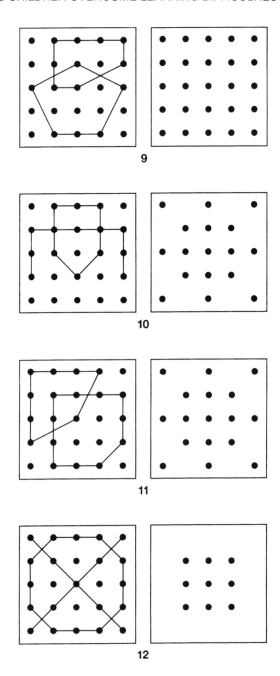

9

10

11

12

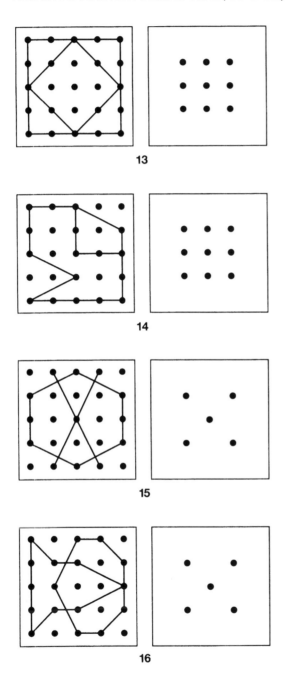

13

14

15

16

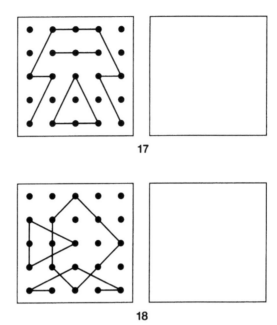

17

18

the same, however. When the child has completed his drawing, score the item and again, *unless he has committed two successive errors,* go on to the next item (item four). Continue in this way until the child has "failed" two successive items or has gotten to item ten.

The instructions change slightly with item ten. The child is now asked to "Copy this design [point to it] here [point to the seventeen-dot map], but notice that some of the dots are missing on your map. Don't draw in the missing dots; just pretend [or 'imagine'] that the dots are there, and draw the lines as though the dots were there."

The test stops when the child has failed two successive items, or completed all items. (In scoring items ten through eighteen, apply the same criteria as with items one through nine, with the additional concern that the child's drawing is positioned reasonably accurately—in other words, "as though the dots were there.")

Sample Scoring

Shown on the following page are four responses, labeled *A, B, C,* and *D.*

A shows a child's incorrect response to test item seven. Can you see why it is incorrect? All the lines are there, but some are positioned on the wrong dots. *B* is a correct response to item nine. All the lines are there, and even though they are not drawn precisely, it is obvious that

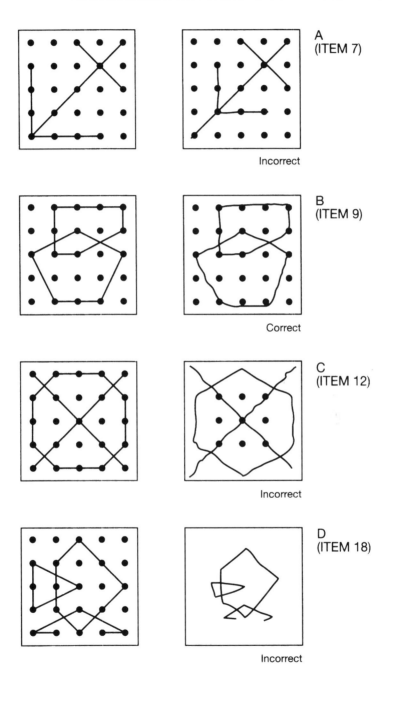

A
(ITEM 7)

Incorrect

B
(ITEM 9)

Correct

C
(ITEM 12)

Incorrect

D
(ITEM 18)

Incorrect

the child was able to identify the correct number of lines and their proper positions on the map. *C* is an incorrect response to item twelve. Although all the lines are there, some are positioned incorrectly—you have to pretend the dots are there when you assess the child's performance. Finally, look at *D*. It is an incorrect response to item eighteen because it, too, is not positioned correctly, even though all the lines are there and the shape is drawn accurately.

Interpreting the Test Results

Scoring the items is not that confusing if you keep in mind what is being tested—the child's ability to analyze a pattern into its separate parts, to read a map of dots, and to construct a map even after most of its landmarks (dots) have been removed.

Now you have to determine whether the child's performance is adequate for his grade level. What is the *number* of the last item he copied correctly before he produced two successive incorrect responses? That is his score on the TVAS.

For example, suppose he copied items one, two, three, and four correctly, but was incorrect on items five and six. His TVAS score would therefore be four. Try another: suppose he copied items one, two, and three correctly, was incorrect on four, correct again on five and six, and incorrect on items seven and eight. The test ends with item eight (two successive incorrect responses) and his TVAS score is six. Now relate his TVAS score to the following chart.

To read the chart, find the child's score in the left-hand column. Opposite that number is the grade level of children who customarily earn this score on the TVAS. For example, if the child's score is five, he performed like a kindergarten child. If, in fact, he is in kindergarten, you can assume that his visual perceptual skills are developing at a normal rate. If he is only in preschool, he is doing better than expected. If, on the other hand, he is in first grade or beyond, you can conclude that his visual perceptual skills are below what they should be and are contributing to his school learning problem. (Ignore, for the present, the third column on that chart. We will come back to it later, when we discuss how to help a child develop better visual analysis skills [chapter 8.])

More Difficult Items for Older Children?

Many people question whether there should not be some more difficult items, items that would challenge fourth graders and above, for example. It is really not necessary. Once a child can respond accurately to the final items on this test, you may assume that his visual perceptual skills are as good as natural development typically provides. In a sense, looking for a

TVAS Score	Expected for Children in:	Level
1	Preschool	1
2	Preschool	2
3	Kindergarten	3
4	Kindergarten	3
5	Kindergarten	4
6	Kindergarten	4
7	Kindergarten	4
8	Grade 1	4
9	Grade 1	5
10	Grade 1	5
11	Grade 2	6
12	Grade 2	6
13	Grade 2	6
14	Grade 2	7
15	Grade 2	7
16	Grade 2	8
17	Grade 3	8
18	Grade 3	completed

more difficult visual perceptual skills test is like looking for something other than a standard measuring device to determine the height of an adult who stopped growing while in his teens.

Achieving full development on the TVAS also indicates that the child's visual perceptual skills are as good as they need be for making satisfactory progress in a standard instructional setting. That does not mean a child who scores eighteen on the TVAS could not be having difficulty in school-related subjects. He could indeed, especially if he developed these analysis skills "behind schedule." But if that is the case, he will be better served if you deal with his problem in the subject areas themselves—reading, spelling, arithmetic, and writing—rather than by trying to teach him more elaborate perceptual skills. This is discussed more thoroughly in chapters 11, 12, and 13.

What next? If the child's performance on the TVAS is not at an expected level, make a note of what he did score. We will discuss how this affects this school achievement and what to do about it later. Right now, we can move on to other, less formal ways of evaluating a child's visual perceptual skills.

Informal Assessment of a Child's Visual Analysis Skills

In most cases, formal testing to identify a lag in visual perceptual skills development is not really necessary. In practical terms, anyone can "test" an elementary school child's visual perceptual skills by observing him devise and execute strategies for working through tasks that require step-by-step interrelated actions and then comparing his performance to others his age.

For example:

• With an elementary school-age child: copying a set of arithmetic problems onto a unlined sheet of paper.

• With kindergarten children: completing a jigsaw puzzle; coloring a picture.

• With preschool children: building a tower of blocks or simply returning toys and other objects to their designated storage spaces.

The child who engages in these or similar activities in a disorganized manner (as compared with other children his age) will almost invariably demonstrate visual perceptual skills deficits on formal testing.

AUDITORY ANALYSIS SKILLS

Just as with visual analysis skills, the normal child will begin to develop fairly sophisticated auditory analysis skills very early in life. He will recognize certain sound patterns—his mother's voice, the family dog's bark, and so on—well before his first birthday.

This is evidence of developing auditory analysis skills, of attentiveness to certain identifying concrete acoustical characteristics. The average three-year-old has no difficulty demonstrating the ability to make precise discriminations of sound differences. He responds correctly to such words as, *go, no, toe, grow, blow,* and so on, and he uses them correctly in conversation.

Yet another three years will probably have to go by before he is able to demonstrate an understanding of the fact that spoken words not only have meaning they also consist of concrete sensory components (sounds) that are independent of semantics. Being able to identify these sensory components and their relative position in spoken words is evidence of auditory analysis skills.

Auditory analysis skills, like visual analysis skills, normally develop on a reasonably predictable schedule. If the child can hear and speak normally and is in an environment that provides reasonable stimulation, if the child is not deprived of the experiences of exploring these stimuli—listening to and saying words, rearranging sounds (as in rhyming, etc.)—and if, again, the child has never had the misfortune of experiencing central nervous system damage, then his auditory perceptual skills will develop. It is yet another characteristic of our species; it is part of our genetic makeup. There is one significant exception to this: children who suffer chronic middle ear infections during their preschool years. They seem to be more at risk to delays in the development of auditory perceptual skills. The speculation is that the delay is due to the sporadic hearing impairment these children experience when fluid accumulates behind the eardrum. The impairment disappears as the chronic infections subside, but they leave their mark on the child.

Like visual perceptual skills, full natural development of auditory analysis skills is achieved sometime around age eleven. True, many individuals continue to develop even more precise auditory analysis skills during their adolescence and adult years, but these are not the consequence of natural development. They are the product of education, of informal and formal experiences that expand their knowledge about a specific domain.

Consider, for example, the professional musician. She hears things that those of us who do not share her vocation miss. Are her naturally developed auditory perceptual skills better than ours? Probably not. What is better is her knowledge of music. This translates into her knowing far more than we do about what to listen for and when. Another example is the skilled, experienced mechanic. She hears things from an idling motor that few of us can detect, again not because of more acute hearing but rather because her experience in listening to motors has given her information we do not have.

TESTING AUDITORY ANALYSIS SKILLS

Some auditory perceptual skills tests investigate the ability to discriminate different nonverbal sounds, such as "dot" and "dash" signals, different pitches (high versus low), different volumes (loud versus soft), and so on. I do not believe that any of these are worth administering to the child with a learning disability. True, learning disabled children may very well have some extra difficulty with such tests, but that information is of no practical use unless you are concerned about the child entering a training program that requires that type of auditory discrimination.

If, as is most often the case, the concern is learning to read and spell, then the test to use is one that investigates the child's ability to analyze spoken words into what reading people call *phonemes*—sounds that can be represented by letters—and to map out the temporal interrelationships among those sounds.

We will look at two such tests: first, the *Wepman Auditory Discrimination Test*, which has been around for some time and is often used by school diagnosticians. Hence, it may very well be cited in a report about a child you are interested in. The second test, the *Test of Auditory Analysis Skills*, is newer and comes closer to testing what needs to be tested. Directions for giving it follow.

The Wepman Auditory Discrimination Test

The Wepman Auditory Discrimination Test consists of forty pairs of words that are pronounced for the child who in turn must indicate whether the two words that constitute the pair were the *same* or *different*. Thirty of the pairs in the test are dissimilar in a specific way, the other ten pairs are identical. For example, the child is asked to say whether the spoken words *pat* and *pit* are the same or different, or the words *than* and *van*, or the words *boy* and *boy*. (None of these were taken from the Wepman test; they are used here simply to illustrate the concept.) Wepman's research showed that children make fewer errors on his list of forty pairs of words as they develop from kindergarten age to about fifth grade level. Therefore, the child's performance is based on the number of errors committed as compared with the number of errors expected from someone of his age.

The test is useful (good readers score better on it than do poor readers), but it has two drawbacks: (1) the young child (kindergartner/ first grader) tends to stop listening before all forty pairs of words have been spoken, thereby leaving the tester in a quandary as to whether the child was unable to perform or simply lost interest; (2) the test does not adequately probe the child's analysis skills. Identifying similarities and differences in spoken words is similar to identifying similarities and differences in drawn patterns. It really depends on how similar or different the pairs are. It is not unlike the example offered in the previous section that compared the relative difficulty of identifying a self-portrait to executing one yourself. I therefore recommend a different test, the TAAS.

THE TEST OF AUDITORY ANALYSIS SKILLS

The TAAS gets closer to what we are interested in: the child's ability to identify the separate sounds in spoken words and the temporal sequence of those sounds. It does this by asking the child to delete sounds and to show that he can do this by voicing what is left after the deletion. My research (and the research of other investigators who have examined this test over the past twenty years) shows that children are first able to grasp this concept at about age four, and become better at it from then on.

Administering the TAAS

The TAAS starts at a relatively simple level; it can be used with kindergarten (and some preschool) children.

Item	Question	Correct Response
A	Say **cowboy**	Now say it again, but don't say **boy**	**cow**
B	Say **steamboat**	Now say it again, but don't say **steam**	**boat**
1	Say **sunshine**	Now say it again, but don't say **shine**	**sun**
2	Say **picnic**	Now say it again, but don't say **pic**	**nic**
3	Say **cucumber**	Now say it again, but don't say **(q)**	**cumber**
4	Say **coat**	Now say it again, but don't say **/k/** (the k sound)	**oat**
5	Say **meat**	Now say it again, but don't say **/m/** (the m sound)	**eat**
6	Say **take**	Now say it again, but don't say **/t/** (the t sound)	**ache**
7	Say **game**	Now say it again, but don't say **/m/**	**gay**
8	Say **wrote**	Now say it again, but don't say **/t/**	**row**
9	Say **please**	Now say it again, but don't say **/z/**	**plea**
10	Say **clap**	Now say it again, but don't say **/k/**	**lap**
11	Say **play**	Now say it again, but don't say **/p/**	**lay**
12	Say **stale**	Now say it again, but don't say **/t/**	**sale**
13	Say **smack**	Now say it again, but don't say **/m/**	**sack**

Demonstration Items

The first two items of the test (items *A* and *B*) are for demonstration, for familiarizing the child with the test. For example, item *A* asks the child to "Say 'steamboat,'" and then, once he has said it (thereby demonstrating that he heard and remembers it, at least for the moment), "Now say it again, but this time don't say 'boat'; just say what's left." The average four-year-old can do this—delete a syllable from a two-syllable, compound word.

If the child does not understand the task, try teaching it to him in the following way:

1. Have the child extend his two hands forward.

2. Repeat the item slowly, emphasizing the two separate syllables (by pausing between them).

3. Touch his left hand as you say the first syllable ("steam") and his right hand as you say the second syllable ("boat"), thereby giving him a visual/spatial reference point for each of the syllables.

4. If he is still unable to comprehend the task, explain to him that "this hand" (touch his left hand) "says 'steam,'" and "this hand" (touch his right hand) "says 'boat.'"

5. Then repeat the item: "Say 'steamboat.'" (Again, touch each hand as you say its syllable.) Then, after he has said "steamboat": "Now

say it again, but leave off 'boat.' Just say what's left.'' (As you say these last two sentences, move his right hand to his side, allowing only the left hand to extend forward.)

If your teaching efforts work, then go on with the test. If it fails to teach him the concept, simply accept the fact that the test is too demanding, that he has not yet developed the basic auditory analysis skills that four-year-olds are normally able to display.

If the child understands the test, as illustrated by his being able to answer items *A* and *B* correctly, you can begin formal testing with item one. This item, like the two demonstration items, asks the child to delete one syllable from a two-syllable, compound word.

If the child does not respond to an item once you have gotten past the demonstration words, repeat the item once but *do not teach*—all teaching must be limited to the demonstration items.

To Score the TAAS

If item one is passed, go on to item two, and continue testing until the child has failed two successive items. His score is the number of the last correct item.

For example, if the child passes items one, two, and three, then fails item four, passes items five and six, then fails items seven and eight, the test stops and his score is recorded as six.

Interpreting the Test Results

Now you have to determine whether the child's performance on the TAAS was adequate for his grade level. The grade-equivalent chart that follows enables you to do this.

To read the chart, find the child's TAAS score in the left-hand column. Opposite that number is the grade level of children who customarily earn this score on the TAAS. For example, if the child's score is six, we would expect him to be in first grade. If, in fact, he is in first grade, you can assume that his auditory perceptual skills are developing at a normal rate. If he is only in kindergarten, he is probably precocious. If, on the other hand, he is in second grade or beyond, you can assume that his auditory perceptual skills are below the expected level and are contributing to his school learning problem.

As you can see from the chart, no item in the TAAS—not even the final ones—should be too difficult for a child in the third grade or above. (Once again, ignore the third column for the time being, we will come back to it when we discuss remediation in chapter 8.)

TAAS Score	Expected for Children in:	Level
1	Kindergarten	1
2	Kindergarten	2
3	Kindergarten	2
4	Grade 1	3
5	Grade 1	3
6	Grade 1	3
7	Grade 1	4
8	Grade 1	4
9	Grade 1	4
10	Grade 2	5
11	Grade 2	5
12	Grade 3	6
13	Grade 3	completed

More Difficult Items for Older Children?

As with visual analysis skills, many people seek auditory perceptual skills tests with items that might challenge children who are beyond third grade. Again the answer is that there is no need for such tests. Once a child can respond accurately to the final items on the TAAS, his auditory perceptual skills are as good as they need be for making satisfactory progress in a standard instructional setting, and as good as natural development typically provides.

This does not mean that a child who completed all the items of the TAAS could not learn more complex auditory analysis skills. However, this would require instruction in a specific context; the skills would not be found in the average normal child. They would be activity-specific, such as learning the concept of meter as it relates to poetry.

Informal Assessment of a Child's Auditory Analysis Skills

Although formal testing of auditory analysis skills is needed in order to make decisions regarding treatment, it may not be necessary for detecting the problem. In essence, you can "test" a child's auditory perceptual skills by observing him do the following things, and then comparing his performance to others his age.

• Early kindergarten children: repeat a list of unfamiliar or nonsense (or foreign) polysyllabic words. Pay attention to how accurately he repeats the syllable order (e.g., *carpuntelon; strackontay; misconskany*).

• End-of-kindergarten children: identify rhyming words.

• Primary grade children: identify (from a list of spoken words) those words that contain a specific sound (located in the initial, final, or medial position) and generate words (from memory) that contain a specific sound; e.g., "Say some words that begin with the /t/ sound; that end with the /g/ sound; that have an /a/ sound in them," and so on.

• All children: listen for misarticulations; these frequently signal auditory analysis skills deficits. (If in doubt about the clarity of a child's speech, seek the advice of a qualified speech/language specialist.)

The child who engages in these (or similar) activities in an inept manner (as compared to other children his age) will almost invariably demonstrate auditory perceptual skills deficits on formal testing.

TESTS OF VISUAL AND AUDITORY MEMORY AND FIGURE-GROUND DISCRIMINATION: ARE THEY NECESSARY?

I do not believe such tests provide any additional, useful information. They do nothing more than investigate the child's (auditory and visual) analysis skills and knowledge base in different ways. They do not tell us anything that can be translated into treatment.

Think about it for a moment. The typical visual memory test consists of looking at something (a picture, a geometric design, etc.) and then demonstrating recall of it a bit later by drawing it, identifying it again upon presentation, or describing it. Performance is then compared with what others of the same age have been found to be able to do. When one performs below the level expected for his age in this kind of test, the popular interpretation is that he is not as good as he should be in remembering what he sees.

The typical auditory memory test consists of listening to something (a sequence of spoken numerals, a list of unrelated words, a meaningful sentence, etc.) and then demonstrating recall of it by repeating it. Once again, performance is then compared with what has shown to be typical of others of the same age. When a child performs below the level expected for his age in this kind of test, the popular interpretation is that he is not as good as he should be in remembering what he hears.

These interpretations inevitably lead to such labels as "visual learner" and "auditory learner" and inferences about how best to teach someone with substandard visual or auditory memory via their ears or their eyes.

I will have more to say about this (incorrect) concept later on (see chapter 10); for the present, let us limit our discussion to the links between visual and auditory analysis skills and visual and auditory memory tests. To demonstrate a "good" visual memory (to do well on the test), one has to

• Identify key features (features that can facilitate recall) of what he is looking at.

• Identify and apply a strategy for not confusing those key features that are potentially ambiguous (e.g., the lowercase *b* or *d*, an arrow pointing in a specific direction, a diagonal line contained within a square). Sometimes this strategy will have to be invented spontaneously; sometimes it will be one that is already well established; for example, the best strategy for remembering the *b* is to be securely familiar with its name, the best strategy for remembering the orientation of an arrow is to know words that accurately describe it (e.g., *up, down, north, east, left, right,* etc.).

To have a good "visual" memory, one must first be able to determine what details to pay attention to and then be able to employ effective strategies for labeling those details in an unambiguous, memorable fashion. The first of these is accurately identified as competent perceptual (sometimes visual, sometimes auditory) skills; the latter, as acquired knowledge.

To demonstrate a good "auditory" memory (to do well on the test), one has to

• Identify the key features (features that can facilitate recall) of what he is listening to.

• Identify and apply a strategy for not confusing those key features that are potentially ambiguous (e.g., the order in a sequence of numerals; the spelling, or function, or some other common feature in a sequence of single words; the syntax and meaning of the spoken sentence).

Sometimes this strategy will have to be invented spontaneously; sometimes it will be one that is already well established. For example, one effective strategy for remembering a sequence of numerals is to identify a spatial pattern in the sequence (e.g., 1, 3, 5, 7); or a similarity to an already known sequence (e.g., a familiar phone number, a work-related formula); or to attach spatial designations to them (e.g., an imagined stairway on which zero belongs on the bottom step, nine on the top step, and so on).

To have good "auditory" memory (as measured on this type of test), one must first be able to determine what details to pay attention to and then be able to label those details in an unambiguous, memorable fashion. The first of these is accurately identified as competent perceptual (sometimes visual, sometimes auditory) skills; the latter, as acquired knowledge.

The point: memory of what you see and what you hear is not analogous to taking a photograph or recording something on audiotape. It is a product of seeing *and* listening analytically and applying what you know in ways that enable you to do what the test requires.

Figure-Ground Tests

The typical visual figure-ground test consists of a picture in which a specified figure is embedded in a background that tends to hide the figure and distract the looker (e.g., a geometric design embedded in a larger, more complex geometric design; a drawing of a human figure embedded in a larger drawing that contains a variety of familiar shapes; a small animal hidden in a dense forest).

To demonstrate capable visual figure-ground discrimination skills (to do well on the test), one has to

• Identify key features in the "figure" (features that can facilitate identification of what is to be looked for (e.g., the number and nature of the angles in a geometric design; the size, shape, and orientation of the small animal, etc.).

• Label these features in a way that enables their recall during the search (e.g., name the design or the animal and—if important—estimate its size).

• Conduct an orderly search for those key features; an inspection that reflects efficient visual analysis skills rather than random behavior that is influenced by the distractors in the background.

To have good visual figure-ground discrimination skills one must first be able to determine what details to look for, then label those features for retention, and then employ effective strategies for carrying out the search. The first and last of these are accurately identified as competent visual perceptual skills; the second as acquired knowledge—not exclusively visual, not exclusively auditory.

The typical auditory figure-ground test consists of listening to a recorded spoken message that is embedded in a noisy background that tends to distract the listener (e.g., cocktail party chatter, street traffic noises, etc.).

To demonstrate capable auditory figure-ground discrimination skills (to do well on the test), one has to

• Identify key features in the figure (features that can facilitate identification of what he is listening to, e.g., voice qualities; the meaning of the spoken message, thereby facilitating expectations of what is to be said next, etc.).

To have good auditory figure-ground discrimination skills one must first determine what to listen for and then be able to label these features in an unambiguous, memorable fashion. The first of these is accurately identified as competent auditory perceptual skills (but not necessarily those tested by the TAAS); the second, as acquired knowledge; not exclusively visual, not exclusively auditory.

The point is identification of something you see or hear that is embedded in a distracting background is not limited to what you see and what you hear. It is a product of seeing *and* listening analytically and then applying your existing knowledge in ways that enhance your ability to meet the requirements of the task.

5
EXPRESSIVE AND RECEPTIVE LANGUAGE ABILITIES

IN CHAPTER 4, we discussed a set of basic learning aptitudes (visual and auditory perceptual skills) that *develop* naturally at a predictable rate in all normal children, and influence strongly how well a child progresses in a standard instructional setting. At the end of that discussion, I stated that perceptual skills combine with one's existing knowledge to facilitate memory and figure-ground discrimination. Existing knowledge can be displayed three ways: IQ (especially the "verbal" items), achievement scores, and general language ability (the ability to understand and use spoken words effectively).

The first two have already been addressed. This chapter focuses on the third: expressive and receptive language and how it is tested. In doing this, we shift our concern from the child's basic analysis and organizational skills to his ability to comprehend and generate semantic information.

The central proposition of this book is that perceptual skills in combination with what the child already knows and how well he can express that knowledge constitutes the foundation upon which a successful school record is built. If both are lacking, the child will not do well in school and it will be explained by a below-average IQ, which is inevitable in such situations. If only one is lacking, the child will not make satisfactory progress in a standard school setting, but, because he will have an average IQ, he will be labeled learning disabled. If both are adequate, and if the factors identified in chapter 3 have been ruled out (i.e., physical, emotional, and neuromotor states), then there is no reason for a child to fall behind in a standard setting. And, in fact, he will not.

LANGUAGE

The dictionary defines *language* as "a systematic means of communicating ideas or feelings by the use of conventionalized signs, sounds, gestures, or marks having understood meaning." Most often, of course, when I use the word *language* here, I am referring to the spoken form or its translated written form.

The subject of language and its development is multifaceted and complex; it goes far beyond the scope of this book. Our discussion will be limited mainly to the kind of language children typically acquire during their preschool years, then expand and apply as they enter formal education.

Language Development and Acquisition

Just as all normal children are expected—indeed, genetically programmed—to develop naturally the analytic abilities we call perceptual skills, so, too, are they programmed to develop the ability to understand and generate language. They are not, however, predestined to speak a specific language and to speak it well. That is determined not by normal growth and development but derived from the experiences they have following birth.

Regardless of where they live, normal children are likely to develop language abilities at a similar rate, babbling "mama," "dada," and other such sounds sometime between six to ten months, using sounds meaningfully a couple of months later, having a three- or four-word spoken vocabulary by their first birthday, doubling this by sixteen to eighteen months, naming pictures of familiar objects and of their major body parts by two years, and so on.

Children do differ, however—some speak earlier, some later—and adults respond to these differences. When a child converses easily, people are inclined to converse with him. They say meaningful things to him that they would not say to the less-verbal child. He responds initially by imitating what they say and later by reacting in various ways, all of which stimulates continued conversation. Thus the child who develops the ability to produce language early tends to get more stimulation toward learning the words of his language early. The opposite is true of the child whose speech development is delayed.

Clearly, a great deal of what we know about our world has come to us through the medium of language rather than through direct experience. Thus the child who becomes fluent in language usage early in life is apt to learn more information earlier than his laconic counterparts. And just as clearly, the child who knows more than average displays his knowledge and the "intelligence" this implies through his language.

All else being equal (including perceptual skills development), well-informed children do better in school than children who do not know very much. One reason is the well-informed child has more ways for organizing information and therefore better strategies for remembering information (e.g., by association, by employing classification strategies, etc.). The uninformed child often has to resort to rote memorization processes to retain information—surely, an inefficient and ineffective method. Hence—and as the Action Plan shows—an important question arises at this point in the process of deciding how to help the learning disabled child, namely, Is the child's present knowledge state (as demonstrated by his receptive and expressive language as well as his school achievement scores) within acceptable limits?

If the child's knowledge state is appropriate for his age, and if the physical, emotional, and neuromotor factors cited in chapter 3 have been ruled out, then the only deterrent to learning to read, write, spell, and do arithmetic *has to be* his substandard perceptual skills. If his knowledge state is inadequate, then the gap between what he should and does know must be reduced if there is to be reasonable hope for overcoming his learning problem, perceptual skills notwithstanding.

TESTING LANGUAGE DEVELOPMENT

Language development is usually tested by speech pathologists, known also as speech and language specialists or speech therapists. All school districts employ them to peform two roles: one, as speech therapists who detect and treat children with faulty enunciation (articulation) or fluency (stuttering) patterns; the other, as language specialists who help children expand their spoken vocabulary and their ability to understand and use language properly.

It would be presumptuous (and futile) for me to attempt to describe here how to conduct a thorough evaluation of a child's language abilities. It is not my specialty, and even if it were there is no need for a technical, detailed discussion of that sort in this kind of book. However, I will identify certain landmark behaviors that a nonprofessional can use as a means of informally investigating a child's language abilities.

The so-called test items listed below identify specific tasks and the ages at which the average child should be able to perform them. Unfortunately, the items stop at about age eight. The normal language abilities and knowledge status of children older than that are so broad and diverse that they cannot be reduced to this kind of format.

If the child you are concerned about is within the appropriate age range, try out the items listed below. If he responds correctly and easily, conclude that his knowledge base and related language abilities are probably within normal limits. If he does not respond correctly and easily, conclude the opposite and plan to do something about it. (See chapter 9.)

If his responses are neither unequivocally poor nor unambiguously good, then it is probably wise to take the cautious route and seek a professional opinion. This can be obtained from the speech and language specialist in your local school, from the speech/language department in a local children's hospital or university, or from a specialist who practices privately. (They are listed in the Yellow Pages of your telephone book.)

It is important to recognize that the "tests" described here are useful because they sample from the very large domain called oral language. The specific behaviors and knowledge they ask the child to display are not important in and of themselves. Teaching a child to pass these test items will not improve his basic learning ability very much. That can only occur if his store of general knowledge is increased.

The Test Items

If the child is two years old, he should be able to demonstrate an understanding of a substantial number of concrete words (action verbs, simple adjectives, prepositions, etc.) and speak some of those words clearly enough to be understood by someone who knows him well; his parents, for example, or his preschool teacher.

If the child is three to four years old, he should be able to respond to and use the following spoken words correctly:

1. *Eyes, ears, nose, mouth, hair, head, hand, fingers, arm, leg, toes, feet.* To test:
   a. *Tell me what this is called.* (point to his eyes, ears, etc.)
   b. *Touch* (or show me) *your eyes, ears, nose . . .*
2. *White, black.* To test, provide a black block and a white block, and say:
   a. *What color is this?* (point to black block, then to white block)
   b. *Give me* (or show me) *the white block. The black block.*
3. *Circle, square.* To test, show the child a drawing of a circle, square, triangle, plus sign, and say:
   a. *What is this called?* (point to circle, then the square)
   b. *Show me a square. A circle.*
4. *On, in, out.* To test, supply a white cube, a black cube, and a box with a removable lid. As the child watches, place a cube (e.g., the white one) in the box, put the lid on the box, place the other cube on the lid, and say:
   a. *Which block is in the box? On the box? Out of the box?*
   b. *Take the white block out of the box and put it on the lid. Put the black cube in the box.*
5. *Over, under, up, down.* To test, say:
   a. *Put your hand over mine.*
   b. *Which way am I pointing?* (point up)

    c. *Put your hand under mine.*
    d. *Which way am I pointing?* (point down)
  6. *Far, near.* To test, use two objects, e.g., one black cube, one white cube. Place one hand on the table surface, and say:
    a. *Put the white cube near my hand.*
    b. *Put the black cube far from my hand.*
    c. Then switch their positions and say, *Which block is near my hand?*
    d. *Which block is far from my hand now?*
  7. *Big, little.* To test, use two objects, one larger than the other, and say:
    a. *This one* (point) *is little. This one is* _____? (point)
    b. Rearrange the cubes and say *Which one is little?*
    c. *This one* (point) *is big. This one is* _____? (point)
    d. Rearrange the cubes and say, *Which one is big?*
  8. *Day, night.* To test, say:
    a. *When do you sleep?*
    b. *When do you eat breakfast?*
    c. *What do you do at night?*
    d. *What do you do in the morning?*
  9. Count two objects accurately? To test, show the child four objects (e.g., one-inch cubes), and say:
    a. *How many blocks are in my hand?* (show child two cubes, then one cube)
    b. *Give me one block. Two blocks.*

If the child is four to four and a half years old, he should be able to respond to and use the following spoken words correctly:
  1. *Chin, thumb, knee, teeth.*
    a. *Tell me what this is called.* (point to chin, etc.)
    b. *Show me your chin. Show me your thumb.* Your knee . . .
  2. *Yellow, blue, green, red.* To test, show the child four colored objects (e.g., one-inch cubes), one for each of the colors listed.
    a. *Give me a red block. A green block.*
    b. *What color is this block?* (point to each of the cubes in turn)
  3. *Draw a circle around; cross out.* To test, show the child a drawing of a circle and one of an *X*, and say:
    a. *What is this called?* (point to circle) *And this one?* (point to *X*)
    b. *Draw a circle around the X.*
    c. *Draw an X over the circle.*
  4. *Front, back, top, bottom.* To test, show child a three-block stack, each a different color (e.g., yellow, white, green).
    a. *This is the front of the block.* (point) *This is the* _____.

     b. *This block is on top.* (point) *This one* (point to bottom block) *is on the* _____.
     c. *This is the back of the block. (point)* This is the _____.
     d. *This block is on the bottom.* (point) *This one* (point) *is on the* _____.
     e. *Stand in front of me.*
     f. *Show me the top block.*
     g. *Point to the back of the room.*
     h. *Show me the bottom block.*

   5. *Behind, above, beside, below, next to, in front of.* To test, show the child two blocks in different orientations, each cube a different color (e.g., one blue, the other yellow).
     a. *The blocks are in front of you.* (now hold blocks behind child's back) *Now they are* _____ *you.*
     b. *The blue block is below the yellow one. The yellow one is* _____ *the blue one.* (place yellow block on blue block)
     c. *Put the blue block beside the yellow one.*
     d. *Put the yellow block below the blue one.*
     e. *Put the blue block next to the yellow one.*

   6. *Middle, center, corner.* To test, fold a sheet of paper into quarters; then unfold and say:
     a. *This is an edge.* (point) (now point to center of paper) *This is the* _____.
     b. *Show me the center of this paper.*
     c. *This is the center of the paper.* (point) (now point to one of the corners) *This is a* _____.
     d. *This is a corner.* (point) *Show me another corner.*

   7. *Short, long.* To test, show the child two sticks (or two drawn lines), one distinctly shorter than the other.
     a. *This stick* (or line) *is short.* (point) *This one* (point) *is* _____.
     b. (rearrange the sticks/lines) *Show me the short stick.*
     c. *This stick* (or line) *is long.* (point) *This one* (point) *is* _____.
     d. (rearrange the sticks/lines) *Show me the long stick.*

   8. Count three objects accurately. To test, show child five objects (e.g., one-inch cubes) organized into two clusters, one comprising three blocks, the other two blocks.
     a. *How many blocks are in this bunch?* (point to three-block cluster)
     b. *Give me two blocks. Three blocks.*

If the child is four and a half to five years old, he should be able to respond to and use the following spoken words correctly:
   1. *Elbow, wrist, chest, back, stomach, neck, ankle.*

    a. *Tell me what this is called.* (point to child's elbow, wrist, etc.)

    b. *Touch your ankle. Stomach. Wrist.*

2. *More, less, too many, too few, enough.* To test, show the child five blocks, organized into two towers—one of three blocks, the other of two blocks.

    a. *This tower has more blocks.* (point) *This one* (point) *has* _____.

    b. *Make this tower* (point to shorter one) *look just like this one.* (point to other tower) *I have two blocks here. Do you need more? Less? Do you have enough? Too many? Not enough?*

    c. *I built this tower with three blocks.* (two cubes remain on table) *Do you have enough blocks to make one just like it?*

3. *Same, different.* To test, show the child four blocks (or other suitable objects)—two that are identical (e.g., same color), and two that are distinctly different from each other (one black, the other white).

    a. *These two are the same color.* (point) *These two are* _____.

    b. (rearrange objects) *Show me two that are different in color* (or size).

    c. *These two are different.* (point) *These two are the* _____.

    d. (rearrange blocks) *Show me two that are the same.*

4. *First, second, third, last.* To test, procure four cubes, each a different color (e.g., yellow, red, blue, green) and say *I am going to put these blocks in a line. I'll start with the yellow one, then the blue one, then the red one, then the green one.* (position blocks as you say this)

    a. *This one was first.* (point to yellow cube) *This one was* _____. (point to blue one)

    b. *If this one was first* (yellow one), *then this one* (point to last cube) *was* _____.

    c. *If the blue one was second, then this one* (point to red cube) *was* _____.

    d. *This one was second.* (point) *This one was* _____. (point to first cube)

5. *Too big, too little.* To test, obtain a container (e.g., jar, drinking glass) and three lids—one too large, one too small, and the third a good fit.

    a. *This lid is too big.* (point) *This one is* _____. (point to lid that is too little)

    b. *Show me the lid that is just right.*

    c. (rearrange lids) *Show me the lid that is too big.*

    d. (rearrange lids) *Show me the lid that is too little.*

6. Child counts five objects accurately. To test, procure eight objects (e.g., one-inch cubes).

    a. *How many blocks do I have in my hand?* (show five blocks)

    b. *How many do I have now?* (show four blocks)

    c. *Give me five blocks.*
    d. *Give me four blocks.*
  7. Count by rote from one to ten.
    a. *Let me hear you count from one to ten. I'll get you started: one, two, three . . .*

If the child is five to five and a half years old, he should be able to respond to and use the following spoken words correctly:
  1. *Triangle, rectangle.* To test, show child drawings of a triangle, a rectangle, an *X*, and a square, and say:
    a. *What is this called?* (point to triangle)
    b. *What is this called?* (point to rectangle)
  2. *Right, left*
    a. *Show me your right* (or left) *hand.*
    b. *What is this hand called?* (point to hand not used in first item)
    (Note: Do not expect child to understand that the right hand of someone facing him is opposite to his left hand; this awareness does not usually come until age seven.)
  3. *Before, after, next.* To test, obtain four cubes, each a different color (e.g., red, yellow, green, blue), and say: *Watch me put these blocks in a row.* (construct row of cubes in this order: red, yellow, green, blue)
    a. *Which one did I put down after this one?* (point to third [green] cube)
    b. *Which one did I put down before this one?* (point to second [yellow] cube)
    c. *I put this one down first.* (point) *Which one is next?*
  4. *Short, shorter, long, longer, tall, taller.* To test, construct four block towers—tower one with two cubes; tower two with three cubes; tower three with six cubes; tower four with eight cubes.
    a. *This one* (point to tower one) *is short. This one* (tower three) *is* _____.
    b. *This one* (point to tower three) *is tall. This one* (tower four) *is* _____.
    c. *This one* (tower three) *is tall. This one* (tower two) *is* _____.
    d. *This one* (tower two) *is short. This one* (tower one) *is* _____.
    e. (Remove all but towers three and four. Rearrange the blocks as rows, one consisting of six cubes, the other of eight cubes.) *This one* (point to shorter row) *is long. This one is* _____.
  5. Name at least three animals in addition to *dog.*
    a. *Can you name some animals? I'll start you. A dog is an animal. What others can you think of?*
  6. Count up to ten objects accurately. To test, show the child ten objects (e.g., blocks, pennies, etc.).

a. *How many blocks* (pennies, etc.) *are on the table?*
b. *Give me six. Eight. Seven. Nine.*

If the child is five and a half to six years old, he should be able to respond to and use the following spoken words correctly:

1. *Wide, narrow, thick, thin.* To test, obtain two objects that are similar, but vary in width (e.g., two sticks).

 a. *This one* (point) *is wide. This one is* _____.
 b. (rearrange sticks) *Show me the thick stick.*
 c. (rearrange sticks) *This one is narrow.* (point) *This one is* _____.
 d. (rearrange sticks) *Show me the thin stick.*

2. *Begin, end.* To test, obtain a pencil and a sheet of paper, and say to the child, *Watch me draw a line.* (draw vertical line on the paper)

 a. *This is where the line begins.* (point) *This is where it* _____.
 b. *Show me where the line begins.*
 c. *Here is the end of this line.* (point) *This is where it* _____.
 d. *Show me where the line ends.*

3. *Near/far, first/last, before/after, long/short.*

 a. *Some things are long. Others are* _____.
 b. *Some things are near. Others are* _____.
 c. *The person who wins a race comes in first. The one who is at the end comes in* _____.
 d. *Breakfast comes before lunch. Dinner comes* _____ *lunch.*

4. *Biggest, smallest, longest, largest, shortest.* To test, show the child four objects, each a different size (e.g., four pieces of paper).

 a. *This one is biggest. This one is* _____.
 b. *This one is longest. This one is* _____.
 c. *This one is largest. This one is* _____.
 d. (rearrange objects) *Show me the smallest.*
 e. (rearrange objects) *Show me the shortest.*

5. Child identifies three parts (for each) of a person, a house, and a dog.

 a. *Name* (or tell me) *three parts of a person.* (If prompt is needed, add: *I'll start you: people have feet. What else?)*
 b. *Name three parts of a house.*
 c. *Name three parts of a dog.*

6. Child solves single-digit addition and subtraction problems, using counters, if necessary; total quantities no greater than six.

Addition problems:

$$1 + 2 = ? \qquad 3 + 3 = ? \qquad 4 + 1 = ?$$
$$2 + 1 = ? \qquad 1 + 3 = ? \qquad 1 + 5 = ?$$
$$2 + 3 = ? \qquad 3 + 1 = ? \qquad 5 + 1 = ?$$
$$3 + 2 = ? \qquad 1 + 4 = ? \qquad 2 + 4 = ?$$

Subtraction problems:

2 − 1 = ?	2 − 2 = ?	3 − 3 = ?
3 − 1 = ?	4 − 3 = ?	5 − 4 = ?
4 − 1 = ?	4 − 2 = ?	5 − 3 = ?
6 − 5 = ?	5 − 2 = ?	6 − 3 = ?

To test, obtain two paper plates, each a different color (e.g., red, blue), and ten objects (buttons, pennies, etc.). Place one counter on one plate (e.g., the red one) and one counter on the other plate (e.g., the blue one), and say

  a. *How many buttons are on the red plate? How many are on the blue plate? Add the buttons on this plate* (the red one) *to this one* (the blue one). *Now how many buttons are there on this* (blue) *plate?* (Explain more thoroughly, if necessary.)

If the child is six to seven years old, he should be able to use and respond to the following words appropriately:

1. *Sharp, dull, straight, curved.*
2. *Hard, soft, heavy, light.*
3. Name the days of the week.
4. Solve addition and subtraction problems involving quantities between six and ten, using counters if necessary.
5. State the number that immediately follows or precedes any stated number from eleven to one hundred.
6. Identify the following money correctly: *quarter, dollar.*
7. Print any/all capital and lowercase manuscript letters from dictation.

If the child is seven to eight years old, he should be able to:

1. Read a relatively simple floor plan or map.
2. Measure relatively short distances (ten feet or less), using a one-foot ruler.
3. State the number that immediately follows or precedes any stated number from 101 to 1,000.
4. Respond correctly to:
   a. How many minutes are there in one hour?
   b. How many hours are there in a day?
   c. How many days are there in a year?

If the child is over eight years old, reliable assessment can no longer be reduced to the ability to respond correctly to a limited set of questions that probe general knowledge. With children this age, try any or all of the following four methods:

1. Have the child describe something he has seen, such as a TV show, a photograph, a book, and so on and try to compare his responses to how other children of his age would respond. Granted, this is not easy to carry out, given that one usually does not have ready access to a group of children of the same age. On the other hand, there is no real need for precise assessment. The rule of thumb is as follows:

An eight-year-old should be able to identify and describe the high points of a story or photograph and enrich that description with some pertinent adjectives and adverbs. His narration is very likely to be limited to concrete aspects; he will probably not do too much inferring and/or deducing (inventing new knowledge out of the events he is describing).

By age nine, a child should be able to provide a more complex description that is not restricted to the concrete; he should be able to draw inferences from facts (demonstrate the capacity to reason that if there is *this* and *this*, then there must also be or have been *that*). A simple illustration: if the story he is telling includes mention of a moon and/or stars, he should know it occurred during nighttime, and so on.

By eleven, the child should be able to respond much like an adult in terms of how well he organizes the information he is relating, albeit with a more limited vocabulary.

2. A second informal method: obtain a few books from your local library that are appropriate for the child's age, and investigate his ability to define some of the words in that book. (Note: This does not include his ability to read the book; if he has a learning problem, that may be too demanding. But it is instructive to determine whether or not he knows the meaning of the words he is expected to be able to read.) If he knows their meaning when you say them, you can interpret it as evidence of adequate language development; if he does not demonstrate understanding of the words, conclude the opposite.

3. A third method: have the child invent similes, and encourage him to use his imagination. For example, have him complete such sentences as (discourage one-word answers; try to elicit more elaborate responses):

    a. The falling rain sounded like _____.
    b. The little boy was as quiet as a _____.
    c. The animal in the field was as big as a _____.
    d. The baby lamb was as pretty as _____.

4. Finally, take a look at the child's school achievement test scores, especially those that reflect his vocabulary and comprehension abilities. If they do not indicate a lag, conclude that the child's language ability is appropriate for his age. Obviously, if they do indicate a lag, interpret it accordingly.

HOW THIS INFORMATION IS USED

Up to this point, we have
• described how the learning disabled child is identified (by comparing his IQ with his achievement test scores (chapter 2) and by ruling out physical, emotional, and neuromotor factors (chapter 3).

• explained that there are only two other factors worth investigating: the child's (visual and auditory) perceptual skills development and his acquired language/knowledge status.

• described ways to evaluate a child's (visual and auditory) perceptual skills and his language/knowledge status.

We now move on to a pivotal question: how do we interpret the information we obtained from assessing the child's perceptual skills and language/knowledge status? How do these two fundamental abilities link up with learning to read, spell, write, and do arithmetic?

6
WHERE THE PROBLEMS ARE: READING, SPELLING, WRITING, AND ARITHMETIC

To TRANSLATE INTO ACTION what the tests tell us, we should understand why and how perceptual skills and language are so important in learning to read, spell, write, and do arithmetic. But before we do that, we should identify what learning to read, spell, and write require of the child. And before we do that, it would be useful to think about how the acts of reading, writing, spelling, and arithmetic came about in the first place. Suppose we start with the last of these and then work our way back to the question regarding how the visual and auditory analysis skills and language influence a child's school achievement.

READING

To begin, we should reach some agreement on the meaning of the word *reading*. As simple as this may sound, it is almost impossible to get consensus among reading experts, probably because their definitions are so all-inclusive and complex. For the purposes of this book, we can settle for a simple (but accurate) definition. When the act of reading is discussed here, it refers to *mapping language onto symbols*. Said another way, it is the *act of reconstituting symbols into their original form*, which, in most cases, is spoken language. (Obviously, the symbols need not be graphic, e.g., Braille; nor need the language be oral, e.g., the deaf. The definition still applies.)

Historical Speculations

It is not difficult to speculate about how reading (and writing and spelling) were first inspired. (We will get to arithmetic shortly.) It seems self-evident that people communicated orally before they attempted to write, and that writing led to reading. Ancient wall drawings in caves suggest that some prehistoric human went for a walk one day, saw something that impressed him—a bull, perhaps—came back home to the cave that served as his dwelling, and, because his family did not understand what he was talking about when he tried to describe what he had seen, drew a picture of the bull on the cave wall. The family then "read" what he had drawn. It was based on a very simple pictographic system that they understood.

Over time, man's spoken vocabulary expanded and, in time, so did his written repertoire. There probably came a time when it became important to someone to express an abstract concept—truth, perhaps, or freedom, or something equally difficult to illustrate with a picture. Perhaps that is when someone was inspired to combine pictures and, in other ways, start to use concrete representations to express something more complicated than just the images themselves. Thus the change from the use of pictographic symbols to ideographic ones.

This system worked fairly well through the era of hieroglyphics, but eventually it, too, caused problems. Man's oral vocabulary kept expanding; he kept discovering new concepts and the words to express them orally. It became obvious that a continuous expansion of the written language in ideographic form would be hampered because the symbol system was so complex and unsystematic. Too few people could commit to memory all of the symbols needed to keep pace with the language explosion.

In all likelihood, that is when a group of individuals got together and decided that it was time for a radical change. Their solution was based on recognizing that a spoken language, regardless of which language, comprises a finite, relatively small number of different sounds that are sequenced in infinite ways. (English, for example, consists of only about forty-four different sounds from which we construct all the words of our language.) Having recognized this, it was but a small (but highly significant) step to recognizing also that the spoken language could therefore be recorded graphically (words could be spelled) by inventing a symbol for each sound.

They did this. No, they did not invent a symbol for each sound, but they came close, designating a written symbol for each of the consonant sounds and for some of the vowel sounds, and leaving to the reader the problem of spelling and reading some of the other vowel sounds, based on his knowledge of the spoken language. The Hebrews called their symbols such names as the *aleph* and the *bet*. The Greeks adopted the concept and called their symbols *alpha, beta,* and so on.

The rest is obvious: it was a brilliant idea. From then on, virtually all of the cultures of the world that sought a written language used one based on phonemics—a system whereby graphic symbols represent the concrete, sequenced sounds of the oral language rather than its semantic values: things and ideas. Some of the Eastern cultures are the exceptions (Chinese, for example), but even they have recognized, if only recently, the need for such a system if literacy is to be widespread.

The point of all this? We spoke before we wrote; we wrote before we read; and today, when we read, we are reconstituting graphic symbols into their original form—spoken words from which we extract information.

Now on to describing in behavioral terms what the child has to be able to do in order to become an efficient, fluent reader.

Language as a Prerequisite to Reading

If our definition of reading is valid—and, despite its simplicity, it is difficult to refute—then an obvious prerequisite to learning how to read is sufficient familiarity with the spoken word form of the language we hope to learn to read.

The child who is not reasonably conversant in English—the child who is not familiar with the oral version of most of the words he is expected to be able to read as he learns that process—will have an extremely difficult time learning to read English. But it would be wrong to label his originating difficulty as a reading problem. Rather, it represents a *language problem* that will cause a reading problem, and that can be overcome only by his becoming more familiar with the spoken form of the language.

Hence, when I discuss what the child has to be able to do in order to learn to read properly, I am assuming a child with appropriate language development. Given such a child, what must he learn? We can identify three basic goals he must achieve as follows:

1. *Identify the symbols and how they are used.* As starters, the child must learn to identify the letters (lower- and uppercase) and the conventions that govern their use: that (in English) the letters are arranged from left to right and from top to bottom, that the words are separated by spaces, that the period designates the end of a sentence, that capital letters are used at the beginning of sentences, and so on.

This does not mean that the child must know *all* of the letters and the conventions before he can take step two in learning to read, but it does mean that he has to know some of them—certainly the letters he is going to encounter in his first reading lessons. Obviously, being able to identify the letters and the rules that dictate their use depends on instruction—formal and informal. But there is more to it than that, as we will see when we get to the role of perceptual skills.

2. *Decode.* Once the child has some working familiarity with the letters and the rules that govern their use, his next hurdle is to learn that letters and (in English) certain strings of letters represent specific sounds. For example, the letters *c-a-t,* when printed in that order, represent the word *cat,* not because, in the aggregate, they look like a cat but because when joined they represent the sounds comprising that spoken word; and

that the letter string (sequence) *t-i-o-n* says *shun,* not because of the individual letter sounds but because of an accepted spelling convention.

Reading people call this ability, which is reflective of word attack skills, *decoding.* It is a crucial ability. Unless one can decode fluently, he can hardly be expected to get meaning out of printed text. Obviously, being able to decode fluently depends, in part, upon almost automatic, correct identification of the different lowercase and capital letters that comprise the printed words. But there is more to it than that, as we will see when we get to the role of perceptual skills.

3. *Comprehend.* The third ability is comprehension—extracting information from text and remembering that information with a fair degree of accuracy. Clearly this requires a complex set of integrated behaviors; it is not simply a case of decode first, remember all the words in the order they occurred, then—having decoded enough—think about meaning. That is not the way to gain information unless you limit your reading to single and simple short sentences.

Competent comprehension ability is contingent in part upon fluent decoding and in part upon the reader's ability to organize information effectively as he decodes it. It is only by processing the language represented by the printed symbols fluently—virtually without conscious effort—that you have a chance to think about and organize what you are reading while you are reading. And it is only through thinking about and organizing what you are reading as you read that you are able to comprehend the meaning of the text. As such, certain perceptual skills again become important, as will become evident when we get to that section of this chapter.

How Reading Used to Be Taught

In a way, the changes in how reading is taught—and there have been many over the years—represent progress, but the route is tortuous. Let's look at what has occurred.

At one time, reading was taught by teaching spelling at the same time—a very effective method because spelling is an analysis activity. To spell accurately, you have to break the spoken word into separate parts, thereby revealing directly the phonemic system (the links between letters and sounds) on which reading is based. (True, spelling requires more than phonemic analysis; more about this later.)

But teaching spelling while you teach reading is impractical because it requires lots of individual supervision, something that the teacher with twenty to twenty-five children in a standard classroom cannot provide. In addition, even if teacher time were not a concern, there are no commercially produced comprehensive programs available for such an approach.

The teacher would have to invent the program and prepare all the materials—a formidable task!

Over time, beginning reading instruction changed to a synthesis approach, a process that starts with the individual letters and attempts to teach children how to transform sequences of letters into spoken words. The phonics concept was emphasized. Children were taught that each letter represented a specific sound, provided with examples of those letter-sound link-ups, and drilled to the point where they recognized the printed words in their beginning reading books without resorting to "sounding them out." (The typical first grade classroom wall displayed memory prompt cards, each containing a single letter and a phonically related picture: the letter *A* and a picture of an apple, for example, or the letter *C* and a picture of a cat.) Then they were taught the exceptions to the rule: that some letters had more than one sound and, in fact, were sometimes "silent."

This was in the pre–World War II days, when not all children were expected to become fluent readers at the same time (and so early) in life; when children could start first grade in January as well as in September; when achievement testing was almost unheard of—teachers identified their problem readers on the basis of day-to-day classroom performance; when children who had trouble learning to read were given more time without labeling; when those children who did not learn to read fluently were not separated from the rest of their class.

Since the end of World War II, major changes have occurred in our attitudes toward education and in our expectations of students. First, educators started to view their profession as a science rather than an art. This was the outcome of advances in behavioral psychology, which asserted that you could teach anything (more or less) to anyone if you described in behavioral terms precisely what it is that you wanted the person ultimately to learn; then analyzed that major accomplishment into subordinate objectives, each of which was also described behaviorally; organized those subordinate behaviors into a valid hierarchy wherein when step one was accomplished, step two was within reach; taught those behaviors in an orderly fashion; and, finally, managed the "reinforcements" (rewards) in a way that kept the learner motivated until all goals were accomplished.

A remarkable advance in educational theory! And, for all practical purposes, probably a valid one. But there was a problem: no one had yet (nor since) been successful in identifying all the behaviors *some* students may need to be taught (and will not learn unless they are taught) in order to be fluent, comprehending readers, and how to teach these behaviors. This is especially true in regard to students who enter the classroom lacking in the basic learning aptitudes described in chapter 4 as visual and auditory perceptual skills. (We will discuss why this is so very shortly.) Teachers of those children need to know the ''art'' as well as the ''science'' of their profession.

Second, during its transformation into a science, educators observed that competent readers did not resort to sounding out words, letter by letter. Rather, competent readers read in larger units from very early on. They read words and phrases; only poor readers had to sound out words. This sponsored the notion that the best way to teach reading to all children was to teach them the method used by the most competent readers: teach them, from the beginning, to read whole words. This means that phonics principles should not be taught because according to this way of thinking it is a ''bad habit,'' a behavior that will soon have to be given up if one is to be a competent whole word and phrase reader.

The *Look and Say* system of the 1940s was developed on this rationale. Teachers were admonished not to teach letter-sound relationships; they were advised to show the children how to use the pictures on the page as clues about what an unfamiliar word might say, to point out to the children that words had shapes that might be helpful. For example, the word *something* is a long word and the word *up* is a short word—not a bad aid if these were the only long and short words. Inevitably, the Look and Say instructional method disappeared; too many children failed to learn with that method and parental reaction was vigorous and effective. (For more about this see books authored by Rudolf Flesch and by Jeanne Chall, listed in the Bibliography.)

This negative parental reaction was fueled by a third change that occurred after World War II: the baby boom. By the early 1950s, schools were extremely overcrowded despite the massive construction programs under way in all regions of the country. Newspapers regularly published articles that warned of forthcoming severe space shortages in our institutions of higher learning. Parents were cautioned that their children would not gain admission to the ''college of their choice'' unless their school qualifications were excellent.

This, in combination with the fact that around this same time achievement testing was introduced and, with it, the early labeling of some children as inadequate achievers, brought us to where we are now. Parents of inadequate achievers commiserated with each other. Soon some discovered that they had another thing in common—their children were not lacking in cognitive ability; they had average or better IQs. Parents joined together, they created lobbying groups, they sponsored the passage of special education laws in state legislatures and in the U.S. Congress. They made progress on standardizing the terms applied to their children.

They legitimized their youngsters' learning difficulties and their roles as advocates of their children. But what they have not yet accomplished is a clarification of just what it is that their children need and how to obtain it. That is what inspired this book.

How Reading Is Taught Now

Reading is currently taught in our schools in a variety of ways, and most children learn to read adequately regardless of which approach is used. But the children we are concerned about in this book are not like most children (although their numbers are substantial); they are children who have extreme difficulty learning how to read adequately under standard instructional conditions.

Today's reading programs tend to differ from each other in one major way—how clearly they show the child that reading is based on a "system," on "rules." Said differently, they differ in how explicitly they link printed symbols to spoken sounds, in how *unambiguous, apparent,* and *regular* (system-based) the relevant information of the lessons is. (The importance of these three characteristics is explained fully in chapter 10.) In this respect, there are four different types of reading approaches used in our schools.

Whole-Word Method

One method—and currently the most popular—is reminiscent of the old Look and Say method with some phonics principles thrown in. The program still places major emphasis on rapid recognition of sight words— words that are spelled in ways that may not follow precise letter-sound relationships.

On the plus side, from the beginning, this method is appealing because it provides stories that are not limited to words that sound more or less all the same. In addition, these programs usually include workbooks and other kinds of desk activities that relate to the lessons and that the teacher can exploit by forming subgroups and assigning seat activities to all but the group she wants to work with directly.

On the negative side, from the first book on, words are introduced that contain letters representing more than one sound, thereby obscuring the letter-sound relationships. For example, the letter *a*; think of the sound of the *a* in the words *man, mane, many, mean, mall, woman.* All different. Yet these words are likely to show up early in reading books. For many children, this presents no problem; they can handle the ambiguities and the lack of an apparent system on the strength of other cues. For some children—those who need phonic cues and, in their absence, have to depend on rote memorization—this results in confusion and, in time, failure.

Phonics-Based Method

At the other end of the spectrum are the phonics-based reading programs. There are not many of these, and they are not popular among teachers for a number of reasons.

First, they are more difficult to use in a standard instructional setting because more individual teacher attention is necessary. Second, the stories they offer are viewed as "boring" (probably more so to teachers than to the children), consisting mainly of words such as *bat, mat, sat,* and the like, all sounding much the same and, except in the hands of very gifted authors, not very interesting. And to make matters worse, there are finite limits on how far one can go in producing stories that use only words that are spelled "regularly," where a given letter represents the same sound in all instances. Usually by second grade, these ambiguities have to be introduced.

Linguistic Method

Somewhere between these two, there is a third instructional approach that attempts to bridge the gap. It is usually identified as a linguistic method and commences with regularly spelled words that highlight phonic principles but rapidly introduces a number of sight words. As such, it contains some characteristics from both the whole-word and the phonics-based methods.

Language Experience Method

There is another method that resembles the whole-word approach and appeals to many teachers. It is usually called the language experience or some variation thereof (e.g., *whole language*) and differs from the whole-word approach in that it attempts to teach and inspire language development through stimulating experiences and discussion, followed by having the students dictate stories to their teacher who then puts them on paper and hands the written material back to the students to read. It is based on the humanistic (and holistic) rationale that these words will have special meaning to the child (and they probably do) because they are "his"; they describe his experiences and thoughts.

This approach is very popular with some teachers, but I am not impressed with its effectiveness with the children who are the focus of this book. They do no better with the language-experience method than with the standard whole-word method and, in my opinion, it would be surprising if they did.

What Each of These Methods Requires of the Child

If we refer back to the three basic abilities that children must learn on the way to becoming competent readers, there are no major differences between the instructional methods in *how the letters are taught.* (There are some reading programs that start off by introducing the letters as having sounds rather than names; for example, the letter *m* is identified as having an "mmmm" sound rather than a name. The reason for this is apparent, but I question its wisdom; first, the general public calls letters by their names; second, identifying letters by their sounds begs the issue of some letters having more than one sound. Both of these spell confusion for the child who is destined to be called learning disabled.)

The second essential ability identified in our behavioral analysis is *decoding*—being able to "say" the words that the letters spell. The child enrolled in a whole-word (or language-experience) program has to be able to deal with ambiguities from the outset; he has to be able to remember what words such as *look, mother, woman,* and *on* "say," even though the letter *o* takes on a different sound in each word.

Children enrolled in a phonics-based program are given a little extra time before they, too, have to cope with these same ambiguities. Is this extra time helpful? Probably, at least for some; but only with short (three- and four-letter) words.

The third key behavior we identified was *comprehension,* which, by definition, depends upon three abilities: one, fluent decoding, so that information is acquired, not just a series of words; second, a reasonable understanding of the vocabulary and concepts expressed in the text; third, the capacity to organize information effectively for short-term and long-term memory storage, so that it can be retrieved with relative ease.

The whole-word and, to some extent, language-experience approaches are probably best for most children in teaching comprehension skills, if only because they introduce richer vocabulary and better-organized stories from the start. Unfortunately, as we will see, these approaches are usually contraindicated for some learning disabled children because of their ineffectiveness in teaching fluent decoding skills.

What Learning Disabled Children Cannot Do

Most destined-to-be-called-learning-disabled children encounter difficulty from the beginning, and the situation deteriorates further as more complex behaviors are called for. (This may not always be apparent to parents. Many first grade teachers are reticent to make negative statements about their students, presumably working on the notion that some children are "slow starters" and will eventually catch up.)

In general, children who have a learning disability in reading lack the ability to identify and employ the strategies needed to do one or more of the following:

• Remember with ease and consistency the identity of printed letters; the lowercase *b* and *d* in particular, but often other letters as well.

• Remember with ease and consistency what the printed words in their reading books "say"; that is, transform the printed word into its spoken form quickly, easily, and almost automatically.

• Remember enough of a story they have just read (or had read to them) to demonstrate understanding of the information contained in the story.

As you read the preceding statements, it becomes evident that a key word is *remember*; this is not coincidence. In essence, one simple but accurate way to think of learning disabled children is that they lack effective strategies for storing information in memory. They try to retain new information the way we try to remember most telephone numbers—on the basis of rote memorization rather than on the basis of effective association strategies. Unless there is some uniquely memorable numeral sequence in a telephone number, it contains nothing salient that enables us to associate it with something we already know. Hence, our capacity to remember a list of telephone numbers is very limited. (Advertisers recognize this; consider how many commercials now present telephone numbers in letter/word form.)

What then impairs the learning disabled child's memory function as it pertains to reading? (1) Neither his instructional program nor his teacher teaches him effective mnemonics; (2) he cannot identify the salient features in his reading lesson that would serve as the bases for effective mnemonics or for associating information; (3) he lacks the knowledge that would facilitate those associations.

The Salient Features Contained in Reading Lessons

What are these salient features that would serve as the bases for associating information? This differs with the type of reading lesson: what it is designed to teach and how that is to be accomplished.

Lessons Designed to Teach Letter Recognition

If a lesson is designed to teach letter identification, then the salient features are the structural elements of the letters themselves: the straight lines, the ovals, the arcs, and their spatial interrelationships and how they are combined to form the different letters.

The prime example is the most commonly confused letters of the lowercase manuscript alphabet—the *b* and the *d*. Why are they so readily confused? Because they are made up of the same structural elements and differ only in the spatial interrelationships between those elements. The child who lacks an efficient strategy for mapping out spatial relationships of this sort when he is first introduced to the lowercase manuscript letters is likely to manifest letter confusion and reversals, early signs of a learning disability.*

Lessons Designed to Teach Decoding

If the lesson is designed to teach decoding—word recognition skills—then the salient features are the sequenced sounds of the spoken forms of the words he is to learn to decode as they relate to the printed forms of those words: the letters and (in English) their left-to-right spatial sequence. The child who lacks the ability to identify the separate sounds and their temporal sequences in spoken words will fail to recognize the relationship between the spoken and printed forms of a word unless, of course, the teacher, or the lesson material itself, makes that information obvious—something that the usual reading lesson does not do. (More about this later.) The result: inept word recognition skills, a prominent indicator of a learning disability.

Lessons Designed to Teach Comprehension

If the lesson is designed to teach comprehension, then the salient features are the things (people, animals, objects) and events and their interactions, as presented in the story. The child who lacks the ability to identify and categorize these things, events, and circumstances as they unfold in a story will lack the ability to comprehend very much unless the lesson itself makes that information explicit—something that the usual reading comprehension lesson does not do. The result: poor reading comprehension, another indicator of a learning disability.

The Links Between Perceptual Skills and Learning to Read

1. *Letter recognition.* We observed that the child who lacks an efficient strategy for mapping out spatial relationships when he is first introduced to the lowercase manuscript letters is likely to display letter confusion and reversals.

Another name for the ability to identify and map out the spatial interrelationships of these structural components is *visual perceptual skills*. The child whose visual analysis skills are lacking when he is introduced to letters (especially the lowercase manuscript letters) is likely to experience confusion because he will employ a less-than-optimal strategy for remembering the orientation of the letters—a problem that

---

*Letter reversals are sometimes interpreted as indicators of ''mirror vision.'' There is no such thing. Children print and read letters/numerals backward because of confusion, not because they literally see them that way. See pages 127–28 for more discussion about reversals and what to do about them.

over time may very well persist as a bad habit, even if his visual perceptual skills do ultimately develop to a satisfactory level.*

2. *Decoding.* There is little question about the importance of being able to identify the separate sounds and their sequences in spoken words as a contributor to acquiring competent decoding skills.

Another name for this ability is *auditory perceptual skills.* The child whose auditory perceptual skills are lacking when he is introduced to lessons that are designed to teach word recognition skills is likely to experience confusion because he employs a less-than-optimal strategy for remembering the words—a problem that over time often persists as a bad habit, even if his auditory perceptual skills do ultimately develop to a satisfactory level.

3. *Comprehension.* We also stated that the child who lacks the ability to identify and categorize things, events, and circumstances as they unfold in a story, will lack the ability to comprehend very much unless the lesson itself makes that information explicit.

Another name for the ability to identify and categorize spatially organized information is *visual perceptual skills.* The child whose visual analysis skills are lacking is likely to have difficulty with reading comprehension because he employs a less-than-optimal strategy for organizing information (abstract and concrete)—a problem that over time often persists as a bad habit, even if his visual perceptual skills do ultimately develop to a satisfactory level.

In review, children with learning disabilities in reading have these problems because they do not remember enough of what their reading lessons are supposed to teach. This stems from their inept ability to identify those aspects of the lessons that would enhance retention. And this in turn stems from an inadequate knowledge base and substantard visual and/or auditory perceptual skills.

SPELLING

Spelling is the act of *converting spoken language into graphic form;* of *mapping symbols onto spoken words* (in ways that satisfy the idiosyncratic letter sequences that emerged when English words were adopted from different languages).

There are many poor spellers. And not all of them have a learning disability. Indeed, a great many competent scholars are poor spellers. Well then, is it worth worrying about, especially when the children we

*Current research indicates that a child should have developed the visual analysis skills typical of a four- to four-and-a-half-year-old before being asked to remember the lowercase letters of the manuscript alphabet. If his skills are not at that level, he is apt to experience the confusion that leads to reversals.

are discussing have so many other problems in school? Yes, it is worth worrying about, *especially* because they have so many other problems in school.

If the child's only problem is his spelling—if he is competent in reading and arithmetic—you might shrug, smile, and acknowledge that no one is perfect. But if the youngster is a poor reader and a poor arithmetic problem solver *in addition* to being a poor speller, no one will smile. They may shrug, but its meaning will be different—"What's the use"—and no one will even try to do anything about it. Besides, good spelling instruction will probably help the child with his reading, and that makes it worthwhile.

The Difference Between Reading and Spelling

Reading and spelling are very much the same in many ways. But there are differences as well. As any experienced schoolteacher will tell you, good readers may not be good spellers but good spellers are always good readers. The implication is that it is more difficult to be a good speller than to be a good reader.

Spelling is an analytic activity; it requires breaking words down into their subcomponents; reading involves synthesis: combining components into whole words. The speller has to hear or think of a spoken word and construct the spelled version from scratch, using a coding system that in the English language often deviates from regular rules.

The reader also has to deal with this deviation from regularity, but he has contextual cues—related information contained in the story—and familiarity with the spoken vocabulary of the language, both of which help him with unfamiliar words. To be a good speller, you have to be able to spell accurately; guessing will not work. You can be a good reader and still do a lot of "educated guessing." In fact, it is difficult to imagine how one can be a fluent reader without doing lots of educated guessing.

The Steps Required in Learning to Spell

To become a good speller, the child has to be able to do three things beyond identifying the letters.

1. *Decode the words he is to learn to spell.* He need not understand the words but, obviously, that is not undesirabie. If he cannot decode the words, then he has an additional cognitive task to contend with, which (in the English language and all of its irregular spellings) is probably insurmountable if he is to learn to spell more than a very few words.

2. *Analyze the words he is to spell into their sounds and represent those sounds with letters.* If there is a perfect match—if there is a sound for each letter in the word and the sounds are specific to those letters and

those letters alone—and if the child already knows those letter-sound combinations, then the task is accomplished. The child will be able to spell the word. He will not have to memorize a thing. Words such as *mat*, *fit*, *run*, and *hot* belong in this category.

3. *Employ effective strategies for remembering the letter-sound irregularities*. If the match is not perfect—if there are irregularities, such as there not being a sound for each letter, or if the letter used to code a sound is one that is not customarily associated with that sound—then a problem arises. The child will have to memorize the spelling of at least that part of the word. He will not spell it correctly if he simply sounds it out and then writes the letters that go with those sounds. There are plenty of words in this category, for example, *field*, *their*, *brought*, *brew*, *through*, and *clothes*.

How Spelling Is Taught Under Standard School Conditions

A school's spelling program usually reflects the school's reading program. Indeed, the first step—decoding—is addressed in the reading program itself. The next two steps also reflect the school's reading program.

If the school teaches reading with a whole-word approach, the spelling program will begin with words from the reading books and sometimes, but not often enough, accompany these with words that belong to the same "family"; words that contain similar sequences of letters: *feast*, *beast*, *least*, for example.

If the reading program leans more toward a phonics basis, the words in the spelling program will reflect this: *cat*, *mat*, *sat*, *bat*, and so on.

The Differences Between Spellers

Suppose we try to imagine, on the basis of what we have just discussed, how a child who learns to spell very easily (a "natural speller") deals with a new word in comparison to the child who is not a good speller.

The Good ("Natural") Speller

Take the word *consistent* as an example. Many adults have trouble with that one, often spelling it *consistant*. The good speller reads the word, pronouncing it clearly. As he does this, he analyzes the word into its separate sounds, matching those individual sounds with individual letters. The word *consistent* turns out to be a fairly easy word for this part of the task; there is a sound for each letter.

There are some potential trouble spots, however. If the child is careful to pronounce the word correctly, he notices that the *o* and *e* stand for ambiguous sounds, sounds that could be coded by letters other than the *o* and *e*. Both of these, in the word *consistent*, are schwa sounds. (The schwa is a very common sound in our language; it can be represented by virtually every printed vowel in the alphabet. For example: *the, above, nation.*) The child (remember, he is a natural speller), having recognized these two potential trouble spots as the only parts of the word that he will not be able to spell with complete confidence, devises a strategy to help him remember that the first schwa sound is coded by an *o* and the second by an *e*. What is his strategy? It can vary. He might pronounce the word to himself incorrectly, giving the *o* a *short o* sound, and the *e* a *short e* sound. Or he might recognize the similarity between the word *consistent* and another word he already knows how to spell—*content*, for example. Either of these would help him remember.

We should try another word, one that has some different kinds of trouble spots. The word *receipt* will do—a sixth grade spelling word in most schools. Again, the good speller reads the word, breaks it down into its separate sounds, and recognizes that two of the letters in that word do not get sounded—the *i* and the *p;* —and one other letter (the *c*) takes on the /*s*/ sound. Having noticed these inconsistencies, he devises a strategy to help him remember them when he writes the word. He does not worry about the rest of the word. He can spell it just by writing the sounds down in correct sequence.

There is one more step in learning to spell a word, this one again something that the natural speller does with virtually no outside assistance. He does lots of reading and spelling (it is predictable that he likes to read and write). In other words, he practices his skills. In time, he no longer has to *think* about the strategies he initially employed. The words become units rather than strings of separate letters.

He eventually memorizes the spelling of words. What originally required his special attention no longer does. He has "chunked" the letters into a word, or into subcomponents of words (spelling units) and now spells the words almost automatically. (The letter sequences *tion, ite, ole,* are examples of spelling units. There are a number of these. Once the child learns that these letters constitute a chunk that consistently represents the same sound, he no longer has to deal with the separate letters.)

In fact, the only time he stops to think about the separate letters is when someone asks him for assistance in spelling a word. Then he has to stop and think for a moment. Indeed, he may even have to write it down. This is not dissimilar to many other skills we acquire. Take the question: Is the vertical line positioned to the right or the left in the lowercase *d?* Most of us would have to stop for a moment and mentally reconstruct the letter, or look at one already in view, even though we are very familiar with the letter. That, in fact, is why we have to stop and reconstruct it.

We are so familiar with the letter *d* that it has become something we print automatically without thinking.

The Average Speller

What about the child who is neither a natural nor a very poor speller—one who falls somewhere in the middle? Suppose he has to learn to spell *receipt*. You show the word to him. Chances are he will be able to read it. He is, after all, a fair student. As he does this, he will also probably be able to analyze it into its separate sounds, and he may even notice that the *i* and the *p* are not sounded in the spoken word, and the *c* is sounded as an /s/.

What happens if he does not notice these things? If his spelling program is a good one, it will be designed to make these inconsistencies apparent to him. *Receipt* will not be taught as an isolated word but rather as part of a group, all of which will share some of the same characteristics: the *ei* sequence. His teacher will call his attention to the similarity of the words in that group, thereby emphasizing it (for example, *receive, deceive*). In addition, she will teach him a way to help him remember, perhaps with the jingle "i before e except after c."

She will also devise one for the silent *p;* perhaps she will have him pronounce the word with the *p* sound included, just to emphasize the fact that it *is* there—recei-*p*-t. Then she will have him practice spelling the word and writing it a number of times to help him memorize it.

The Poor Speller

Now, what about the learning disabled child whose spelling skills match his inept reading skills? What does he do when faced with the task of learning how to spell the word *receipt*? First, he probably cannot read the word; his teacher has to read it to him. Thus he is in trouble from the start. Because he is a poor reader, it is predictable that he will be a poor sound analyzer; he will have difficulty breaking down the word into its individual sounds. He will also have real difficulty matching sounds to letters, even when the match is a regular one.

In addition, the fact that this word is being taught as part of a group of words, all of which share some of the same characteristics, will not help him be aware of those characteristics. He will have trouble with all the words in the group, so no one of them will help him with the others. There is too much to be aware of, let alone to memorize.

Finally, when his teacher shows him some strategies for keeping the irregularities straight in his memory, they are promptly forgotten. He is coping with a major and basic problem; he does not know how to match the regular sounds very well; talking to him about irregularities is useless.

It is over his head—he has no way of understanding it, let alone using it. (It is a little like talking to a beginning skier about how to hold his arms so that he gets a little extra speed. He is devoting all his attention to staying on his feet; he has little time and energy available for thinking about an elaboration of that act.)

At any rate, suppose he has had the prescribed instruction and his teacher now tells him to practice writing the newly learned word. He practices and may even manage to write it accurately a few times. But he is depending completely upon rote memorization of the entire word, not just certain strategic parts of it. It is just too much to remember for very long. Even though he spells it correctly in the Friday afternoon spelling test, the word will be gone by the following Monday.

The Links Between Perceptual Skills and Spelling

To be a good speller, one must have competent visual and auditory perceptual skills. The importance of the latter is evident. The ability to analyze spoken words into their phonemic elements is simply another way of defining *auditory analysis skills. Visual perceptual skills* are important in that these are the skills used to identify the spelling patterns that enable us to relate the irregular spelling in one word to another word containing the same pattern.

WRITING

When we write, we are—at a fundamental level—simply *translating spoken words into a graphic form.* It is a mechanical (motor) act. When we write to express information, we go beyond the mechanical level; we translate *information* into a graphic form. Clearly, this second level of performance depends, at least in part, upon being able to carry out the mechanics of writing easily and efficiently almost without conscious effort.

How Writing Is Taught: Cursive versus Manuscript

Almost every kindergarten child is taught the manuscript letters. Cursive is not introduced until second or third grade.

This was not always so. In pre–World War II days, cursive was taught from the beginning, and good penmanship was an important educational goal. Then, along with the educational revolution in reading, manuscript replaced cursive as the first written symbol system the child learned. The rationale: the beginning reader has to learn to read books printed in the manuscript alphabet so he may as well learn also how to print that alphabet. In addition, it was argued, the transition between manuscript and cursive would not be difficult; children merely had to learn to connect the separate manuscript letters with arcs or loops.

The reasoning seemed valid at the time, so the change was made, much to the detriment of the children who are the subject of this book.

One immediate effect from the change: less effort was devoted to penmanship and to neatness. Because manuscript letters require less motor adeptness (it was reasoned), there is no need to insist on as much practice as was needed with the cursive system. Thus teachers started to place less stress on neatness and on the preferred way to construct the letters. The children were given more leeway in inventing their own printing systems; their printing was judged satisfactory as long as their final product—the individual letters—was identifiable and formed correctly.

Another outcome is directional confusion between certain letters. Clearly, it is much easier to distinguish and remember the differences between the cursive *b* and *d* than their manuscript counterparts.

And yet another difference between cursive and manuscript is that the latter is less efficient—more demanding on fine-motor processes and more time consuming. Cursive calls for a continuous, rhythmic act; manuscript is a series of starts and stops.

Nonetheless, despite all these differences that seem to favor cursive, the manuscript letters continue to be the ones children learn to print first.

The Link Between Perceptual Skills and Writing

Visual perceptual skills have a direct effect on the ease with which a child will learn to print neatly; auditory perceptual skills have no effect.

Children whose visual perceptual skills are not adequately developed (approximating at least the four- to four-and-a-half-year-old level) when they are taught to print are likely to have poor printing skills. In practical terms, this means that *children whose visual perceptual skills are below the four-year-old level should not enter into a program designed to teach them to print the letters of the alphabet.* (More about this in chapter 10.)

True, they will learn some of the letters, but not all, and not securely enough to enable them to achieve the "automatic" stage of printing, where they do not have to think about how to form the letters and can devote their attention to the information that they want to express. The outcome is that they develop bad habits—poor writing skills (at the mechanical level)—that remain with them forever (unless forced to give them up somewhere along the line).

Some may assert that the problem should not last forever because the children will eventually develop better-than-four-year-old visual perceptual skills. The latter portion of that statement is true, but their poor handwriting will persist even after they have developed adequate visual perceptual skills. It is the case of developing a bad habit in order to compensate for a deficit and then retaining the bad habit after the underlying deficit is eliminated.

ARITHMETIC

Arithmetic is a branch of mathematics that pertains *to carrying out calculations that involve numbers.* Mathematics in turn is *the mapping of language onto symbols.*

As you will recall, this latter is the same definition we applied to reading. And, in fact, it is accurate in both applications. What makes mathematics different from reading is its symbols and the language those symbols code.

The Origin of Arithmetic

Just as with reading, it is not difficult to imagine the circumstances that spawned arithmetic. Man calculated by applying mathematical principles—by recognizing the fundamental properties and interrelationships of quantities and magnitudes—long before he was able to represent his calculations orally, let alone record them on paper.

Certainly, the caveman who tracked game, who anticipated the animal's path and moved diagonally to head him off, or who adjusted the aim and force of his weapon in accord with the animal's speed and direction of movement, was making calculations based upon the recognition of the properties and interrelationships of certain quantities and magnitudes present in that situation.

Eventually there came a time when man felt a need to have a graphic record of his calculations—possibly because his commerce required it. At first, he used a crude but logical system of drawing a mark or using an object, such as a rock or a bone, for each unit he wanted to record. In time, as he tried to improve upon his methods, he figured out how to represent groups of objects with single units such as using the X to represent 10 and C for 100. He was forced to do this in the interest of time and space.

Eventually he came to the idea of Arabic numerals and their remarkable power to represent complex conditions with relative simplicity.

Just as with reading, there had to be agreement on the meanings of these symbols among the users of the system. But once accomplished, numerical communications were possible, and one basic code came to be accepted by virtually everyone, regardless of the verbal language we use—testimony of the remarkable efficiency of this system and its power to express complex information simply.

The Languages of Mathematics: Prerequisites to Mastering Arithmetic

There are two languages in mathematics: verbal and nonverbal. The former is the language we employ when we use the spoken words *one, two, three,* and so on, to specify quantities; when we use such phrases as *first, second,* and *third* to express order/position in a series; when we say *the same as, greater than, less than* to express relative magnitude; and when we use such terms as *twice as much* to express relationships.

The nonverbal language of mathematics is what we use when we identify the salient features of quantity, magnitude, orientation, and relationships in spatially organized, concrete information.

The nonverbal language of arithmetic is a language of exact, unambiguous conditions. It is a universal language. It is not altered by the code we use to represent it. We do in fact use a variety of codes, written and spoken, and though they may vary, the conditions they describe remain constant.

In sum, then, we can conclude that the child who attempts to learn arithmetic without first being familiar with both its *verbal and nonverbal languages,* is in the same position as the child who attempts to learn to read a language he cannot speak. He will have to memorize the information; he will not recognize the underlying "system"; arithmetic will not "make sense."

Children who are already familiar with the two languages of mathematics when they enter an instructional program in arithmetic will not have to memorize very much; they will be able to associate new facts with knowledge acquired through exposure and experience. The system will make sense.

The Steps Required in Learning Arithmetic

In order to make satisfactory progress in arithmetic, the child has to

1. *Learn the symbols and their meaning:* learn to count and to relate specific quantities to specific numerals.

2. *Decode efficiently:* translate arithmetic problems into actions that employ counting algorithms, and do this often enough so that the answers to a set of basic calculations become so familiar that they are immediately available without employing the counting algorithm: They become memorized *number facts* that can be called upon as needed, without resorting to a counting algorithm.

3. *Apply these number facts in the solution of more complex calcu-*

lations: reduce the number of steps required to arrive at an answer (e.g., regroup numbers, employ the concept of commutative properties, etc.).

How Arithmetic Is Taught in Our Schools

Although there are many variations, arithmetic instructional programs tend to follow one of two approaches: *math concepts* and *math facts.*

Math Concepts

In this type of program, children are taught that arithmetic is based on concepts that may be proven by counting. Once the concepts are learned (the reasoning goes), the rest is "simply" a matter of application and, with practice, arithmetic fluency is attainable. This rationale resembles, in many ways, the whole-word approach to reading instruction.

Math Facts

In this type of approach, number facts are taught as units to be remembered, with instruction regarding the underlying concepts introduced afterward. This is much like the phonics-based reading instruction approach.

The Link Between Mathematics and Perceptual Skills

Visual perceptual skills are critical to mastering arithmetic. When you test a child's visual perceptual skills, you are testing his knowledge of the nonverbal language of mathematics—of what numerals represent: the fundamental properties and relationships of quantities and magnitudes.

The four-year-old who copies a plus sign with reasonable accuracy (as is expected from children his age), is illustrating that he grasps the concepts of perpendicular lines of equal length that intersect at their centers so that all segments are of equal length. This does not imply that he can express in words what he has portrayed on paper, or that he knows how to code these concepts with numerals, but it does show that he is close to being ready to learn the latter.

The Link Between Perceptual Skills and Arithmetic

The child who knows the number fact "2 + 2 = 4"—who is so familiar with that fact that he does not have to do the calculation—and who comprehends the basic concept of spatial relationships (part of the nonverbal language of arithmetic, evidence of competent visual analysis skills), will have little difficulty solving the calculation problems of $2 + 3 = ?$ and $3 + 2 = ?$.

The child who does not appreciate spatial relationships (whose visual analysis skills are deficient) will, in contrast, have to deal with these last two problems as separate and unrelated to the first; each will have to be solved independently of the others. Similarly, the child who lacks the ability to employ spatial analysis strategies to arithmetic "word problems," will have to resort to keeping the problem in memory in its entirety, then organizing it into a solvable problem—a very difficult task, to be sure.

Simply stated, satisfactory progress in arithmetic depends upon adequate development of visual perceptual skills, regardless of whether the instructional program stresses concepts or facts. If the child's visual analysis skills are not appropriately developed, learning difficulties in arithmetic are inevitable; arithmetic cannot be mastered through memorization.

Auditory perceptual skills, on the other hand, make no direct contribution to arithmetic achievement.

Why Primary Grade Children with Poor Visual Perceptual Skills May Not Have Trouble with Arithmetic

Surprisingly—in light of what has just been stated—it is not unusual to encounter a first or second grade child who has very poor visual perceptual skills yet is making satisfactory progress in arithmetic. This can be explained by the fact that in the first and second grades arithmetic calculations involve small numbers that children can solve by counting on their fingers or "in their heads."

The situation changes markedly by third or fourth grade, when the children are confronted with arithmetic that involves large numbers. It is one thing to be able to solve $3 + 4 = ?$ by counting, and another to solve $7 \times 8 = ?$ Hence, satisfactory arithmetic grades in first and second grade do not always mean that the child is learning the concepts of arithmetic, only that he has learned to count accurately.

It is also important to understand that poor arithmetic skills do not predict poor visual analysis skills, even though the former may have been caused by the latter. This apparent dilemma is also easily explained. Most children outgrow a visual perceptual skills deficit; they acquire the basic set of skills, albeit later in life than expected. But they do not outgrow the substandard arithmetic abilities that stem from their originally substandard visual perceptual skills.

Therefore, if you assess the visual perceptual skills of a group of high school children who have significant difficulties in math, you will discover that a good number of them have adequate visual perceptual skills. The explanation is that they were late in acquiring these skills, but they finally did develop them, thereby leaving them only with the arithmetic deficit.

7
TREATMENT OPTIONS

THERE USUALLY ARE three ways to help the learning disabled child overcome his learning problem: *remediate, compensate,* or simply *wait.* In some cases, only one option is worth considering; in other situations, more than one should be implemented simultaneously. I will get to the decision-making process in a moment and, in later chapters, discuss how to put those decisions into action—what to do and when. First, the options themselves.

REMEDIATE

To *remediate* means to cure, to alleviate or eliminate a problem; in this context, to help the child overcome his perceptual skills and/or language deficits so that he is equipped to make satisfactory progress under standard instructional conditions; in other words, to change him and to improve his skills so that special school conditions will not be necessary.

COMPENSATE

To *compensate* means to accommodate, to counterbalance, to provide a means for counteracting a situation. In this context, therefore, it means providing nonstandard instructional conditions that enable the learning disabled child to make satisfactory school progress despite his perceptual skills and/or language deficits.

WAIT

To *wait* does not mean to ignore. Rather, it means to watch as you wait, to defer any advancement in grade level until the child has developed the perceptual skills and/or learned the language required for satisfactory performance in a standard instructional setting; in other words, to consider retention of the child who is already in school, or to delay entry if he is a preschooler.

DECISION-MAKING GUIDELINES

How do you decide among the three? First, notice that none of these approaches depends on identifying and eliminating the underlying cause of the child's learning problem. Instead, the three alternatives assume several things.

First, the underlying cause of a learning disability, whatever it is, significantly impairs the development of certain key abilities.

1. *Perceptual skills,* as they pertain to being able to identify the bases of the coding and decoding systems we call reading, writing, spelling, and arithmetic.

2. *Language,* as it pertains to providing the child with the information that the coding systems code.

Second, we are able to identify and assess these key abilities; and third, we are able either to remediate the deficits we identify and/or design instruction that effectively accommodates them.

In essence, the choice among the three options should be based on pragmatics—on which approach is likely to be the most effective in helping the child overcome his school learning difficulties and the least expensive in terms of physical and emotional energy and time as well as money.

In some cases, *wait and see* is the treatment of choice; sometimes it is *remediation;* sometimes it is *accommodation;* sometimes it is some combination of the three.

PROGNOSTIC FACTORS

There are three factors that we have to look at when making a decision about treatment. These are

1. The probable cause of the language and/or perceptual skills deficit. Is there reason to believe that it was caused by some permanent, albeit very subtle, injury to the child's central nervous system rather than simply being a normal variation in his development?

2. The age of the child and the extent of the lag he displays in school achievement. That is, his present grade placement and how far behind he is in the different subject areas.

3. The availability of the emotional and physical resources needed to engage in a remedial program; the time and energy needed to keep up

with a program that requires about one-half hour of daily participation for perhaps as long as four or five months.

Why These Factors Are Important and How to Interpret Them

Let's start with the first factor. Language and/or perceptual skills deficits usually originate from one of two main sources. The most common is a normal variation in development—a temporary lag, a deficit that will disappear in time. Just as some children grow tall early in life and others "bloom" later, some children—for no apparent reason—develop language and/or perceptual skills a bit more slowly than is usual.

The other (and, fortunately, less common) source is an event and/or a circumstance that caused subtle central nervous system damage and, as a result, limited potential in this aspect of development. For example, premature delivery, an at-risk status at birth, a very high fever during the first six to nine months of life, a seizure—explained or unexplained—during the preschool years, or any other event of that nature.

If it can be established that the source of the child's language and/or perceptual skills deficit(s) is simply a normal variation in development, then prognosis related to remediation or to a "give him time" approach is favorable. If the second factor—an organic cause—is implicated, then the likelihood of benefiting from a wait-and-see approach or from remediation is reduced. Something else will have to be done.

There are also those cases in which a central nervous system problem can only be *suspected* but not documented. A bit more optimism is justified in these cases, but, once again, you simply cannot ignore the possibility of long-lasting effects and a resistance to remediation.

In any case—good prognosis or not—the proof is in the doing. When remediation is indicated, I usually suggest that the first month of treatment be viewed as a trial period. If, at the end of that month, you observe improvement, then you may assume a more sanguine attitude and make a more securely optimistic prediction about the benefits to be derived from a remedial program. Give it a try and see what happens. As long as you do not delude yourself or the child, then there is nothing wrong (and much correct) about this reasoning.

The second factor refers to the child's age and the extent of his school achievement deficit. If he is very young—in preschool, say, or kindergarten—and therefore not very far behind where he should be in school, then the prospects improve for two of the treatment options: remediation and wait and see. There should be little if any need to change the instructional conditions.

On the other hand, if the child is in third grade or beyond, and is a year or more behind in his achievement test scores, then clearly, time has run out for the wait and see option, and there is little reason to support remedial treatment other than as an adjunct to *compensatory* treatment.

How about those in between: children in first, second, and perhaps early third grade who are less than a year behind in school achievement? They are probably best served by a *remediate and accommodate* approach and, sometimes, with the opportunity to repeat a year in the same grade rather than push on to ever increasing challenges.

Think of it this way: school is like an automobile race in which children come in first, last, or somewhere in between. It is a long race, usually lasting twelve years.

Children who enter the race with "substandard equipment" (inadequately developed perceptual skills and/or inept language abilities) will start to slip behind very early in the race.

To continue with the analogy, if the substandard equipment is identified and the problem eliminated early in the race—if the child can then start to make progress at an appropriate rate before he gets very far behind—then he will probably be able to catch up. He may not have much chance of coming in at the head of the pack, but at least he will not be left behind.

If the opposite is true, if the substandard equipment is not identified and the problem not eliminated until the race is long under way (third grade, say), it is certain that the child will have fallen far behind. It is unreasonable to believe that repairing the equipment and bringing it up to the standard of the others in the race at that late date will be all that is needed. Repairing the equipment will not automatically enable the child to catch up in the race. At best, he will not slip any farther behind, but neither will he catch up. (In fact, he *will* slip farther behind because his daily lessons—when given in a standard classroom—are designed on the assumption that he does not have an educational deficit, that he knows and can do all that his classmates know and can do.)

Thus we come to the only feasible conclusion about treatment in these situations: improve the equipment—remediate—as best and as early as you can, but not at the cost (in time and effort) of slipping farther behind in the race. Instead, provide the child with a track that offers less impedance—a track that is modified a bit to accommodate his less-than-perfect equipment—and give him a helping hand once in a while, thereby making it possible for him to stay in the race.

Obviously, this approach would not be acceptable in an auto race, but it is appropriate in education where, traditionally, instructional methods are modified extensively to serve children with other difficulties, such as those who have visual or auditory impairment. Schools do not ask those children to function competitively under standard instructional conditions; they modify conditions to accommodate the deficit. The same should hold true for the learning disabled child.

The third prognostic factor was the availability of the emotional and physical resources needed to engage in a remedial program. The auto race analogy just presented makes clear the value of early identification and the desirability of remediation under proper circumstances. However, there are times when remediation is not the best recommendation, even for the first grade child with perceptual skills and/or language deficits who is not that far behind in school.

When is this true? When it is evident from the outset that no matter how motivated a remedial effort cannot be sustained long enough to produce the desired results.

Remediation requires effort and time and the involvement of an adult, either in the home or in school, who will supervise the effort on a regular basis. It is not like taking a prescribed medication for a fixed time period, and then being cured. Even in the best situation, you have to plan on about four months of sustained effort before the established goals are achieved.

Four months is a long time; keeping a child "in the race" for four months while he is struggling (probably unsuccessfully) to not fall farther behind in school, requires a committed supervisor, someone who is able to communicate effectively with the child, someone whom the child trusts, someone who is secure enough to keep at the task even on those "bad days" when the child (and perhaps his teacher as well) wants to give up. If such a person is not available at home or in the school or even if there is such a person available but he/she does not have the time and energy to devote to the task, then remediation should not be tried; compensatory instruction should be instituted.

SUMMARY

Three treatment options are available when considering how best to help the learning disabled child. These have been organized into a set of directives as follows:

CRITERIA FOR SELECTING A TREATMENT OPTION FOR THE LEARNING DISABLED CHILD

Select *wait and see* (i.e., give him more time; retain him in his present grade level)
• When child is very young (in kindergarten or younger), *and* his academic and/or aptitude deficits are minor, *and* there is reason to believe that he will soon overcome the deficits without intervention.
and

• When it appears that the problem originates from a developmental rather than a neurological factor.

Select *remediation plus retention*

• When the child is very young (in kindergarten or younger), but his academic and/or aptitude deficits (albeit apparently stemming from a developmental rather than a neurological factor) are such that retention in grade alone is not likely to be enough.

Select *remediation* only

• When the child is very young (in kindergarten or younger), *and* when it appears that the problem originates from developmental rather than neurological factors, but retention is ruled out by parent or school. (Many schools now subscribe to the principle that if early retention is needed, it should occur in first grade, not in kindergarten. In my opinion, this is not a wise decision.)

or

• When the child is in grades kindergarten through two, and his academic deficits are not great (less than a six-month lag).

Select *remediation plus classroom accommodation*

• When the child is in grades kindergarten through two, and his academic deficits are in excess of six months.

and

• When the child is in grades kindergarten through two, and, although his academic deficits are not significant, there is reason to believe that his basic aptitudes deficits stem from neurological rather than developmental factors.

Select *remediation plus classroom accommodation plus retention*

• When the child is in grades one through three, *and* his academic deficits (achievement scores) are in excess of one year, *and* there is no reason to suspect an underlying neurological problem.

Select *classroom accommodation* only

• When the child is in third grade and beyond, and qualifies for the learning disabled designation.

or

• When remediation has already been attempted and proven to be unsuccessful (perhaps because of an unrecognized neurological factor), regardless of the child's age/grade.

or

• When there are insufficient resources (time, energy, and/or emotional) to implement an effective remedial program.

8
IMPROVING PERCEPTUAL SKILLS

THERE ARE A NUMBER of perceptual skills training packages on the market. Some are better than others and, in many cases, more than one might be needed. In essence, the good ones share the following characteristics:

1. They identify the ultimate behaviors the child is to learn as a result of engaging in the training program and what desirable things he will be able to do at the end that he could not do at the outset. In good programs, these goals are representative of general skills. As the child improves in the program, he should also demonstrate improved classroom-related skills.

2. They identify the behaviors that are subordinate to the ultimate goals—the steps along the way.

3. They provide ways to determine the child's location within that hierarchy of subordinate goals, that is, ways to find out what he already can do as well as what he cannot do.

4. They provide methods/materials for teaching the youngster how to proceed from where he is at present to where he should ultimately be. The program should offer different levels of instruction, allowing the child to start, if necessary, at a three- to four-year-old level and progress as rapidly as he can through the higher levels.

VISUAL PERCEPTUAL SKILLS TRAINING

A full-scale visual analysis skills training program should be organized into four stages.

Stage one can best be characterized as simple *hand-eye coordination activities that have to be worked through in a step-by-step sequence.* For example, such activities as coloring pictures, cutting out shapes, pasting shapes together into patterns, folding (paper, towels, etc.), drawing on chalkboard, connecting dots, stacking blocks, stringing beads, moving levers, pushing buttons, turning handles, managing eating utensils, and so on.

Stage two comprises activities that foster the development of *visual discrimination skills*, with special emphasis devoted to the (spatial) perceptual features of size, shape, orientation, quantity, and distance. There are a number of different ways to design these activities. Probably the most common format employs kindergarten and first grade workbooks that ask the child to find the one (a picture, a letter, etc.) that is different or the ones that are the same. These are sold in many places, including supermarkets, drugstores, and school supply stores. (A word of caution: some workbooks are very good; some are reasonably good, and some are simply not good at all. And to complicate the choice even more, some are very good for some children, but not others. In other words, the activities cannot be judged independent of the child who is to use them, especially if they are not sequenced in a way that allows you to determine what is appropriate for the child of concern. A rule of thumb is to look for activity books that challenge but do not frustrate; too easy is no good, too difficult is even worse. How do you identify the ones you want? Consult with others and try some out as you watch the child. Make your decisions accordingly. There is no better way.)

Another approach in this stage is to employ common household objects to provide the child with experiences in *matching, sorting,* and *organizing*. For example, have him sort and/or organize

- buttons according to size, color, etcetera
- eating utensils according to shape, size, etcetera
- playing cards according to suit, number, etcetera
- shoes according to size, color, etcetera
- nuts, bolts, and other hardware items according to size
- socks according to color, size, etcetera
- food containers (e.g., cans) according to size or color

Stage three consists of activities that lead to the discovery of strategies for *analyzing spatially organized patterns to the degree needed to reproduce them*, for example, activities that teach the child how to go about copying unfamiliar geometric designs, mosaic patterns, block constructions, and the like from concrete as well as drawn representations.

Stage four consists of activities that foster the development of *strategies for solving spatial reasoning problems*. (Remedial programs that stop short of this last stage will not produce the effects you want.) For example:

- Draw (copy) designs the way they would look if he were sitting opposite rather than in front of them.
- Complete patterns (sequences of designs) that already contain

enough clues to make this possible such as: *"Look at this row of shapes* [or letters, numerals, etc.]. *The first is a circle, the second is a square, the third is a circle. What should the next one be?"* (Note: This need not be limited to visual stimuli; you can carry out the same activity by naming rather than showing; see chapter 9. Obviously, there is no limit on the number of different patterns that can be generated, and these can range from simple to complex.)

THE VISUAL ANALYSIS SKILLS PROGRAM

The program described below, which provides activities at all stages, was first published in 1975, in the first edition of this book. The information on which that remedial program was based comes from my clinical experiences obtained between 1950, when I first got interested in children with enigmatic learning problems, and 1968, when I started the Perceptual Skills Research Project at the University of Pittsburgh's Learning Research and Development Center (LRDC). I have revised it since 1975 (and these revisions are included here), but its fundamental principles remain unchanged.

My research goals during those seven years at the LRDC were to answer the following questions:

1. Are any of the behaviors we call perceptual skills truly correlated with school learning in some specific ways, or are they simply general indices of development that overlap school performance?

The answer: our research showed that visual and auditory analysis skills are closely correlated with school learning (in the ways discussed in chapter 6). We also discovered (in contradiction to what was conventional wisdom at that time) that although gross and fine-motor skills sometimes correlate with academic performance, the correlations are weak and not exploitable in any practical way.

2. Is it possible to improve these basic visual and auditory analysis skills through controlled experiences, or must one wait for them to develop naturally?

The answer: our research (and that of others) showed that visual and auditory analysis skills can be improved (in children who are lagging in that aspect of development) by *instruction,* if the lag is not due to a neurological deficit.

3. If you improve a child's perceptual skills through instruction, are the effects observable in the correlated school behavior? In other words, if you are able to improve a child's auditory analysis skills, will his word attack skills also improve? Or, if you are able to improve a child's visual analysis skills, will his arithmetic abilities also improve?

The answer: yes; we found that *if* you provide the training early in the child's school career *before* he has slipped too far behind what the lessons assume he already knows.

4. Is it possible to describe the perceptual skills instructional program in a way that makes it possible for others (parents, teachers, etc.) to obtain the same results?

The answer: yes, the method can be described; the results can be replicated.

The program that evolved from all this information was published in 1973 under the title Perceptual Skills Curriculum. It was field tested and validated in a number of schools in the United States, Canada, and Australia. It was updated in 1982 under the name PREP. Both programs were published by Walker Educational Book Corporation.

The Connection Between the TVAS and the Training Program

The Visual Analysis Skills training program is directly related to the Test of Visual Analysis Skills (TVAS) described in chapter 4. It is designed to remediate visual perceptual skills deficits.

It does this by defining a set of goals that, when achieved, enable the child to "pass" the TVAS. Based on my research and experience, you can expect that as he does better on the TVAS, he will also do better in other perceptual skills tests as well as in classroom-related activities.

That is the unique feature of the TVAS. The other tests become invalid if you set about teaching the child how to pass them. Not so with the TVAS; we will see why when we examine the training program.

The Training Program

1. The child's starting point in this program is determined by the score he obtained on the TVAS (see pp. 33–40). As pointed out when we discussed that test, the table on p. 40 enables you to convert that TVAS score to a Level 1 to 8, and its grade equivalent.

2. Now look back at the table on page 40 and locate the grade that the child is in presently. This shows the level (the range of TVAS scores) expected from children in his grade and the level he should be in.

3. You have now determined "where he is" and "where he should be." It is now time to get started in the activities. (Obviously, if he is where he should be, then there is no good reason to implement the training program.)

4. Appendix A provides two hundred teaching patterns that are very much like the TVAS test patterns. The training program is based on teaching the child how to copy these two hundred patterns under different conditions. As the child learns to do this, his TVAS score will improve. And, as his TVAS score improves, so, too, will his performance in the

correlated school behaviors *if* the qualifying statements about prognostic factors (pp. 86–90) are interpreted correctly.

5. Also in the appendix are instructions for teaching each level of the training program. To start, simply identify the procedure that fits the child's entering level (as designated by the table on p. 40), and go to work.

6. The procedure identifies the teaching patterns you will use and explains how to use them. If the child's TVAS score was eight or below, you will need a simple device called a *geoboard*. The geoboard was originally developed for teaching geometric principles or, more accurately, helping children discover these principles on their own. Although geoboards can be purchased from school supply companies, I suggest you make your own—a ten-inch square of perforated plywood (holes are one inch apart) will serve nicely. It can be assembled in different configurations of five, nine, or twenty-five bolts (secured by nuts), "pins" on which rubber bands may be stretched to construct geometric shapes. (Instructions for assembling the geoboard are shown in Appendix A on p. 169.) The number of pins needed in the geoboard is specified in the procedures.

7. To be effective, the training program should be implemented five days per week, about thirty minutes per day. However, it is also important to recognize that the training program is not like a diet; missing a day or two of activity now and then will not make the child slip behind—he just will not move ahead. (And even that is not completely true because once a youngster starts to acquire better visual analysis skills, he begins to exercise them in different situations, thereby getting better without the benefit of specific lessons.)

8. You will also need one or two maps (depending on the procedure) comprising five, nine, seventeen, or twenty-five dots. These, too, are in Appendix A, p. 171.

9. Within a month or so you should be able to document the child's progress in a number of ways. First, of course, he should be moving through the program and making a better score on the TVAS. Second, his printing/writing should be showing signs of improvement and his papers should be better organized. Third, he should be starting to demonstrate a more orderly, methodical approach to a number of day-to-day situations, such as organizing his time/efforts better, noticing things that facilitate learning, and so on. (Note: do not expect major improvement in his school subjects unless he was not that far behind to start with or unless he is not very far along in school—kindergarten or first grade, for example. Improved analysis skills does not mean increased knowledge; it means that the child will be easier to teach. He will still have to be taught, and he will still have to learn.)

10. Continue until the child reaches the training level (and achieves a

score on the TVAS) that is one step beyond what his present grade level predicts; this extra step serves as a safety measure.

Why Not Go Beyond the TVAS Limits?

There are times when it might seem desirable to continue the training program into levels more difficult than what I have defined here, especially when the child is beyond elementary school. I do not advise it. Any energy available at that time should be devoted to the school skills/knowledge that he lacks. His improved visual analysis skills will enable him to respond better to compensatory instruction efforts. In fact, his perceptual skills will also continue to improve even though the training program is stopped. Why this occurs will become clear when we get to chapter 10 and talk about effective compensatory instructional programs.

AUDITORY PERCEPTUAL SKILLS

There are a number of auditory perceptual skills training packages on the market—not quite as many as there are programs designed to improve visual perceptual skills, but enough. As always, some are better than others for the same reasons as was noted. Once again, good auditory programs are typically organized into four stages of activity.

Stage one. Vocal-ear coordination. Mimicking speech patterns. Generally, this falls within the province of the speech and language therapist and, like hand-eye coordination tasks, stresses the skills needed to produce a sequence of sounds accurately and in correct order, for example, simple voice-ear coordination activities (e.g., talking, singing, etc.).

Stage two. Discrimination tasks. Identification of precise similarities and differences in spoken words. Typically, these subdivide into beginning sounds, final sounds, and medial sounds (e.g., "Listen to these words—pen, pin, pen. Which word is different? Which are the same?")

Stage three. Replication tasks. Listening to and repeating clusters of sounds that do not constitute meaningful words (e.g., "Repeat what I say: 'flib,' or 'linderplan,' " etc.). The complexity of the clusters (length, sound sequences) may be varied. In all cases, the child is taught to listen, analyze, and repeat. (Foreign language recordings may be useful in this activity if the words are spoken clearly and slowly.)

Stage four. Problem-solving tasks.
• Delete a single sound from a sequence (e.g., "Say 'boat.' Now say it again but don't say the 'b' sound." (Note: If you do this, do not use words that are included in the TAAS; see p. 45).
• Identify the sound that should be deleted to generate a related word

(e.g., "Say 'sprite.' Now tell me what sound you have to take away from sprite to make spite.")
 • Substitute sounds (e.g., "Say fit. Now say it again, but instead of 'f' say 'm.' ")
 • Reorder sound sequences (e.g., "Say 'cat.' Now say it backward.")
 • These activities, in turn, foster the development of strategies for solving reasoning problems that involve spoken words (e.g., "Listen to these words: 'cat,' 'fat,' 'can.' What word should come next?")
More examples:
cat, cot, bat, _____
cat, coat, bat, _____
cat, can, fat, _____
hat, hot, fat, _____
cat, can, tack, _____
can, clan, pan, _____
trick, track, click, _____
trim, trip, dim, _____
fin, spin, fan, _____
clip, clop, chip, _____
slack, sack, black, _____

THE AUDITORY ANALYSIS SKILLS PROGRAM

Like the visual analysis skills program, the auditory analysis skills program was also first described in the first edition of *Helping Children Overcome Learning Difficulties*. It, too, is based on my clinical experiences and the research conducted at the University of Pittsburgh's Learning Research and Development Center. It, too, has been field tested, validated (not only by me, but by many other researchers as well), and updated; it works.

The Training Program

1. The child's starting point in this program is determined by the score he obtained in the TAAS (see p. 47). The table enables you to convert that TAAS score to a level (1 to 6) and a grade equivalent.
2. Now look back at that table and locate the grade the child is in presently. This shows the range of TAAS scores expected from children in that grade. (There is no practical reason to implement a training program if the child's present auditory analysis skills are at the level expected for his age and grade.)
3. Appendix B contains the procedures (levels 1 through 6) that are designed to teach the child how to do better on the TAAS. As he progresss

through the levels, his TAAS score will improve, and so, too, will his performance in the correlated school behaviors (especially decoding skills), *if* the qualifying statements regarding prognosis (chapter 7) were interpreted correctly.

4. Each procedure has a level designation. To start, simply identify the procedure that fits the child's entering level (as designated by the table on p. 47), and go to work.

6. To be effective, this training program should be implemented five days per week, about ten minutes per day. (Just as with visual skills training, recognize that the program is not like a diet; missing a day or two will not make the child slip behind—he just will not move ahead. And, here again, that is not completely true because once a youngster starts to acquire better auditory analysis skills, he will begin to exercise them in different ways, thereby getting better without the benefit of specific lessons.)

WHAT PERCEPTUAL SKILLS TRAINING DOES AND DOES NOT DO

Just a few reminders:

1. Visual and auditory analysis skills are important because they enable the child to identify those (concrete) features of spatially organized patterns and of spoken words that the symbolic codes of the classroom (letters and numerals) code. As such, they enable the child to recognize that reading, spelling, writing, and arithmetic are based on *systems* (rules) and therefore can be mastered by associated reasoning rather than by rote memorization.

2. Visual and auditory analysis skills are developed naturally by all normal humans, and the rate of that development is reasonably predictable.

3. If visual and/or auditory analysis skills development is lagging, and if that lag is not caused by a neurological impediment, it can be enhanced by specific experiences—activities that lead to improved analysis skills.

4. Such experiences need not be programmed; they may be provided by a vast number of different activities. In all cases, the important ingredient is that the activities should have the potential to enhance the child's ability to recognize the sensory (structural) features in information and, through this, to recognize that many objects/words in our environment contain these same features.

The central point is that perceptual skills training is not like a medicine that "cures" a child. Perceptual skills training cures nothing. If effective, it enhances the child's analysis skills and makes him better equipped for a standard instructional environment because he is able to identify and relate what he is to learn *today* to something he has already learned; hence, he will not have to depend on memorization.

If the child's perceptual skills are deficient (and his language development is not deficient), then training that is effectively implemented before the child has slipped behind in school will enable him to make satisfactory school progress under standard instructional conditions.

If training is delayed for this child until after he has slipped behind in the classroom, then his school performance will not improve even if the training program is remarkably successful. The only way to overcome a deficit in school achievement is by learning the information/skills that represent that achievement; and that can only be accomplished through direct (and, usually, directed) experiences with the school material itself.

AVOID "MIRACLE CURES"

Some of you may have gotten to this point and begun to wonder why I have ignored some of the other learning disability treatment programs that are currently being talked about around the country. This is reasonable; I will get to the ones I know something about very shortly.

First, however, we should spend a little time getting historical perspective on the subject. As you know, one great advantage of knowing history is that it might prevent you from making a similar error.

Séguin

People have been trying for at least three centuries to devise treatments that will improve a child's cognitive abilities. I will not go back that far; we will begin our retrospective search with Édouard Séguin, an early nineteenth-century French physician who had an active interest in retarded children. His theory was that because so many retarded children also displayed poor gross and fine-motor skills—remember, this was at a time when retardation was detected on rather imprecise criteria; there were no IQ tests—perhaps the best way to help them improve their intellectual skills was to help them improve their motor skills.

Séguin devised a set of gross motor-training exercises (e.g., climbing a rope ladder, walking up and down stairs, balancing on a board) that he called the "physiological" method. In fact, he wrote a book about it, *Idiocy, and Its Treatment with the Physiological Method,* which was translated into English and published in the United States in the mid-1800s. Séguin also tried to invent a method for monitoring the effects of his treatment using form boards, wherein the child was asked to fit different wooden shapes into their proper slots in a board. Séguin never proved his theory, but he remained committed to it throughout his life, and wrote a number of papers about it.

Montessori

Some of Séguin's work came to the attention of an Italian physician who was very interested in children: Maria Montessori. Montessori practiced in Rome at the end of the nineteen hundreds at a time when Italy was experiencing an economic depression and many men were unemployed. Women could get work as maids, but they had no place to leave their children; there were no day care facilities.

Montessori seized the opportunity: she succeeded in convincing the owner of a large apartment complex to donate one of his empty apartments as a *casa de bambini*—a "house for children" or a day care center. This allowed the mothers to go to work. And, more to her purposes, it gave Montessori the opportunity to demonstrate the validity of a theory she supported strongly: that children did not really have to be taught, they simply needed the opportunity to learn through stimulating experiences. She stocked the casa with a number of different toys and other interesting devices and activities, all intended to stimulate the senses of the children, and she trained her teachers to guide rather than teach. (In many ways, the open classroom concepts of the 1960s were based on these principles.)

As we all know, Montessori's theory appeals to lots of people; today there are hundreds of Montessori schools in this country and abroad, some staffed by teachers who were trained at the Montessori center in Switzerland, some simply trading on the name.

Interestingly, Montessori never provided any scientific evidence that her theory was valid. To those who have observed it and watched how different children responded to the type of environment she advocated, there is little doubt about its value with the right type of child. The Montessori classroom is a wonderful place for the child who enters it with appropriately developed analysis skills and language abilities; it is not very good for the learning disabled child. He needs something different; he literally needs to be taught.

Gesell

Arnold Gesell was a pediatrician who spent his entire professional life (and it was a long one) observing children and describing how they changed from birth on. He and his co-workers published a long list of articles and books on the subject, identifying the milestones of social, adaptive, language, and motor development.

Strictly speaking, Gesell did not attempt to devise methods for hastening development for children who were lagging. But, in 1948, in a book called *Vision and Its Development in Infant and Child*, he allowed himself to speculate a bit about the possibility that visual development could be "guided." The term *vision*, in the context of this book, went beyond eyesight and implied "perception": the ability to interpret what was seen. He offered no treatments, no methods, but the notion was interesting to many people. (Remember, this was just when the baby boom was getting under way, when schools were very overcrowded, when annual achievement testing was being adopted by schools all over the country, and when the popular press was full of articles about the forthcoming space crunch in our colleges. Parents worried about whether their first grader would get into college, especially if his achievement test scores were low. It created a climate for innovative thinking, and the inevitable happened.)

Developmental Programs

Lots of people from lots of professions joined the movement. Lots of treatment methods were spawned and though they all lacked supportive scientific data, each had its share of believers. In general, they all were based on the loosely integrated rationale that (1) human development is a predictable phenomenon; children can be expected to do certain things at certain ages, regardless of race, religion, and socioeconomic status; (2) many children who encounter difficulty in school also showed some deviation from the expected in their preschool development; (3) in order to improve the child's present developmental status, one had to deal first with those earlier deviations.

For example, if the child had missed the crawling stage (not an unusual situation) and had gone instead from "sitting unaided"—a developmental milestone—to standing and walking, then the first treatments had to focus on providing the child with those missing crawling experiences. (If the child stayed with the program long enough, he eventually got into activities like those described in chapter 8. So it was not without merit, but it certainly was drawn out.)

To many parents, it was the answer. They embraced it with fervor, and became strong vocal advocates of the practitioner and the profession he or she represented. Unfortunately, very little research was conducted; everything was based on reason, and enthusiastic supporters. There are vestiges of it still around, but it has lost much of its early appeal.

Drugs and Diet

There are a number of so-called drug treatments and controlled diets for learning disabled children. These range from large doses of vitamins, to "pep" pills that have a paradoxical calming effect on some children, to diets that avoid artificial food colorings. Diet is the only treatment that has been researched properly, but it has not met the test. (As already noted, certain drugs—Ritalin, for example—have been shown to have a settling effect on some hyperactive children and are therefore much appreciated by their parents and schoolteachers. However, despite its positive effect on some children, there are no studies showing that Ritalin improves school achievement.)

Eye Dominance

The notion that learning disabled children are what they are because of "crossed dominance" keeps appearing on the scene. It was popularized during the 1930s (indeed, there were sponsors of the theory long before then), came back into popularity during the 1960s, and was reintroduced in the past decade. In essence, the rationale is that right-handed children should be "right-eyed"; that is, when asked to look through a paper tube, or a hole in a sheet of paper, they should sight with their right eye. If a right-handed child sights with his left eye, he is said to have crossed dominance, implying that the wrong hemisphere of his brain is being used and, therefore, it is not surprising that he tends to "see backward." Treatments were devised: Their main approach was to patch the interfering eye and force the correct eye to take over the dominant role. (There were other treatment components as well, but I was never able to figure out whether these were also viewed as essential or merely served as "window trimming.")

It is a seductive theory; it seems to "make sense" to the layperson. But it is not valid for a number of reasons. First, both eyes are represented in both hemispheres of the brain; it is not analogous to motor functions, where the right arm is managed by the left brain. Second, and even more convincing, a few researchers have examined the validity of the theory by testing large numbers of children and analyzing the relationship between so-called crossed dominance and school achievement. In every case, the theory has been found lacking: crossed dominance does not predict school learning problems, and the opposite—unilateral dominance—does not guarantee satisfactory school progress.

Eye Movements

This is another resilient theory, and for the same reason. Despite a lack of supporting scientific evidence, it is appealing because it makes sense to the layperson; and it has particular appeal to the anxious parent of the learning disabled child because it explains his difficulties on the basis of fine-motor function rather than on the basis of an intellectual deficit.

Eye movement treatment programs have been offered for many years. In the main, they comprise different activities that engage the child in following a moving target (e.g., a swinging ball that is suspended from the ceiling, a target on a rotating device). These too often have adjunct components that involve hand-eye activities, and it is difficult to determine whether the motivation for including these is meant to be therapeutic or cosmetic. In any case, there is no research evidence to support the theory.

Colored Filters

This is another fetching idea. Years ago someone invented a device that shone different colored lights into the eye. In essence, it was a light source and an assortment of different-colored lenses that could be positioned in front of the light source. The inventor, whoever he was, called the instrument a Syntonizer and made elaborate (and unsubstantiated) claims about its power as a treatment not only for visual disorders but for systemic disorders as well. It all but disappeared in time, but now it is back. A new version of the device is being produced and syntonic treatments are being offered for a variety of ailments including learning disabilities.

About thirty years ago, someone proposed that children had learning disabilities because they could not focus appropriately on the blue letters that were characteristic of ditto sheets. (This was just before the era of black-and-white photocopying; classroom materials were duplicated with carbon stencils in a process called mimeographing.) The idea took hold and dittos were discarded, but the learning disability phenomenon remained.

More recently, a new variation has been introduced, based on the following facts: when one reads, the eyes "hop" (move in quick jumps) across the lines of print. Remarkably, we do not notice movements in our visual field as this occurs. The reason we do not see movement is complicated and not worth going into here.

What is worth noting is the proposition that learning disabled children have difficulty learning to read because their eyes do not function normally and because they do see movement in their visual field when they move their eyes across a line of print. The proposed treatment is colored lenses or colored transparent plastic that is placed on the reading material.

The theory has great appeal, especially to the anxious parents of learning disabled children. But the research is lacking. I have not seen any data that could lead me to recommend colored filters (or transparencies) for the learning disabled child.

Summary

I have not mentioned all of the "miracle" treatments currently available, but I trust that I have made my point: learning disabled children are best treated on the basis of an educational rationale. There is no evidence to show that these children have scrambled neurological systems, or highly idiosyncratic visual systems, or remarkably sensitive digestive systems. But there is plenty of evidence to show that their parents are willing to try anything that sounds halfway reasonable. And when that circumstance exists, there are always individuals who are ready to offer "help" for a fee.

Most of us believe that the age of miracles is past. Do not waste resources looking for an esoteric cure. Look instead for ways to convince schools about the importance of a child's perceptual skills and language development and his entering knowledge base as these influence his ability to make satisfactory progress in a standard classroom. And look also for ways to convince schools to provide appropriately designed instructional programs for those who need it.

9
IMPROVING A CHILD'S
LANGUAGE SKILLS

I HAVE REPEATEDLY STRESSED that both perceptual skills and language skills are prerequisites to making satisfactory progress in a standard instructional setting. I have also differentiated between perceptual skills and language abilities, describing the former as fundamental organizational skills—the ability to analyze spatial and oral information on the basis of its concrete (structural) features—and the latter as the ability to analyze abstract (semantic) information on the basis of those aspects of the information that facilitate retention and recall.

As such, perceptual skills and language are different yet similar. Perceptual skills evolve naturally and achieve full development within the first decade or so following birth. Language is learned through experiences and never achieves full development—we can learn new words and ways to use them until the day our brain ceases to function normally. On the other hand, the former—albeit quite circumscribed—provides the basis for the latter. Perceptual skills are the tools that enable us to relate units of semantic information to other units that contain similar concrete features, and language enables us to relate units of semantic information to other units that contain similar abstract features.

It has been said (and I believe) that a human's basic cognitive behaviors are really quite simple; it is experience that provides us with the knowledge to use these behaviors in increasingly complex settings. Translated to this discussion, we can say that the process of organizing concrete information is really quite simple and provides the basis for our being able to exploit language in an effective way. The child who knows the meaning of lots of words but lacks basic spatial analysis skills will not be able to take full advantage of his learned vocabulary to organize information. The child with good spatial analysis skills but poor vocabulary will not be able to exercise his basic organizational skills fully because of inadequate language. Both limitations are problems; both have to be addressed. Treating one effectively will not eliminate the need to treat the other.

In chapter 5, I offered a number of test items that could be used to determine the child's present knowledge state (as illustrated by his language). If you go back and look at those items again, you will notice that they really investigate two sets of abilities.

Those designed for younger children focus mainly on vocabulary development and on how many common words the child understands as compared with what is expected for his age. Those designed for the older children concentrate not so much on the meaning of specific words but rather on the child's ability to obtain and organize information (regardless of whether it is received by eye or by ear) and express it orally.

Obviously, these two sets of abilities are interrelated; the first—knowledge of vocabulary—facilitates the second. Thus when we set about attempting to improve a child's language skills, we should be concerned about both, paying more attention at first to the child's vocabulary and adding to this, when appropriate, a component devoted to improving his ability to communicate (receive and express information) in an organized manner.

VOCABULARY IMPROVEMENT

What Words Should He Know?

As mentioned in chapter 5, the best source for a list of words that should be in the child's spoken vocabulary (considering his age) is your local library. The librarian will be able to identify books written for the child's age, and an examination of those books will yield a list of words that the child should understand and be able to use. (The library will probably also have a reference book that lists words organized in accord with grade levels.)

Having acquired such a list, set about teaching him the words he does not yet know. This can be done in a number of ways, some of which are described as follows.

To Teach Vocabulary

As you look through the following activities you will realize that the beginning ones are rather easy and therefore usually inappropriate for children beyond first or second grade. However, as you read over these activities, you will see that most of them can be modified so that they are applicable to the very young preschooler as well as challenging to the competent high school student.

The trick is to keep the level of demand appropriate for the child you are working with. How do you do that? Do some trial and error experimenting; in addition to using the words you find in books written for his age level, introduce some more difficult ones. If he can respond success-fully, then fine; if he cannot, so be it. Failure to respond correctly does not injure a child's ego; punishing him (implicitly or overtly) for respond-ing incorrectly does. So if you confront him with words that are beyond his reach, simply accept the responsibility for making the error of select-ing one at too difficult a level. Scale down a bit, and start again.

Activities

1. *Show and tell.* Have the child describe an object (e.g., a toy) that he likes and that is within his view. Ask him questions. Try to structure the questions so that they are meaningful and help organize the informa-tion he is trying to convey; ask questions that focus on, rather than lead away from, the matter being discussed. (Although this is usually a kindergarten activity, it is easy to see how it can be adapted to a much higher cognitive level. Inspiring a high school youngster to talk about his day, or something else in his life, can stimulate significant vocabulary development.)

2. *Tell me what you see.* Show the child a photograph or a short video, and have him describe and/or summarize it. Encourage him to go beyond simply listing things. Try to get him to express a main idea, supporting related information and, if possible, some inferences he drew from it. For example, given a photo of a wintry scene in which a house is shown with Christmas decorations, even the young child should be able to infer the holiday and build some story on that. (Again, it is not difficult to recognize how this same activity can be used with an older child, simply by selecting a more complex situation that he is to describe.)

3. *Finish the sentence.* State the beginning segment of a sentence and ask the child to complete it in a meaningful way. Encourage him to make his responses lengthy and interesting. (Once he shows some ability in this activity, it is useful to ask him to complete it in a silly way.) For example:

  a. "The little boy jumped when _____."
  b. "There was thunder and lightning; the moon was _____."
  c. "The dog's bark was as loud as _____."
  d. "When I wake up, I think about _____."

You can make this more challenging by urging the child to invent similies to complete the sentences.

4. *Colors.* Teach the child to identify the primary colors. This is best accomplished with the following sequence:

  a. Have the child match colors without naming them, for example, "Show me another crayon that is this same color."
  b. Have him match colors as you name them, for example, "This

is a red crayon. Show me another crayon that is this color and tell me what that color is.''

c. Have him identify a color that you name but do not also show, for example, ''Which of these crayons is red?''

d. Have him name the color, for example, you point to a color: ''What color is this?''

(With older children, expand the range of colors used in the exercise and delete those activities that are too easy.)

5. *Body parts*. Teach the child the names/locations of the major body parts: head, arms, legs, feet, hands. Then teach him that these parts contain other parts, for example, the eyes, ears, nose, mouth are all located in the head; arms have elbows, wrists, and so on. This can be accomplished in a number of different ways. To name but a few:

a. Nursery rhymes/songs (e.g., ''If you're happy and you know it . . .''

b. Play Simon Says (''Simon says touch your nose,'' etc.).

c. Drawing figures and marking the major body parts with distinctive colors.

(With older children, convert the activity to a memory exercise by having them touch sequences of named body parts. The goal is to follow the sequence correctly. For example, ''Touch your nose, then your knee, then your left ear with your right hand.''

6. *Spatial words*. Teach the meaning of the following words by having the child relate them to actions; have him both respond to your words and describe your actions in words.

in (''Put your penny *in* the box'' and/or to stimulate his use of the word: ''Where did I put your penny?'')

on
over
under
out
near
far
up
down
little
big
in front of
behind
center
corner
long
short
middle

forward
backward
(With older children, use such words as diagonal, orthogonal, perpendicular, parallel, etc.)
7. *Words that compare.* Teach the child how to use the following words correctly. (Again, have the child relate the words to actions; have him respond to the spoken words and describe situations you create.)
more than
less than
same
different
lower
higher
first
second
bigger
smaller
enough
not enough
8. *Count to ten*
   a. By rote; teach with nursery rhymes; by clapping as you count, etc.
   b. Count specific quantities using concrete materials, such as blocks.
   c. "What number comes just after _____?"
   d. "What number comes just before _____?"
   (With older children, delete the counting activities and introduce questions *c* and *d* using higher numbers.)
9. *Geometric shapes.* Teach the child the names of the familiar geometric shapes.
circle
square
rectangle
triangle
cross
plus
oval
semicircle
octagon
   Don't expect him to be able to draw all of these, although he might. Follow this sequence:
   a. Matching: show the child a shape (it can be cut out of cardboard or drawn), name it, and ask him to find another just like it. (If you wish, you may introduce size and color concepts at the

same time by using different sizes and colors of the same shape.)

b. "Show me a _____." Place an assortment of shapes before the child and ask him to identify a specific one.

c. "What do you call this?" Show the child a shape and ask him to name it.

(With older children, introduce more complex shapes, such as polyhedron, rhomboid, etc.)

10. *Synonyms. Tell me another word that means . . .*

big
small
many
bright
nice
naughty
thin
pretty
(Use more difficult words with older children.)

11. *Antonyms. Tell me a word that means the opposite of . . .*

hot
small
thin
bad
heavy
bright
funny
top
here
stop
first
high
(Use more difficult words with older children.)

12. Say words that begin with the _____ sound.

(With younger children, use single sounds, such as /c/, /t/, etc. With older children, use consonant-vowel combinations, such as *ca* [candy, cantaloupe, cap, castle, cantilever], *ro* [road, roast, roaming, rodeo], *be* [benefit, belt, benevolent, beggar].)

13. *Say words that have a _____ sound in them.*

(Again, with older children use letter combinations rather than single sounds unless, of course, single sounds are sufficiently challenging.)

14. *Say a word that rhymes with*

cat
cut

cot
fin
tan
cold
run
boy
man

15. *Make up alliterations.* Identify a sound and have the child try to invent an alliterative sentence—the longer (and sillier) the better.

16. *What am I thinking of?* Describe, little by little, an object, person, or word that the child is familiar with and have him identify it, encouraging him to identify it as early in the process as possible. Then switch roles and have the child do the describing, for example, "I'm thinking of something that is good to eat. It is sweet. It grows on a tree. Its color is orange."

17. *Stand up* (or perform some other motor behavior) *when I say the magic word* (e.g., *to*). Child sits and listens as you speak. He gets a point if he responds correctly. For example:

    a. "fun, go, listen, three, see, do, boat, to, make . . ." (Child should have stood up when you spoke the word *to*.)

    b. "My horse is gray. He runs very fast. I like *to* ride him."

(With older children, the activity may be modified to having the child respond when he hears a specified sound embedded in a more complex context. For example, "Respond when you hear a word that has the 'ad' sound in it: lap, dash, flag, dad, mit, mat . . ."

18. *What word comes next?*

    a. small, smaller, _____

    b. short, _____

    c. bad, _____

    d. white, _____

    e. high, _____

    f. funny, funnier, _____

    g. tall, taller, _____

19. *Embedded words.*

    a. Identify a short target word and have the child identify words that contain the spoken form of that word. (Forget spelling; think only about the sounds.) Ask the child, "Is the word _____ hidden in the word _____ ?"

Examples:

ate   lately
          slate
          slave

        grate
        migrate
        blame
        grave
        berate
        eliminate
        debate
        delight

ane   Spain
        line
        flame
        stain
        blame
        sane
        Jane
        instantaneous
        claim

ite   delight
        flight
        tight
        white
        slight

b. Show the child how to generate words that contain the smaller word (spoken sounds). Then say, "Tell me a word that has the word _____ in it." For example:

oat   wrote
        gloat
        oatmeal
        float
        coat
        goat
        coated
        dote
        doting
        moat
        smote
        note
        denote
        notation
        tote
        totem

total
vote

aim   same
defame
claim
aimless

20. *Expand the child's vocabulary* by selecting words from his spelling lists, his textbooks, and so on. Encourage him to use the dictionary to learn the meaning of words, and to use them in his conversation. In addition, you can

a. Select a new word each day and ask him to try to fit it into conversations. (Have him record his new words in a "word book.")
b. Select a word and encourage him to try to figure out its meaning, based on its parts (root, prefix, suffix, etc.).
c. Encourage him to try to work crossword puzzles.
d. Play anagrams
e. Play Scrabble and other word games.

21. *Read to him.*

22. *Discuss things with him* and give him ample opportunity to express his thoughts.

IMPROVING LANGUAGE-BASED ORGANIZATIONAL SKILLS

The chief objective of the following activities is to teach the child how to use words to organize thoughts so that they are easier to remember.

Activities

1. Teach the child that information can be organized according to one or more characteristics. *Show him;* do not assume that he is able to do it without your direction until after you have clear evidence that he can. For example, show him (using pictures as well as words) that

a. *Animals* can be organized according to
  • size
  • color
  • food preference (carnivores vs. herbivores)
  • noise they make (bark, roar, squeak)
  • habitat: land, in the house, on the farm, in the wild, in the sea. fresh water versus ocean, air
  • number of feet: two, four, none

    • friendly versus hostile
  b. *Individual animals* (e.g., dogs) can be organized according to
    • size
    • color
    • personality
    • size of ears
  c. *Food* can be organized as
    • eaten hot or cold
    • eaten raw or cooked
    • eaten with a fork or a spoon
    • taste (good/bad, spicy/bland)
    • animal, vegetable, or mineral
    • fruit, vegetable, meat
    • liquid, solid
  d. *Light* can be organized according to
    • color
    • brightness
    • position of source
  e. *Automobiles* can be organized according to
    • color
    • size
    • number of doors
    • age (old/new)
    • license plate
  f. *Miscellaneous:* furniture (size, function, color), houses (size, location, color), trees (size, deciduous/evergreen), television programs (long/short, funny/sad, for children/adults). As is evident, the list is almost endless.

    2. Once the child seems to understand the concept, you name the class (i.e., identify a thing, animal, etc.) and have him identify ways to categorize them. Have him take over from you.

    3. Once he is able to perform the previous task satisfactorily, have him identify different characteristics that lend themselves to categorizing. For example, "How many things [objects, animals, and so on] can you think of that differ in size, in color, in shape? Give me some examples."

    4. Once this concept appears to have been mastered, have the child invent his own classification systems (for example, have him organize a photo or story into persons, animals, objects, events, circumstances, etc.). To start, you may have to show him how to design an organizational structure. Map it out for him on paper or a chalkboard so that he can see it as he thinks about it; then work toward eliminating the visual support.

    5. Teach double classification strategies, using vertical and horizontal columns and/or Venn diagrams (overlapping circles). For example, show the child how to organize ("file") information that has more than one

major characteristic: animals that differ in habitat *and* size, automobiles that differ in the number of doors *and* color, and so on. Work through the same sequence as before.

    a. First, you illustrate (demonstrate) the entire process; then

    b. you construct the organizer (lines and columns, or overlapping circles) and the categories, and have the child fill in the cells; then

    c. you construct the organizer and have the child identify the categories and what belongs in the different cells; then

    d. have the child carry out all the steps, inventing the organizing structure and all else.

  6. Teach triple classification strategies, following the same sequence as before.

  7. Have the child name as many things as he can that may be described as

    sweet
    sour
    pretty
    ugly
    hot
    cold
    soft
    hard
    and so on

  8. Have the child identify things (animals, objects, etc.) that can be the same in one way and different in another. For example:

    a. Automobiles all have a steering wheel yet may differ in color.

    b. People are all humans yet may differ in height, and so on.

    c. Apples all grow on trees yet may differ in taste and appearance.

  9. Unscramble a sentence. Say a list of words to the child and have him organize them into a meaningful sentence. For example, "Listen to these words: 'boy,' 'my,' 'John,' 'is,' 'seven.' Make a sentence out of them." (If necessary, show him the words as you say them in order to reduce the memory demand, then gradually eliminate the visual support.)

    a. *windy, was, a, day, it*

    b. *can, turkey, see, hear, and, I, a*

    c. and so on

  10. Deduction skills. Teach the child how to play twenty (or any number you designate) questions: "I'm thinking of a _____. What is it?" (All questions must be phrased so that they can be answered either yes or no. The best strategy, obviously, is to identify large classes first, thereby narrowing the possible choices as rapidly as possible.)

    For example: "I'm thinking of a number."

        Child: Is it higher than 100?   Answer: "No."
                "Is it higher than 50?"   Answer: "No."
                "Is it higher than 25?"   Answer: "Yes."
And so on.

Some suggestions: "I'm thinking of a . . ."
friend
animal
food
dairy product
drink
president of the United States
country
river (It does not detract to have him look at a map as he plays this game; in fact, it probably helps to provide him with reference sources.)
state
city
piece of furniture
song, book, or movie title
and so on

10. Teach him the concept of a pun.

11. Keep on a lookout for riddles, jokes, and other interesting word-related activities.

12. Teach him (and have him practice) how to file information according to

    a. alphabetic order (e.g., give him a stack of index cards, each containing a word, and have him organize these alphabetically, starting off by sorting into large subgroups [e.g., words that begin with the letters *A* through *M* and words that begin with the letters *N* through *Z*] and then subdividing these into smaller groups as appropriate). You can give this a contest format by measuring how long it takes him to find a designated telephone number in a phone book.

    b. numerical order (e.g., give him a stack of canceled checks, each showing a number, and have him organize these numerically, starting off by creating large subgroups [e.g., checks showing the numbers 1 through 50, another group showing the numbers 51 through 100, etc.], and then subdividing these as appropriate).

    c. size (e.g., give him an assortment of round disks that vary in size and have him organize them).

    d. shape.

    e. color.

 f. monetary worth (e.g., give him an assortment of coins and have him figure out different ways of organizing them: i.e., according to their worth, in clusters of value [a dollar's worth in each cluster], and so on).

13. Remembering lists. State a list of words that he is to remember. Start with short 2- and 3-word lists, and gradually make them longer. Develop the lists so that they may best be organized according to their

 a. beginning sound (e.g., bed, butter, bread; cake, cans; or apple, bun, can, dog, etc.).

 b. size (e.g., bee, ant, elephant, hippopotamus, etc.).

 c. color (e.g., carrot, orange; banana, lemon, etc.).

 d. location (e.g., location within your local supermarket, within the home, within some other geographical area, etc.).

 e. function (e.g., knife, pen, fork, pencil, spoon).

Show him the best way to remember these lists (i.e., how you would do it), stressing that there is no single way that works best for all situations and that the trick is to figure out the best way for the task at hand.

14. Map reading. Identify three or four specific sites on a map, along with a "home base," and have the child

 a. identify and compare the distance between home base and each of these.

 b. the shortest route between home base and any two or three of these.

 c. the shortest round-trip route.

 d. the longest round-trip route.

It would also be helpful to teach him the concept of longitude and latitude as they are employed in maps.

 a. Locate a specific place on a map in terms of its longitude and latitude and have the child find and name that place.

 b. Then change roles; have him locate a specific place on a map in terms of its coordinates, and you identify that place.

15. Remember the location. Once the child has gotten familiar with the map, have him close his eyes (or blindfold him), spread the map on a table in front of him (or on a wall), place his finger on home base, and have him attempt to locate (by moving his finger) one of the other sites he has been dealing with. The goal is to be able to visualize relative positions in space based on a mental map.

16. Play strategy games, such as

 a. pen the pig.

 b. ghost (or hang the . . .): spelling.

 c. checkers.

 d. submarine (sometimes called warships).

 e. card games: cribbage, casino, rummy.

f. tic-tac-toe.

17. Robot. Have the child tell you (words only; no hand movements) how to

a. draw a specific geometric design.

b. construct a design with blocks.

c. put on an article of clothing (e.g., a sock).

d. get from one location in the house to another.

e. obtain an item from a closet, refrigerator, etc.

f. get from one outdoor location to another (e.g., from the garage to the front door).

(The general goal is to teach the child how to analyze an activity and express it in verbal form. Follow his directions verbatim (but avoid bodily harm), thereby revealing to him the shortcomings of his analysis. This is a difficult activity. Trade places with him once in a while, to give him the opportunity to see how you would analyze the task.

18. Visualize a scene. Ask the child to describe

a. his room.

b. the exterior of his house.

c. the family automobile.

d. the kitchen.

e. a familiar toy.

f. and so on

19. It should be apparent that the preceding list could be extended with variations. The key concern in all of this, however, is not *more* activities but rather activities that *show* the child how to organize verbal information effectively, and then give him the opportunity to practice what he has been shown and to apply the principle in other contexts.

10
COMPENSATORY INSTRUCTION

THE GOAL OF CLASSROOM ACCOMMODATIONS

ALTHOUGH TREATING DEFICIENT perceptual skills and/or language abilities and doing nothing else will not spontaneously eliminate a child's school achievement deficit, teaching him in a way that is effective despite his deficits will improve his perceptual skills and language abilities. Why this is so will become understandable as we get farther along in this chapter.

The goal in modifying instructional conditions is to *enable the child to learn what he will not be able to learn under standard conditions*. This does not mean lowering the standards and judging him on a less demanding set of criteria, or limiting the learning goals; nor does it mean simply repeating a lesson or doing the work for him. It means changing one or more of the components that comprise a standard classroom and modifying instructional conditions in ways that facilitate learning.

THE COMPONENTS OF A STANDARD INSTRUCTIONAL SETTING

In chapter 1, I identified the three critical components of a standard instructional environment: the *teacher*, the *instructional program*, and certain other *environmental factors* that have significant effect on the learning disabled child's academic performance. We now have to consider these three components and try to decide which should (and can) be changed, and how.

The Teacher

What kind of teacher is best for the learning disabled child? What are the characteristics of a teacher who will be most effective with him?

Odd as it may sound, the best kind of teacher for this type of child is one who tends to be pedantic (in a benign sense) rather than stimulating—

someone who is patient, explains things slowly and adequately, and clarifies the explanation if necessary; someone who accepts the fact that the child will have bad days as well as good days, days when it appears that there is no hope.

In addition, this teacher must know her craft and be secure enough to persist for more than a week or two with the instructional approach she knows to be correct.

And finally, this teacher must be able to motivate the child, gain his trust, and inspire his continued effort in the face of periodic failure.

Teachers like this are not easy to find, but they do exist. Usually they are very experienced; only rarely are they beginners. The kind of knowledge and skills they have are not acquired in teacher preparation programs; they are the outcome of repeated experiences that are instructive because the teacher was motivated to learn, to profit from her mistakes, to analyze her successes, and to become a *teacher*.

How do you find such a teacher? And, having found her, how do you see to it that the child you are concerned about is placed with her? These are difficult questions.

One place to start is to contact other parents in the child's school who have been through the same process; experience is a good teacher. Many of these parents belong to the Association for Children with Learning Disabilities (ACLD) and are great sources of information. It is worth seeking them out. There are local chapters in many cities and towns. The national offices are at 4156 Library Rd., Pittsburgh, PA 15234; they will be glad to provide a listing of chapters near you. (It also might be worthwhile to look at your telephone directory. Most ACLD chapters have local listings.) Another possible source of support is the Orton Dyslexia Society. Their national headquarters is at 724 York Rd., Baltimore, MD 21204. They might be able to identify a parent-member located near you.

Now to the other question: having found what you hope is the right teacher, how do you see to it that the child you are concerned about is placed with her? If it is a teacher who is working in the child's school, then the best way to obtain her services is to negotiate with the school's principal. In doing this, be assured that the old cliché "the squeaky wheel gets the grease" is valid—be assertive, be persistent, be emphatic. Nothing is likely to happen if you behave otherwise. Obviously, if it is a teacher who is not working in the child's school, then the only feasible solution is to contract with her for tutorial services. This is not an ideal circumstance but it is better than nothing.

One more practical question: what do you do if, in addition to your not being able to identify a teacher who displays the desired traits, you find that the child is assigned to a teacher who has traits that are completely contrary to the child's needs? This does not mean that she is a bad teacher, only that she will be a bad teacher for this child. She may very well be a wonderful teacher for another type of child.

You again negotiate with the school's principal for a different teacher. You do not simply shrug, complain about the situation to yourself and close friends, and let the child bear the brunt of the situation. Each day that a child does not make progress in school is like placing him in a pit that keeps getting deeper; each day of no progress increases the hopelessness of his situation. Be the child's advocate. Do it politely, of course, but do it firmly; and do it before it gets too late, before the pit gets too deep. Remember, a learning disability is an educational problem; a key ingredient in solving the problem is the teacher.

The Instructional Program

This topic is discussed in detail in chapter 11. But before we get to that, there are some general, introductory comments to be made.

In the simplest of terms, the kind of instructional program the learning disabled child needs (regardless of subject) is one in which the key elements of the information presented to him (and that is expected to lead to learning) are as *apparent, unambiguous,* and *regular* (system-based) as possible. An illustration or two will help here.

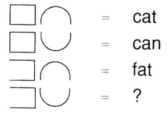

Look at the symbols in the preceding figure. Pretend they are part of a new system for reading and spelling. As you can see, the first set of symbols represents the spoken word *cat;* the second, the word *can;* the third, the word *fat.* Although the figure does not show what the fourth set of symbols represents, you will conclude that it *must* be the word *fan.* How did you accomplish this; why *must* it be *fan?*

You did this by exercising your visual and auditory analysis skills in combination with your language abilities. Relevant to perceptual skills, you identified the pertinent differences and similarities in the visual patterns and related these to the key differences and similarities in the sounds of the words. Relevant to your language abilities, you knew that there was such a word as *fan.* Hence, your decision that it *must* be *fan* was reasonable.

But we also have to acknowledge that this was not a difficult task because the salient information in this lesson was

1. very *apparent*—it was not embedded in a lot of distracting information.

2. *unambiguous*—the letters retained the same sounds in each example.

3. *systematic*—the examples linked up neatly, each containing features that highlighted similar pertinent differences and similarities in all four words; you were able to formulate a "rule" from the examples.

In addition and more important, the lesson did not assume entering knowledge that you did not have; I assumed (correctly) that the word *fan* was in your vocabulary and that you understood the other words in the lesson.

Let's have a look at another illustration.

$$
\begin{array}{ll}
\bigcirc \ = \ 1 & \bigcirc \ = 10 \\
\square \ = \ 4 & \square \ = \ ? \\
\triangle \ = \ ? & \triangle \ = \ ?
\end{array}
$$

Pretend this is a lesson in using a new symbol system for arithmetic. As is shown, the small circle represents the quantity one; the large circle, the quantity ten; the small square, the quantity four. You are not told what the large square represents, yet you will probably be secure in concluding that it represents the quantity forty. If we could speak to each other at this point, you would assert that *it had to* represent forty; it could be nothing else.

How did you accomplish this; why *must* it be forty? You did this by exercising your visual analysis skills in combination with previously acquired knowledge.

Relevant to visual perceptual skills, you identified the salient differences and similarities in the patterns and related them to the facts I supplied. You recognized that a circle consists of a *single* line, that the square comprises *four* lines, and that the size differences between the designs were also germane.

Relevant to the knowledge you brought to this lesson, you recognized the one to ten ratio represented by the two circles and were secure therefore in concluding that the large square *must* represent ten times four, or forty.

Once again, we have to acknowledge that this was not a difficult task because the salient information in this lesson was

1. very *apparent*—it was not embedded in a lot of distracting background information.

2. *unambiguous*—the salient characteristics of the symbols were easy to identify.

3. *systematic*—the circles and squares linked up neatly, each containing features that were readily associated with the quantities they represented. You were able to construct a "rule" from the examples. In addition, the lesson did not assume entering knowledge from you that you did not have. I assumed (correctly) that you would be able to understand my instructions and to infer the one:ten ratio from the lesson.

How about the two triangles? Is it obvious to you what they represent? Perhaps. I am certain that you are willing to argue that one of the triangles represents the quantity three and the other the quantity thirty. But which is which? What is different about this lesson that was not present in the other? Obviously, it is the relative positions of the two triangles.

You will probably decide that the small triangle represents the quantity three, and the larger one the quantity thirty. But if I disagreed, if I said that it was the opposite—that the large triangle represented the quantity three and the smaller one the quantity thirty—you would probably not be comfortable in arguing strongly against that statement. You would simply come to the conclusion that relative size was not salient and that relative position was; that the larger triangle represented the quantity three because it was to the left of the small triangle, and that the size difference had nothing to do with it. In other words, I introduced an ambiguity that made you less secure in concluding what it *must* be.

That same phenomenon occurs often in the classroom, especially in the standard classroom where the instructional programs are designed to be effective with the average child who can cope with a fair amount of ambiguity because his perceptual skills and his knowledge base are developed to the point where he can deal effectively with exceptions to the rule.

The child whose basic analytic aptitudes and/or knowledge base are not adequate is not so fortunate. Exceptions to the rule are mind-boggling to him because he cannot even generate the "rule" to start with. This leaves him with the impression that the only way he will be able to learn is to memorize the information—an impossible task. And to compound his problem, he sees the vast majority of his classmates learning and moving ahead. It is not difficult to imagine the demoralizing effect this has on him.

That is the essence of classroom accommodation—compensatory instruction that takes into account the child's needs. It reduces to the following set of guidelines. (I will repeat these again in chapter 11, along with relevant examples, as we explore how to apply them in the specific subject areas of reading, spelling, writing, and arithmetic.)

GENERAL GUIDELINES FOR COMPENSATORY INSTRUCTION

1. Be certain that the child really does have the factual knowledge he will need in order to learn from the lesson. *Make sure* that he knows what the lesson assumes he knows.

2. Limit the amount of new information presented in a lesson and present it in small bites. Keep explanations short and simple; complex explanations get in the way of learning.

3. Present information in a way that highlights plainly what is especially pertinent (what the child *must* pay attention to if he is to learn), and unless it cannot be avoided stay away from what is potentially ambiguous.

4. Make explicit the *system* that links up the new information in the lesson with something the student already knows. Do not assume that the child will be able to figure out an effective system from appropriate examples. (In other words, leave as little as possible to guesswork; learning disabled children are very poor guessers in the classroom.)

5. As the student becomes familiar with the system and with using small units of analysis, introduce him to larger units ("chunks") that he has not yet identified on his own, and illustrate these through analysis rather than synthesis processes. Teach the larger units by presenting and identifying them, and then show the child that the smaller units (those that he is already familiar with) are embedded in those larger ones.

6. When exceptions to the system are to be taught—as is inevitable in the written form of the English language—these, too, must be made obvious, and the student should be shown an effective way to remember the exceptions. Do not leave it to the child to invent the mnemonic. As already noted, learning disabled children are very poor rule inventors.)

7. Provide enough repeated experiences to establish new information securely in the child's long-term memory. Once you have constructed effective associations for him, have him practice these until he can identify them "on sight," instantaneously and automatically. Have the child practice applying the method you taught him until he no longer needs to use that "method" and until he no longer has to "figure it out" but simply "knows it" and has the information at his fingertips.

8. Drill and practice exercises are most effective if the child is required to *say and write* as he *looks and hears*. Multisensory activities are helpful, not because of some magic effect they have on the brain but rather because saying and writing (or printing) requires the child to pay more precise attention to details than does seeing and hearing.

11
COMPENSATORY
INSTRUCTION METHODS

READING

IN CHAPTER 6, I defined reading as *mapping language onto symbols*. I also speculated on how reading originated, how it eventually became phonetically based after having started as pictographic and then ideographic, and how language is now coded on the basis of its oral sounds rather than on its meaning. I then described the various reading instruction methods that were and, in varied formats, still are used in standard instructional settings.

It is now time to talk about the kind of reading program the learning disabled child needs. It is obvious that he needs something other than the standard; indeed, he probably earned his learning disability designation *because* he did not learn satisfactorily from that standard approach. Let us apply the guidelines listed above to teaching a learning disabled child to read.

Applying the Guidelines to Reading

Guideline 1. Be certain that the child really does have the factual knowledge that he will need in order to learn from the lesson.

How does that apply? What factual knowledge does a child need in order to learn to read, and what should be done if he lacks that knowledge?

1. By definition, he needs to be conversant in the language he is trying to learn to read. As emphasized earlier, if he is not conversant—at least with the words in his reading book and the general rules of grammar that apply—then his learning efforts will be to no avail.

If his knowledge of the language is lacking, then the only option you have is to increase it: use the procedures listed in chapter 9, and use them vigorously (and/or consult a speech therapist).

2. He needs to know enough about the subject matter he is reading

to be able to organize the information in ways that enable him to remember and take meaning from it.

This is not a very common problem with young children, as long as they are conversant in the language they are trying to learn to read. But it may be a problem with older children who are having difficulty reading a technical text, not only because they are inefficient readers but also because they do not know enough about the subject to fill in the inevitable gaps. The only way to deal with this is to see to it that the gaps are filled in. There is no easier way.

3. He needs to be familiar with the printed letters and the conventions that govern their use. True, certain letters are more important than others. Clearly, the letter z is not that critical, nor is the q. Neither one shows up often enough in beginning reading books to make much difference. But, the letters b, d, g, and p do show up, and it is important that the student knows securely which is which so that he does not have to interrupt the reading process in order to figure it out each time he encounters one of them.

What do you do if the child has persistent difficulty keeping those (or some of the other) letters straight in memory? You teach them—or, more accurately, reteach them—in a way that eliminates the confusion. Rather than describe here a method for doing that, I refer you to guideline 4 to illustrate this method.

4. If the information in the lesson you are teaching today can be linked with something that was taught in previous lessons (e.g., if the lesson attempts to teach recognition of the word *book* on the basis of the child already being able to read the word *look*), check to see if the child recalls that reference word (the word *look*). If he does not, then return to that point and teach it again, rather than go on.

Guideline 2. Limit the amount of new information contained in any lesson, and offer it in small bites.

What does this mean in practical terms? Just what it says. Be satisfied with learning that occurs in small increments and do not try to build on to these too rapidly. It is always tempting to try to take advantage of a successful learning breakthrough by following it up immediately with another lesson, especially with a child who is lagging behind and has a fair amount of catching up to do.

Do not do it; allow the child to savor his success and, if he has any energy left, use the moment to establish the newly learned knowledge more securely in long-term memory.

Similarly, when explaining something—a concept, a rule, and so on— try hard to keep your explanations short, simple, and easy to follow and remember. (See guideline 6 for more discussion about this in respect to generating mnemonics.)

Guideline 3. Present information in a way that highlights plainly what is especially pertinent (what the child must pay attention to if he is to learn), and unless it is pertinent avoid what is potentially ambiguous.

1. If the child's visual perceptual skills are deficient, avoid introducing the lowercase *b* and *d* at the same time. Logic might suggest that the opposite is desirable, because the differences between the two letters will be most apparent to the child when they are presented side by side. The child's problem, however, is not in *seeing* that the two are different but rather in *remembering which is which.*

Work on one of these letters only and ignore the other until the one you started with is learned securely. Once the first one is learned, the other one will not present a problem; it will simply be "the other one." (See guideline 4 for more specific suggestions.)

2. If the child is confused about the spatial orientation of the letters (if he sometimes prints right to left instead of left to right), provide a spatial reference point—a heavy red line (drawn with a felt-tip pen) down the left-hand side of the page works well, explaining to the child that he should always start at the upper left-hand corner of the page as he goes across and down.

3. If the child has difficulty with reading comprehension (and if you know that this is not due to a language impairment), take steps to help the child organize the information he is reading. Show him how to identify the main idea and how it relates to subordinate ideas. Illustrate as clearly and as concretely as possible (using pictures, charts, and so on—not just spoken words) how information can be organized by classification and categorization strategies. (See chapter 9 for some examples.)

4. If the child's auditory perceptual skills are deficient, avoid introducing words in which the same vowel represents different sounds; try to teach one vowel sound (e.g., the short *a* sound as in *cat*) so it is well learned before introducing words in which the letter *a* represents a different sound. (Remember the discussion about teaching the lowercase *b* and *d*. Exceptions to the "rule" are learned most successfully after the rule itself has been learned securely.)

Guideline 4. Make explicit the *system* (the "link") that relates the new information in a lesson you are teaching with the information he already knows. Do not assume that the child will be able to figure out an effective system from appropriate examples. (In other words, leave as little as possible to guesswork.) For example:

1. When attempting to help the child who confuses the *b* and *d*, identify an effective mnemonic, a related reference point that the child already has well established in memory.

One way is to find out if the child ever reverses the capital *B*. (Do not ask; have him print it.) If he does not, then use it as the mnemonic for the lowercase *b* by showing him (on a chalkboard) how the lowercase *b* is embedded ("hidden") in the capital *B*. Then have him find and mark the lowercase *b* in all the capital *B*'s he can locate in a book, or a newspaper, or other types of printed material. (Remember, ignore the *d* until he has the *b* securely learned.)

If the child is not secure on the spatial orientation of the *B*, then look for another reliable reference point—the *P*, for example, or the *E*.

Similarly, if you decide to try to teach the lowercase *d* (which means that you should ignore the *b* until the *d* has been securely learned), try to find an already established reference point. One that often works well *for right-handed children* is to first teach them the lowercase *c*.

This is easy to do with right-handed children by showing them that the hand that holds the paper (their *left*) defines the letter *c* when it is placed palm down on the paper they are going to write on. (The space between the fingers and the thumb is open to the right, just like the letter *c*.) This then leads to the orientation of the *d* by showing the child how the addition of a straight line that closes off the opening in the *c* transforms it to a *d*.

(Note: the child should have established a consistent hand preference before you try to teach him the letters. Most children demonstrate a consistent hand preference, that is, they are right-handed or left-handed before their fourth birthday. However, some children enter kindergarten still inconsistent about which hand to use for printing, coloring, and other fine-motor tasks.

No one seems to know why this occurs, but it is apparent that (1) it is usually accompanied by a delay in other aspects of development, and (2) it is important that the child begin to use one hand consistently if he is to remember the spatial orientation of the letters.

How can this be accomplished? *You* select his preferred hand. Examine samples of his printing when done with the right hand and the left, identify which hand provided the better [i.e., neater, more accurate] product, figure out a way of helping the child remember *that* hand [use a wrist ribbon, or a toy wristwatch, or something else of that nature], advise him and his teacher of that decision and the importance of establishing a "habit," and have him do all his printing with that hand. The habit will be established within a few weeks and, as it emerges, the child will experience significantly less confusion with such letters as the *b* and *d*.) I have used this approach for many years and have never observed any undesirable effects from it.

2. If the child's auditory analysis skills are deficient, anticipate that he will not recognize the link-ups between certain sets of words—*cat, catch,* and *catcher,* for example. Point these out, by explanation and with a marking pen that highlights the letter sequence *c-a-t* in all three words. Then have him search for the same letter sequences in other words.

3. Alternative instructional approaches have been designed to make the system evident. There are a number of published reading programs that are designed to make clear the system that underlies reading. For example:

- *initial teaching alphabet* (ita). There are no capital letters in this system, only large and small letters of the same format. Hence the use of lowercase letters when referring to the program.

    ita attempts to solve the mismatch between letters and sounds by using an expanded alphabet—forty-four symbols in all: the twenty-six of our standard alphabet (called by ita "traditional orthography" or "T.O."), plus eighteen new ones. These new symbols are mainly variations and combinations of the T.O. lowercase manuscript letters. By adding these eighteen letters, ita provides a graphic symbol for each sound in the spoken English language, which makes it possible to spell each word just as it sounds.

    However, ita has a couple drawbacks. One is that some of the letters that are unique to ita are too much like some of the lowercase T.O. letters, differing only in their left-right orientation or in some other subtle (and therefore, ambiguous) way. As such, the child with substandard visual analysis skills often has trouble keeping the ita letters straight in memory. Thus the system—the method intended to be helpful—often becomes a major obstacle in itself.

    The second major drawback is that there are very few books available in ita—just those that have been produced specifically for use with the primary grade school reading programs. As a result, the child does not have very much opportunity outside the classroom to practice what is being taught in the classroom. He does not see ita on TV or on billboards or in supermarkets, or anywhere there are things to read.

    This is not a trivial problem. Good beginning readers are good readers because they practice. If the instructional program limits their opportunity to practice, they will not progress as well as they should. The conclusion is that ita is probably a good idea, but not if its use is limited to the first grade classroom.

- *Color coding.* There are a number of reading instruction programs on the market that use color as a way of indicating a letter's sound. For example, the program may initially teach the child to give a specific vowel a "long" sound when the letter is printed in green and a "short" sound when red ink is used.

There are problems, however, the main one being that these programs violate guideline 2. The color-coding system is not simple enough; too many colors are needed to take care of the many vowel sounds in our language.

As a result, the system often turns out to be as difficult to master as learning to read itself. In addition, as with ita, the color-coding system is not universal. When the child goes to the supermarket with his parent, or looks at television and magazines, he sees print in all colors, none of which signal their sounds. The result? Color-coding reading programs do not work very well.

· *Modality preference.* This is not really a reading program but a concept that attempts to forge a link between the child's "modality strengths" (visual or auditory "channels") and the way reading is taught. It is based on the *erroneous* concept that children will learn best if taught via their "stronger" sensory channel. For example, if a child has reasonably good visual analysis skills and poor auditory analysis skills, then he is a "visual" learner and therefore according to the theory will learn best if taught by a so-called sight or whole-word approach. Or if the child has adequate auditory analysis skills and substandard visual analysis skills, then he is an auditory learner and will progress best with an auditory or phonics-based reading program.

This all sounds sensible (and is therefore easy to remember), but it is completely wrong. It does not work, and every research effort to demonstrate its validity has failed—for good reason. It ignores what reading is: *converting (visual) symbols back into their original (oral) form.*

It obviously stems from the rationale that inspired the reading programs for the blind and the deaf. Blind children are taught to read via an intact sensory modality: touch. Deaf children are taught to read with standard visually presented letters, but with modifications that compensate for their very poorly developed language abilities. But in neither of these situations is there an altering of the basic definition of reading: *mapping language onto symbols.* To adopt the modality preference concept in deciding how best to teach the learning disabled child is to invite failure; it is wrongly conceived and it does not work.

Guideline 5. As the student becomes familiar with how the system works with small units of analysis, introduce him to larger units of analysis (chunks) that he has not identified on his own, and illustrate these through analysis rather than synthesis processes.

It is not enough to teach a child that single letters have sounds and that these single sounds can be blended into words. Blending single letter sounds into words works only if the words are short—consisting of three or, at most, four sounds—and spelled exactly the way they sound. If the child is to learn how to sound out longer words, it is necessary to teach him that certain *strings of letters* also have specific sounds. This is best taught by taking words apart rather than by blending. For example:

1. Start with the word *late*, by *showing and telling* the child that these letters "say" the word *late;* that the *l* says / *l* / (the *l* sound) and the *ate* says /*ate*/. (Underline and point to these letters as you say this.)

2. Once he demonstrates that he remembers what you have told him (check this to make certain), show him another word that contains the *ate* letter string (e.g., *mate*) and have him demonstrate that he understands the concept in this context as well. (And if he is not able to demonstrate the concept with this new word, teach it to him again using the new word. Then, again, check to see if he has learned it.)

3. Then go on to other words (the same length and longer) that contain the *ate* sequence (e.g., *rate, grate, grateful, inflate*, etc.) and show him how the letter sequence *ate* always (in the examples you have chosen) represents the sound that is voiced in the word *late*. As he is taught letter chunking, and if he grasps and is able to apply the concept, the child's reading ability will improve.

Although this sounds like an enormous task, it is not. There are only about 100 such letter strings in the English language (for example, *an, and, ad, ade*, etc.), and research shows that not all of them have to be taught thoroughly; what has to be taught is the *concept* that certain sequences of letters take on a specific sound, just as single letters do; that although *ate* comprises three letters, it represents a single sound: /*ate*/. Most children will generalize from that. (See Appendix C, "List of 108 Common Decoding Units," pp. 221–22, for a listing of these letter strings. See Appendix C for specific information about this instructional method.)

Guideline 6. When exceptions to the system are to be taught—as is inevitable in the written form of the English language—these, too, should be made obvious, and the student should be shown effective ways to remember them. (Do *not* leave it to the child to invent the mnemonic.) For example:

1. When words containing the *ough* letter string are to be taught, organize them into consistent groups ("families") and teach them in isolation and in the context of sentences and poems: for example, *rough,*

enough, tough. Avoid introducing words in which the same letter string takes on a different sound (e.g., *though*) until the first set has been learned securely.

Guideline 7. Provide enough repeated experiences to establish new information securely in the child's long-term memory. Have him practice using the system you taught him until he no longer needs to use the system to figure it out, but simply knows it and has the information at his fingertips.

Think back to when you learned to drive a car. At first, your attention was almost completely devoted to the mechanics of operating the vehicle safely; there was no time for extraneous thoughts, conversation, or enjoying the scenery. Once you learned to drive, and practiced that skill to the point where you did not have to devote all of your mental energy to the activity, you were able to think complex thoughts, converse intelligently, enjoy the view, and so on. The physical act of operating the vehicle became virtually automatic (unless an emergency arose), thereby freeing your mind to engage in more complex activities.

In essence, this means that breaking information down into subunits—seeing the "trees in the forest"; the *ate* letter string in the words *late* and *lately*—is not enough. The child also needs lots of practice in combining those subunits into larger units—forests instead of individual trees—and working with those larger units until he can deal with them almost automatically.

An illustration might help. Read the following "words" aloud: *plastopine, nipsuntake, clasmatran.* Based on experience, I would bet that you read these without very much hesitation, just as though they were familiar words. Yet they are not familiar words. How is it, then, that you were able to read them so fluently? You exercised a long-established reading habit: you identified components of the word that were very familiar to you, and blended these into whole words with ease. That is your goal with the child; it can be accomplished if (1) he knows what to do, and (2) he practices doing it often enough to become adept.

Guideline 8. Drill and practice exercises are most effective if the child is required to "say" and "write" while he "looks" and "hears."

Consider how much easier it is to read certain words (e.g., *embarrass*) than to spell them. Why is that? Simply stated, it is because reading is not as demanding of attentiveness to detail as is spelling. Hence, writing (or printing) words on paper greatly reinforces your capacity to read those words.

Summary

Reading is a complex cognitive act. It involves a process (translation of graphic symbols into words) and cognition (understanding and remembering the information that the words convey). The instructional method should be compatible with the child's existing abilities.

If a beginning first grader's language abilities and his visual and auditory analysis skills are developed to the level expected of a six-year-old, and if he is familiar with the manuscript letters, then he will probably learn to read with any program found in a standard classroom. (I have heard a good teacher describe such children this way: "You can teach them to read with a telephone book.")

If he is lacking in one of the aforementioned basic abilities, he will encounter difficulty unless (1) time and effort are devoted to helping him acquire the abilities he lacks and/or (2) the instructional program is modified to accommodate his substandard abilities. This section has been devoted to the latter.

SPELLING

In chapter 6, I defined spelling as mapping graphic symbols onto spoken words in ways that satisfy the idiosyncratic letter orders that were produced when English words were adopted from different languages. I also noted then that a good speller is a good speller because (1) he is able to analyze spoken words into their separate sounds and represent these sounds with letters (i.e., spell phonetically); and (2), he has effective strategies for remembering the letter sequences in those words where phonetic spelling does not work. A poor speller is a poor speller because he tries to memorize the full spelling of all words—an impossible goal.

It may not be logical to try to turn a poor speller into a "natural" speller, but it certainly is reasonable to spend some time and energy converting a poor speller into a better speller. The general guidelines presented earlier apply here in specific ways, as follows:

Applying the Guidelines to Spelling

Guideline 1. Take time to make certain that the child has the factual knowledge he will need in order to learn from the lesson: *make sure* that he knows what the lesson assumes he knows. For example:

1. Assure yourself that the child is able to read the words he is expected to learn to spell. Obviously, that is a major order, one that may force you to put aside your spelling objectives for a while. But there is no alternative. If the child cannot read a word, you can bet that he is not

going to be able to identify its sounds and their temporal sequences when he hears it. On this basis, you can conclude that learning to spell that word will require rote memorization of the most difficult type. On the other hand, if you deal effectively with the child's reading problem—if you are able to teach him to do what I outlined in the previous section— then not only will he acquire better reading skills but he will also become a better speller.

2. Check on the child's auditory analysis skills. This is critical. If he lacks these, he will not be able to do adequately either of the two things that good spellers do: spell phonetically and identify those parts of words where the spoken sounds don't match the spelling.

3. Check also on his visual analysis skills. Although these are not quite as critical as auditory analysis skills, they are important in that they facilitate retention of those parts of a word that are not spelled phonetically.

Guideline 2. Limit the amount of new information presented in a lesson and present what is offered in small bites. This needs no elaboration.

Guideline 3. Present information in a way that highlights plainly what the child is to pay close attention to, and unless it is highly relevant, avoid what is potentially ambiguous. For example:

1. Teach *word families,* group of words that share certain visual and auditory characteristics. There are many of these in the English language and they become easier to spell if they are taught at the same time (e.g., *bought, thought, sought; receive, deceive, conceive;* etc.).

Guideline 4. Make explicit the *system* that links up the new information in the lesson with something the student already knows. In other words, teach him ways to identify and remember the letter-sound mismatches in words, the irregularities in their spelling. There are different ways to accomplish this. For example:

1. Show the child a word he is to learn to spell and have him read it aloud. (If he cannot read it, he is in an activity that is beyond his abilities.) Have him say it first the correct way, then incorrectly, pronouncing every letter.

2. Now have him copy the word, saying the letters as he prints/writes them. Repeat this at least five times. (Actually, there is no magic number; he should repeat this until it appears that he can do it without thinking. It also helps to identify the salient letters with a transparent color marker; for example, the *t* in *listen.*)

3. Have him print/write the word again, but from memory rather than by copying it. Repeat this as indicated before. When he appears to be able to do this without thinking, go to the next step.

4. Have him print/write the word with his eyes closed, spelling it aloud as he does this, and thinking about what his hand is doing. Repeat as much as necessary.

5. Finally, have him write a sentence or two, using the word appropriately. If he can make up the sentence himself, all the better.

Guideline 5. As the student becomes familiar with the system you are teaching, using small units of analysis (single letters and sounds), introduce him to larger units (chunks) that he has not yet identified on his own, and illustrate these through analysis rather than synthesis processes. Teach the larger units by identifying them in the printed word, and then showing the child that the smaller units (those that he is already familiar with) are embedded in those larger ones. For example:

1. Once the child learns how to spell the words *steam, beam, dream,* and so on, introduce the words *streamline, moonbeam, steamboat,* and so on, making sure that the child recognizes that those longer words contain the smaller one he has already learned to spell.

2. When the child displays some competencies with this task, encourage him to identify additional "long" words that contain the *eam* sound.

Guideline 6. When exceptions to the phonic-analysis system are to be taught—as is inevitable in the written form of the English language—these, too, must be made obvious, and the student should be shown a way to remember the exceptions. There is no single strategy. Rather, there are such things as

1. pertinent jingles; for example, "i before e except after c." Keeping guideline 2 in mind, do not identify the words that are exceptions to the rule, such as *foreign* and *vein*. That introduces an undesirable ambiguity. Let the child think, for the while, that the "i before e" rule is something he can rely on. He will be able to cope with the revelation of exceptions later on.

2. enunciating an irregularly spelled word to himself precisely the way it is spelled (e.g., *knife, ghost. listen,* etc.). This also illustrates the value of multisensory involvement or of saying as you see.

3. figuring out a way of remembering where double consonants belong (e.g., saying to yourself "ok-kasion," pausing between and stressing the two c's).

Guideline 7. Provide enough repeated experiences to establish new information securely in the child's long-term memory. Have him practice the activities you have shown him until he can perform them automatically. Use such activities as

1. games: Scrabble, anagrams, Spell-it.
2. computer programs such as *Spell.*
3. finding small words in long ones. Show the child a long word (e.g., *caterpillar*) and ask him to construct as many words as he can from the letters in that word. For example:

cat	pill	pact	part	lip
let	tell	car	cap	pet

Guideline 8. Drill and practice exercises are most effective if the child is required to say and write as he looks and hears. This requires no elaboration.

Summary

We often view inept spelling skills as something not too worrisome, an idiosyncrasy, something that a "secretary" or a computer will take care of when he gets older, something not worth a lot of extra effort.

I do not agree with this attitude. Poor spelling need not be a permanent condition. It can be remedied and it is worth the effort. Do it. The poor speller will not become a good speller overnight. But poor spellers can be taught to be better spellers.

WRITING

This section is limited to penmanship—the production component of writing. The cognitive aspects of writing fall more correctly (and are dealt with) under the heading of comprehension (see p. 74). Thus we can put aside the instructional guidelines and focus directly on teaching the child better handwriting skills. But before we do that, we have to look at a few prerequisite skills.

1. Assess the child's visual analysis skills and, if they are not yet at the early kindergarten level, do something about it. The child with significantly delayed visual analysis skills will experience marked difficulty

    a. spacing letters appropriately on the page, organizing letters into readily discernible words with spaces between the words, and so on.

    b. differentiating between the ambiguous letters (the *b* and *d,* for example), and remembering the orientation of the others. (Note: this is not because they have "mirror vision"; they do not see things backward. There is no such condition. It is only because of an inability to remember the key spatial features of the letters.) If the child displays this deficit, take time off to improve his visual analysis skills before investing too much effort into teaching the lowercase manuscript alphabet.

2. Determine if the child understands the positional relationships of the different letters; that is, that the lower case *p* differs from the lower case *b* in the relative position of the vertical line in those letters. Use three-line, primary grade paper to assess this, thereby providing a structure that defines clearly the cogent spatial landmarks, something you can then use if necessary to teach these relationships to the child.

3. Determine if the child knows that letters in words are printed from left to right and, if needed, teach it to him. (Note: this does not mean that the child has to know how to use the spoken words *right* and *left* correctly; it is acceptable if he knows simply how to locate the starting [left] side and the relative location of the letters that follow.)

4. Having done this, initiate daily sessions to improve penmanship, using a chalkboard and a large stick of chalk (kindergarten size). This is far less demanding than paper and pencil.

    a. Engage the child in "rhythmic writing" activities; have him draw repetitive patterns across the chalkboard in a fluent, rhythmic fashion. It is not necessary that the patterns be letters. Stress the importance of smooth, fluid performance. (See patterns in the following example; these are merely suggestions; feel free to add to the array but do not make them too complex).

    At the start, you draw the pattern across the chalkboard (somewhat above his eye level) and have the child draw one just like it below yours.

    b. Show him how to hold the chalk (resting across the four fingers and secured by the thumb).

    c. Urge him to move his whole arm freely. True, he is to strive for neatness, but not at the expense of fluent, efficient movement. (Music sometimes helps stimulate rhythmic movement.)

    d. Have him erase his drawing and try again. Remind him to think about what his hand is doing, but again not at the expense of fluency.

    e. After about five or ten trials, his pattern should begin to approximate yours. When it does, have him repeat the activity with his eyes closed.

    f. Then, if his performance is reasonably good, go on to another pattern. There is no need to stay with a pattern until it is

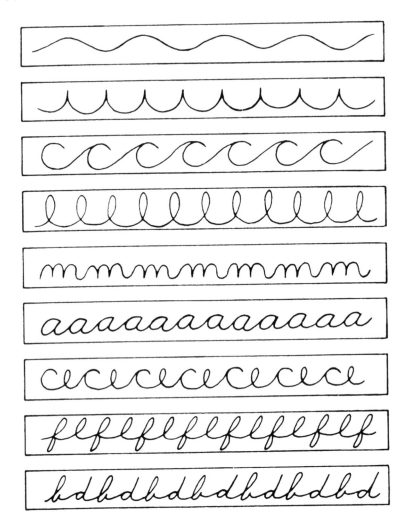

perfect, although you might want to go back and review patterns from time to time if only to give the child some direct evidence of his improvement.

5. Once he shows improvement at the chalkboard, begin some paper and pencil activities. (Note: at this point, a visit to your local school supply store or elementary school will probably lead you to at least one well-designed writing instruction program. Examine what you find there and choose the one that seems to make sense to you.)

    a. Show the child how to hold the pencil with thumb and index finger. Do not allow him to pinch the pencil at its point. His index finger should not extend beyond the painted portion of the pencil. It often helps to begin with a big (kindergarten size) pencil; far less dexterity is needed to control it.

b. Show him how to position the paper—angled so that it aligns with his writing hand.

c. Show him how to hold the paper in position by placing his other hand at the top edge of the paper. If he cannot do this easily, secure the paper to the desk in its correct position with masking tape.

d. Make certain that the child is seated comfortably and properly. The desk top should be below chest level. He should be able to place his feet flat on the floor. A slant-top desk is desirable, but not essential.

e. Use primary grade paper—the kind that has a middle line in addition to a top and bottom line, thereby facilitating accurate positioning of the letters on the line.

f. Have him draw letter elements: circles, ovals, vertical lines, diagonal lines, arcs open upward (as in the letter *u*) and downard (as in the letter *n*).

6. When he has improved sufficiently in these activities, have the child engage in writing chains of letters, which are letters linked together as in cursive writing. (Note: given a choice, children who enter school with substandard visual analysis skills benefit from being taught cursive from the outset. It is far easier for them than manuscript not only in the mechanical aspect of the task but in the letter recognition aspect as well. There are far fewer potentially confusing letter pairs in the cursive alphabet.)

7. Practice until these newly acquired skills become almost automatic and until they can be demonstrated without much conscious effort, for example, while talking.

Summary

Penmanship can be improved with controlled, properly designed activities and sufficient, appropriate practice. If the child's only problem is poor penmanship, do not spend a lot of energy trying to find out why it exists; go ahead and work on improving it.

ARITHMETIC

In chapter 6, we observe that arithmetic is a branch of mathematics that pertains to carrying out *calculations involving numbers*, and mathematics, in turn, as *the mapping of language onto symbols*. We also examined the standard approaches to teaching arithmetic and identified those abilities that the child must learn if he is to make satisfactory progress in school.

This section addresses the question: How can we help the child who despite at least average intelligence does not make satisfactory progress in a standard mathematics program? What can we do to accommodate his deficits effectively? The same guidelines apply.

Applying the Guidelines to Arithmetic

Guideline 1: Be certain that the child really does have the factual knowledge he will need in order to learn from the lessons.

1. By definition, he needs to be conversant in the languages of mathematics. (You will recall that there are two languages in mathematics: verbal and nonverbal. The former is the language we employ when we speak words to specify quantities, relative position, relative magnitude, and relationships. The nonverbal language of mathematics is what we use when we identify quantities, magnitudes, orientation, and relationships in spatially organized patterns.) If the child is not conversant in both languages, he will not progress as he should. Your first step therefore is to assess the child's knowledge of these languages.

- To test his knowledge of the verbal language, probe informally using the words listed in activities 6, 7, and 8 on pp. 108–9. If the child's verbal language is lacking, teach him what he has to know, as described in those activities.
- To test the child's knowledge of the nonverbal language of arithmetic, assess his visual analysis skills. The youngster who responds to the TVAS at an age-appropriate level is demonstrating an adequate knowledge of the nonverbal language of arithmetic. If the child's visual analysis skills are deficient, apply the criteria described on pages 89–90 to decide whether to attempt to improve those skills and/or modify the instructional approach.
- If this leads you to the decision to improve his visual analysis skills, follow the suggestions offered in chapter 8. If the decision is to modify the instructional approach in ways that accommodate his deficits, follow the guidelines in this section.

2. He needs to be familiar with the printed symbols and the conventions that govern their use: the numerals, how they are combined to represent numbers that exceed nine, and the operational signs (e.g., $+$, $-$, $=$).

What do you do if the child has persistent difficulty remembering the numerals and the conventions for using them to represent numbers greater than nine? You teach them in a way that eliminates the confusion. Rather than describe here a method for doing that, I refer you to guideline 3, where the example will illustrate this suggestion.

3. If the information in the lesson you are teaching today can be linked with something that was taught in a previous lesson (e.g., if the lesson is designed to teach the number fact $5 + 4 = 9$ on the basis of his already being able to respond quickly and accurately to the problem $4 + 4 = ?$ [without employing a counting algorithm]), then check to see if he recalls the solution to the latter problem. If he does not, then return to that point and teach it again, rather than going on.

Guideline 2. Limit the amount of new information presented in any lesson, and offer it in small bites. Keep explanations short and simple. This means just what it says. Be satisifed with small, steady gains; avoid trying to push the child too quickly; make your explanations easy to follow and remember. (See guidelines 5 for more discussion about this in respect to generating mnemonics.)

Guideline 3. Present information in a way that highlights what the child must pay special attention to if he is to learn, and unless it is pertinent avoid what is potentially ambiguous.
1. If the child is confused about the spatial orientation of the numerals (if he sometimes prints or reads them in reverse direction), provide a spatial reference point similar to what was suggested for letter reversals: a heavy red line (drawn with a felt-tip pen) down the left-hand side of the page along with an explanation to the child that he start at that side of the page.
2. If the child has difficulty comprehending a mathematical concept, illustrate it in concrete form. For example, show him that reorganizing quantities does not alter their total.
  • Use pennies (or any other counter) and two (or more) plates (or any other appropriate container) to illustrate how the quantities on each plate can be redistributed without altering the sum: how $8 + 14$, for example, can be reorganized (without changing the total) as $10 + 12$; or how $8 + 7$ is the same as $7 + 8$.

Guideline 4. Make explicit the system (the rule) that links up the new information in the lesson you are teaching with information the student already knows. For example:
1. When attempting to help the child who is uncertain about the spatial orientation of the numerals, identify an effective mnemonic—a pertinent reference point that the child already has well established in his memory.
  • Find out if the child ever reverses the capital S. If he does not,

then use it as the reference point (the mnemonic) for the 5 and the 6.

- Determine if the child ever reverses the capital *B*. If he does not, it can serve as the reference point for the numeral 3. To do this, have him print the *B*, but leave space between the vertical line and the rest of the letter (which, of course, is very much like the numeral 3).
- Once he has learned this, introduce the numerals 2, 7, and 9. The similarities in shape between these and the 3 are self-evident. Now show him the similarity between the 4 and the 7.
- Obey guideline 2. Do not introduce the numeral 2 until the 3 has been well learned. Similarly, do not introduce the 7. and the others, until the one you are teaching now has been learned securely.
- This leaves only the 8, a numeral that cannot be reversed and, therefore, is never a problem.

2. When teaching number facts, teach the child how to exploit what he does know in order to solve problems that are not yet familiar to him. For example:

- Given the addition problem 4 + 5 = ?, determine if the child already nows (that is, has memorized) the answer to 4 + 4 = ? or to 5 + 5 = ? If he knows either of these two number facts, then use counters and two plates to show him the link between the problem he has yet to solve and the one he already knows. Illustrate how the removal (or addition) of one counter from (or to) one plate translates the problem from something he does not know into something he does know.

Guideline 5. As the child becomes familiar with the system involving small units of analysis, introduce him to larger units of analysis (chunks) that he has not identified on his own, and illustrate these through analysis rather than synthesis processes.

It is not enough to teach a child that single numerals represent specific quantities, and that two such quantities can be combined into a greater quantity. If the child is to learn how to "think mathematically," he will have to learn the power of regrouping or restructuring a calculation problem into quantities that facilitate solution. For example:

1. Given the problem 7 + 8 = ?, illustrate (using counters and two plates) how this problem can be restructured as 5 + 10 = ?; certainly an easier problem to solve.

2. Apply the same principle (and concrete materials) to teach the concepts of subtraction, multiplication, and division.

3. Introduce the concept that a single counter can represent a quan-

tity greater than one; for example, how one size disk can represent one, and a larger disk ten.

Guideline 6. When exceptions to the system are to be taught, these, too, should be made obvious, and the student should be shown ways to remember them. This guideline is superfluous to arithmetic; arithmetic is very systematic; there are no exceptions to the system: 1 always means one, 2 always means two, and so on.

Guideline 7. Provide enough repeated experiences to establish new information securely in the child's long-term memory. Have him practice using the system you taught him until he no longer needs to use that system to figure it out, but simply knows it and has the information at his fingertips.

1. In practical terms, this means having the child carry out calculations with concrete materials until he can start to "pretend" he is using these materials.

2. In time, he will reduce this mental arithmetic process until he simply "knows" the answer to many problems and be able to use that knowledge to solve unfamiliar problems without resorting to the counters.

3. Do not interpret this to mean that you should encourage the child to memorize his number facts. On the contrary, discourage overt memorization efforts. The only method that will serve effectively is for the child to engage in translating the symbols into concrete quantities and recognizing how what he already knows subserves knowing more. Do this often enough for the process to be condensed and less dependent upon the separate operational steps. The eventual outcome of this is memorization.

Guideline 8. Drill and practice exercises are most effective if the child is required to "say" and "write" as he "looks" and "hears."

This directive has already been stressed amply by the emphasis placed on the importance of using concrete materials to represent the abstractions of numerals.

Summary

Arithmetic is a relatively uncomplicated aspect of mathematics. It involves the processes of translating symbols into finite quantities and carrying out calculations involving those quantities. The child who grasps the fundamental concepts of mathematics—the child who is already adequately familiar with the verbal *and* nonverbal languages of mathematics when he enters arithmetic instruction—will encounter no confusion with arithmetic and will make satisfactory progress in school.

The child who is not familiar with those languages—and the one most crucial is the nonverbal, visual analysis skills—progresses adequately in arithmetic only if he knows how to employ the counting algorithm and is confronted only with problems that present relatively small numbers.

This child will inevitably try to master arithmetic by memorization (a futile objective) or by counting, also an ineffective method. It is important to teach him with an instructional approach that depends very little on his basic abilities being established at least until he has developed those basic abilities, until he no longer needs that special consideration.

12
THE INSTRUCTIONAL ENVIRONMENT

THERE WAS A TIME when all schools resembled each other: they had classrooms of equal size, each set up to accommodate thirty to fifty children, a chalkboard, bookshelves, a desk for each student (typically arranged in precise lines and rows and bolted to the floor), and a desk and chair for the teacher.

The teacher directed the activities of the class from her desk. The children all worked on the same lesson at the same time. When a child wanted to speak or leave his desk for whatever reason, he raised his hand, got his teacher's attention, and requested permission to do what he wanted to do. When the children moved about the school building, they remained in orderly lines and noise was kept to a minimum.

Report cards were issued every nine weeks or so. These contained letter grades that reflected the teacher's opinion of the child's classroom performance.

Homework was standard. A moderate amount was assigned daily. The teacher checked over these assignments regularly and speedily, then returned it to the students along with her judgment and comments.

Lesson preparation was done after hours. Teachers devoted many evenings to designing activities that would enhance learning.

Discipline was usually managed locally by the teacher. The child who misbehaved was kept after school and assigned some type of punitive task (for example, write an apologetic statement on the chalkboard a countless number of times), which he did as his teacher worked on something else.

The school principal visited each classroom at least twice each semester (usually more often) in order to observe the teacher and her class, and offer constructive comments. Beyond that, the principal was unknown to the children, unless one committed an act that warranted serious "disciplinary action"—a principal's responsibility.

Was all this good? Should we yearn for the "good old days"? No. They were not good old days for the child with a learning disability, at least not unless he was simply a "late bloomer" who caught up on his

145

own before he had slipped too far behind his class. If he was truly learning disabled, he started to fall behind in the primary grades and continued to slip even farther behind as time went by. He failed, and that was that.

But they were not all bad days either. Education had not gotten "modernized"; educational programs had not yet been taken over by the psychologists who were expert in describing what had to be learned, but who were lacking in the ability to describe how to teach that material to children who really had to be taught, children who would not learn unless they were literally taught what they were expected to know.

It is time for education to take a serious look at what its so-called modern methods have produced. But it has to be done sensibly, methodically, in a way that takes the individual differences of the students into account. It is time to recognize that some children not only do better with certain types of programs and teachers but also do better with certain sets of conditions. It is time to start constructing school environments that accommodate these differences among children, rather than simply introducing change for the sake of change itself or because it is different and appears to work well with children who are lucky enough to have all the abilities prerequisite to learning. (Note: here again is that same old trap. If a certain school arrangement works well with the achieving child, then it is reasoned [erroneously] that the thing to do is to provide that arrangement for all children, thereby making them all good achievers.)

We all know that there are no panaceas in education. We now have to translate that knowledge into practical terms. There is no single program that works best with all children and no one type of teacher who reaches all children equally well; neither is there one school environment design that suits all children. But that does not mean that there are not any optimal conditions for different kinds of children and that these cannot be determined and provided within the context of a regular public school. It is in fact the only reasonable thing to do. It is not reasonable to keep doing what has been customary to date: meeting the needs of the average child, applauding the better than average achievers for their performance, and failing the others.

This brings to mind another of society's current misinterpretations. We like to say that children go to school to learn. This is incorrect. It is a distortion of what society had in mind when it started the institution of school. *Children go to school to be taught.* We send our children there for that express purpose—to be taught to read, write, do arithmetic, spell, and to apply those abilities in the acquisition of more knowledge. The extent to which they learn depends on how well they are taught or how readily they can be taught and the type of instruction they receive.

Children do not elect to go to school. The law mandates their attendance. How then can we justify the position that, once they are enrolled in school, the responsibility for learning becomes theirs? Obviously we cannot, yet we do.

What are the important factors of a school environment, beyond the teacher and the instructional programs? I will list and discuss them separately, and try to identify which conditions suit the learning disabled child.

CLASS SIZE

This is a very important concern. The learning disabled child needs explicit, unambiguous instruction that is offered in limited portions and accompanied by more than the usual amount of drill and practice. This cannot be done in a classroom where twenty-five children congregate with one teacher. There is just not enough time in a school day for this teacher-student ratio to be effective for the learning disabled child.

The learning disabled child should not have to share his teacher with more than six to eight other children, at least not during those portions of the day when the key subjects—reading and arithmetic—are being taught. Granted, this adds to the cost of education, but it is important and there probably are ways to solve the added expense problem.

First, some of the expense could be absorbed by assigning a counterbalancing (extralarge) number of children—not learning disabled ones to be sure—to another teacher. True, the children will have to be those who do not need very much direct instruction and the program they use will have to be one that provides lots of interesting, self-instructional opportunities and materials. The teacher would have to be the type who can deal with such a program and the dynamics of a classroom where thirty-five or more easily stimulated, active children are busy doing things that maintain their interest and add to their store of knowledge. But it is possible.

Another suggestion is to provide this special class-size arrangement for only sixty to ninety minutes per day, just for arithmetic and reading, say. This, of course, calls for special scheduling and regroupings, but it can be done. (Note: indeed, many schools provide a resource room that fits this description. Ordinarily, a resource room is staffed by a specially trained teacher and an aide. Children are assigned there for specific portions of the school day to receive special help instruction. Obviously, what goes on in these rooms varies from school to school, but the concept is good and should be supported.)

CLASS HOMOGENEITY

Most school administrators believe that the classroom should mirror society. It should comprise a mixture of all kinds of children, rich and poor, black and white, male and female, learning disabled and overachievers, thereby providing conditions that will influence the children, making them more democratic and, as a result, shaping the society of the future.

I have no quarrel with a class being made up of children from various socioeconomic levels or from different racial groups and different neighborhoods. But I do not agree with the indiscriminate mixing of learning disabled and non–learning disabled children. A teacher cannot do justice to all of her students if they vary widely in their ability to make satisfactory progress under standard instructional conditions. Regardless of her knowledge, temperament, and commitment, it just cannot be done. Children will have to take their turn at being ignored, and the ones who can least afford this are the learning disabled children. They need much more time than the others. Hence even if they are fortunate enough to get the same number of minutes of direct instruction as the others, they will learn less and their deficits will compound daily.

Heterogeneous classroom makeup does have its positive features. It is a fine thing for the learning disabled child to listen to (and learn from) his classmates responding in such classes as social studies and language arts, for example. But it is a total waste of time for that child to listen to his more fortunate classmate read in a way that he can neither begin to approximate nor even figure out how his classmate does it. It demoralizes him; it does him no good at all.

OPEN CLASSROOM VERSUS TRADITIONAL CLASSROOM

In 1967, Joseph Featherstone wrote a series of articles in the *New Republic* magazine about innovations in some English elementary schools. He described how the children in those schools seemed to learn how to do arithmetic while engaging in pleasurable activities, like measuring and building things, keeping score of game events, and so on.

They also seemed to learn to read and spell in fortuitous, undirected ways—reading what they could on their own, asking their teacher to help decode a word now and then, writing stories, and so on.

According to Featherstone, each child worked at his own rate and level. The teachers did not teach, at least not in any traditional sense of the word. They simply asked pointed questions, answered children's questions, made suggestions, and in general functioned as interested adults who were there to help.

The open classroom concept captured the imagination of U.S. education. It was imported, translated into American "educationese," and put into operation. "Classrooms without walls" were built all over the country. They appealed to the budget-minded because, lacking many interior walls, they were relatively less expensive to build. They appealed to the progressive parents because the programs sounded and looked as though they were fun. It was how school should look—active, dynamic, children working independently and learning through self-inspired investigation and discovery. No sitting quietly and listening to "boring" lectures. Large spaces with children all over the place, conversing with each other. What a nice scene.

Many teachers, especially the older, experienced ones, were a bit skeptical and slow to get on the bandwagon. They were classified as old-fashioned, committed to archaic ideas. To most progressive parents and teachers, the open classroom was evidence that all children can learn if they are given the kind of stimulating environment that does not interfere with their natural intellectual curiosity and growth.

Books and articles were written on the open classroom. Educational writers praised it. England attained the position of instructional exemplar. Teacher-training programs were designed and put into operation.

Then what happened? Some children did very well in the open classroom. They were the ones who really did not need much direct instruction. They thrived under conditions that allowed them to move at their own pace, to pursue their own interests, to devise their own structure, to set up their own learning goals and achieve them. Some others did not do all that well. They needed a bit more structure, a bit more direct instruction. And if they got it, their learning problems usually disappeared.

And the children we label learning disabled? They were totally out of their element, utterly confused by the lack of structure. They wandered about—literally—often getting into trouble because they did not know the rules (no one had told them) nor did they know how to figure them out on their own, at least not without first creating some kind of crisis that necessitated it.

I am not proposing that the open classroom concept be discarded. On the contrary, the open classroom is a wonderful thing for children who can learn adequately in such a setting. It simply is not for the learning disabled child.

GRADED VERSUS NONGRADED

The term nongraded means that what the child is to learn is laid out in clear, behavioral language and the only thing that is "reported" is which goals have been accomplished and which remain to be achieved. Qualitative differences in children's work are neutralized in this kind of approach. Children are not evaluated in terms of how well they master the objectives, only in when they master them.

Nongraded therefore means an elimination of the traditional stratification of grade levels. Children are not identified as second graders, for example. Instead they are located somewhere in their arithmetic program, somewhere else in their reading program, all of this determined by the mastering of learning objectives rather than years spent in school and annual promotions in grade level.

It is not a bad idea in theory. It is based on the notion that since children progress at different rates, they should be given instruction that accommodates those individual differences. Hence, even if one year after entering school, Child *A* is much farther ahead than child *B*, the long-term results should not be affected. All child *B* needs is more time. He will get there, and once he does, both children will be equally educated.

It is not a good idea in practice. Same old problem. Good achievers move along at a rapid pace. In fact, many progress too rapidly, moving into levels of work that may not be appropriate for them. The child with average skills? He does as well as you would expect. And the learning disabled child? He plods along, working through lessons that fail to make the links between them adequately obvious, and he ends the year far behind his classmates.

What has not been taken into consideration is that although you can call a school nongraded, there is always a starting date and a termination date, and if the school comprises six grades (or, to maintain the nongraded theme, if the child is expected to enter seventh grade once he leaves this school), then the terminal date usually comes along six years after the starting date.

Thus the learning disabled child looks up from his desk five years and nine months after he started and either discovers that his classmates are leaving him behind, or, perhaps even worse, he joins them despite his lack of accomplishment.

HOMEWORK VERSUS NO HOMEWORK

This is a trivial concern in comparison with the topics just discussed. But it is worth a little consideration. Should homework be assigned? Yes, but for a specific purpose only. Homework should be designed to give the learning disabled child *practice* in something he can already do, but not do as easily as he should. It should not be designed to teach him new information; that should be done in school. He needs consistency. His parents may teach differently than his teacher. This, in itself—putting aside the undesirable emotional dynamics that arise when parents attempt to do what the teacher could not do—is enough to rule out attempting to teach new information under the guise of homework.

STRUCTURE

We now come to the general and pivotal topic of structure. I have used the term a number of times without defining it. Structure means *something arranged in a definite pattern of organization.*

Learning disabled children require more structure than their more successful classmates. That does not mean that they need harsh, totalitarian conditions. Hardly. It means that there has to be some order, some predictability in their environment, that they have to be able to anticipate what they are expected to do and how they are expected to do it. This can apply to where coats and hats are to be stored in the classroom, to where on the paper they are to write their name, to how to go about getting permission to go to the bathroom, and so on. At a somewhat less concrete level, it pertains also to how reading and arithmetic are taught, and how thoroughly the steps are covered in the instructional situation.

Schools vary in the degree of structure they provide. To the extent that structure is lacking, the learning disabled child will suffer. He will do best if there is organization and if his work is mapped out—what he is to do, when he is to do it, and in what sequence—and shown how what he is doing today links up with what he did yesterday. Structure is based on supports. Provide these supports and he will progress.

HOW LONG WILL THE CHILD NEED SPECIAL HELP?

This is a logical question, and one that is often posed by teachers. It is usually accompanied by the statement: "After all, this can't last forever. He will have to learn to operate independently if he hopes to survive in the real world."

I agree. You cannot provide a child with individual attention forever. But forever is a long time. Rarely will a learning disabled child—as we have defined him—need special conditions "forever." How long then will he need special help? Perhaps for years, but, if managed successfully, with the need diminishing steadily. As children receive what they need in the classroom, their special needs—for an extraordinary teacher, for highly organized lesson material, for small group instruction—diminish.

How does this happen? How does the child overcome his special needs in a reading program? For one thing, if the reading program is designed appropriately, it not only makes clear the link between spoken sounds and printed words but it also serves to enhance the child's auditory perceptual skills. As this occurs, the child becomes less dependent upon a hand-fashioned reading program.

Similarly, in arithmetic if the instructional program is properly designed, it makes clear to the child how to symbolize the quantities and properties of magnitudes and relationships—the characteristics of the space that numbers code. It also teaches him how to identify those characteristics, thereby improving his visual analysis skills and, as a consequence, making him less dependent upon specially tailored instruction.

And just as important, as children get older, they are allowed to specialize more in school. Consider, for a moment, the plight of the child in the primary grades where uniformity is demanded. If he is to be perceived as progressing satisfactorily in first, second, or third grade, he must read, spell, and print at some basic level of competence at least as good as that of the average student in his class. As he gets older, a child is allowed to devote more energy to certain subject areas and ignore others; poor handwriting and spelling are tolerated better in high school and college than in elementary school. It is important therefore that we see to it that these children do not "drop out," do not get "written off," and are not allowed to see themselves as failures. This is not easy to accomplish but it is critical.

Summary

Schools are more than buildings divided into classrooms. School means schedules, room assignments, teacher assignments, methods for evaluating student progress, and more. There was a time when the rules for designing a school's physical and instructional environment were so fixed and accepted that all schools looked the same, no matter where you went. Then with the end of World War II and the arrival of the era of boundless optimism that grew out of rapid technological advances, schools changed. They changed drastically and to the point where there did not appear to be any common rules. A school administrator designed an environment that suited him and redesigned it a year later if he felt like it, especially if something new came along that sounded interesting.

Now we are in a backlash era—a "back to basics" period. Society is trying to recover all those good things we once had, then threw out in our fit of optimism.

The truth of the matter is this: (1) no single approach suits all children adequately; (2) the child who enters first grade with appropriately developed basic learning aptitudes (perceptual skills) and language abilities does well in any environment but thrives in an environment that allows him to make some of the decisions himself; (3) the learning disabled child needs structure but cannot generate it on his own. In effect, his progress in school, if he makes any, can be charted in terms of his relative dependency on others to provide that structure. The more he progresses, the less he will need that help.

How does this translate operationally? Schools should be organized according to the students' instructional needs. They should provide self-directed learning environments for the children who can cope effectively with this. Such children should be placed in the hands of good, knowledgeable, committed teachers who have the temperament to allow the children to do most of the teaching for themselves, teachers who will not mind the children milling about, talking to each other and to themselves, advancing at uneven rates, becoming distracted by an irrelevant topic for a while, and asking more questions than one would necessarily welcome.

Moderately structured learning environments should be provided for children with average abilities, at least for part of the day.

And highly structured learning environments should be provided for learning disabled children for part of the day.

Bring all the children together, in various combinations, for instruction in those topics where a mixture is beneficial.

Can this be done? Sure it can. But it requires certain conditions: a large enough student body to provide enough children with different levels of ability; a competent faculty; and a school administrator who accepts that his chief concern is to make certain that the students are taught to the extent needed to meet the requirements society has set for schools. All else—school buses, cafeterias, paper clips—matters only as it contributes to this process.

WHAT PARENTS CAN DO

It is one thing to describe the kind of teacher a child needs and the kind of school environment that will benefit him. It is another matter—and no small accomplishment—to make it happen when what the child needs is not readily available in his school.

I have no simple, pat answer. There are too many variables involved here, too many differences among school districts in terms of size, money, available classrooms, and a host of other factors, to lay out a specific plan of action. I suppose that the best I can do is to suggest that parents seek out the counsel of other parents who have preceded them along this path, and build on what they can learn. Progress is slow, but it is being made.

All public schools in this country are mandated by federal law to provide children between the ages of three and twenty-one whatever assistance they need in order to achieve their educational potential. This opens up a remarkable number of debatable issues such as, How do you determine a child's potential? How do you decide what he needs to achieve that potential? And so on.

But the fact remains that the mandate is there. School administrators know it is there and the child's parents, therefore, have a right (and an obligation) to insist that something be done.

13
PREVENTION

THE FIRST STEP IN PREVENTION is to identify the child *before* he starts to have difficulty in school, before he becomes a candidate for the learning disabled label. Look back at the list of signs/symptoms in chapter 2 that signal "at risk." Then look at the list of language test items in chapter 5 that pertain to the age of the child you are concerned about. And finally, if the child is four or older, administer the TVAS and TAAS (see chapter 4). This will give you the information you need to make proper decisions. The preschool child who displays deficits in any of these areas should be looked at more carefully.

FORMAL TESTING

Health

Follow the Action Plan. If in doubt, take the pessimistic view and work your way through the steps defined in chapter 3; ask your family physician or pediatrician if some health factor could explain the at-risk signs you have noticed. If he identifies something, act accordingly.

Development

Find out if the youngster is achieving his developmental milestones on schedule. Getting a developmental assessment should not be difficult or costly. If you cannot get it from your pediatrician, call your county medical society or public health agency and find out who in your region provides that service; then visit them. (Indeed, your local school system might provide it.)

Specifically, you will want to know if the child's social, language, motor, and adaptive behaviors are emerging as expected. If they are, good. If they are not, go into action. Ask for help from whoever did the testing, and if the problem lies in adaptive behaviors, start to use the

154

simplest of the activities described in chapter 8. If the problem lies in language, seek professional help from a university-based or hospital-based speech clinic or from the public school in your area.

Vision and Hearing

Have his eyes examined by an optometrist or ophthalmologist. Do not settle for an eye chart visual screening. Look for an eye doctor who will do more than evaluate the health of the child's eyes and the clarity of his eyesight. Both factors are important of course, but they do not go far enough. Find someone who will investigate visual function—if he is farsighted and to what degree; how well and efficiently he uses his eyes, coordinates them, shifts and sustains focus.

Both optometrists and ophthalmologists can do that if they will take the time and trouble. Impress upon the one you select that you want him to take the time and trouble, and do not settle for less. If no visual problem is found, good. If a problem is identified, follow the doctor's advice, but make certain to inquire about the link between the problem he identifies and the problem you are concerned about. If there is not a direct link—if the vision problem is independent of the general development one you have observed—then think through your decision about treatment before you act.

Then have his hearing tested. In my experience, this need not be done by an audiologist; a responsible school nurse can do a valid hearing screening. Obviously, if a hearing loss is detected, then a consultation with an ear/nose/throat doctor will be needed.

Perceptual Skills

Who should assess these? The TVAS and the TAAS, described in chapter 4, are not designed to be used with children younger than age four, and although I could suggest some other tests for this age group, I hesitate to do so. Very young children are notoriously unreliable test takers, particularly if the tests are administered by nonprofessionals.

If the child's visual and/or auditory perceptual skills are to be tested, and if he is younger than four, have a professional do it. Some optometrists and some psychologists test visual and auditory perceptual skills. So, too, do so some speech and hearing specialists. See if you can find someone competent in your community. If you can, good. If you cannot, then I think you should again take the dim view: assume that the child's perceptual skills are not adequate as you design your plan of action.

In other words, take nothing for granted. If it turns out that you underestimated the child (that his perceptual skills and language abilities are adequate), then you caused no harm. That is certainly more desirable than neglecting a deficit that ultimately will cause him to fail in school. In short, it is preferable to be overcautious than to ignore a significant problem. And do not delay. Act early.

Preschool

These days, most children are enrolled in some kind of school well before their fifth birthday. Many begin school at age two or three; some even earlier. A preschool should be chosen carefully, whether the child is at risk or not. Some preschools do not do well with distractible, inattentive children. They may be excellent schools, but not for that child. He will taste failure there; he will gain very little.

Look for a nursery school that meets his needs. Look for a school whose staff knows how to (and is pleased to) handle an at-risk child, directing his limited attention in productive ways, teaching him skills when the opportunities arise, and helping him at all times to feel like an acceptable member of his group.

Age to Start Kindergarten

As a general rule, children should not be enrolled in a standard kindergarten until they have passed the five-year, six-month mark. True, there are exceptions to this rule. The child not yet five and a half, who displays superior social, language, and adaptive development, will probably do quite well in a standard kindergarten. But there are few of these children.

Do not be deceived by the statement "Just listen to him talk! Surely he is ready for school." Many children have good language abilities yet lag in the development of social and/or adaptive behaviors. They should not be placed in a competitive setting where they will be compared to children older and farther along in development than themselves.

(Note: some interesting data. In a retrospective study of the last 150 healthy, normal-IQ children seen in a Houston-based teaching clinic where patients are referred because they display signs of LD, ADD, and dyslexia, more than half had June, July, and August birthdays. In other words, more than half of them were younger than five years, three months when they entered first grade. Was that the cause of their LD? Probably not, but it surely contributed. Their immaturity, in conjunction with whatever other deficits they had, influenced strongly their ability to make satisfactory progress in school.)

SUMMARY

Children develop many skills and learn much information during their preschool years. Standard school instructional conditions are designed on the assumption that the students will have achieved a certain level of ability (in terms of perceptual skills and language) by the time they enter school. This is not always the case.

It is important therefore that parents and preschool teachers know how to (and do) look carefully at all children, and identify those who are lagging in one or more aspects of their development and early learning. They must also know how to follow up identification with appropriate actions. What actions? Try to change the child by eliminating (or substantially reducing) the deficiencies through direct intervention or by delaying entry into school, and/or place the child in a nonstandard instructional setting, a classroom where the teacher and/or the teaching program and other factors have been modified to accommodate the child's deficiencies. How to do these things has already been covered in this book.

14
CONCLUSIONS

CHILDREN, LIKE ADULTS, differ one from another. None (with the exception perhaps of identical twins) looks exactly like someone else, none has a voice that sounds exactly like someone else, none has a body build or moves exactly like someone else, and none of them thinks exactly like someone else. The brain comprises billions of neurons; it is unrealistic to believe that any two brains are exactly alike in structure, organization, and function.

Schools are very much like one another. True, no teacher is exactly like another teacher, but most instructional programs are very much alike (indeed, many schools purchase and use the same instructional programs), most school buildings are organized much the same, and most schools use the same achievement tests (hence, the same instructional goals) that scale the children against national norms.

What happens when an unusually tall child enters a standard first grade classroom and the teacher finds that there are no desks that can accommodate him? She informs someone in the building that she needs a larger desk for this child. She does not feel the need to have a series of consultations and apply a label ("extra tall," perhaps) before she submits her request; the school custodian responds without questions. A larger desk is brought to the classroom and life goes on.

What happens when a left-handed child enters a standard first grade classroom that contains desks for right-handed children only? The teacher—without seeking someone else's opinion and without having a panel of experts testify that the child is truly left-handed—has a left-handed desk brought to her room.

What happens when a six-year-old with immature visual or auditory perceptual skills, or inept language ability, shows up in a standard first grade classroom? The teacher—usually unaware of the deficits—starts off by attempting to teach this child the standard curriculum in the standard fashion. By midterm, the teacher has become sufficiently frustrated and concerned that (if the school is located in a middle-class neighborhood) she requests conferences with the school diagnostician and the child's parents. (If the school is located in a poor neighborhood, she might simply shrug and accept the situation as not unusual. Isn't that unfortunate.)

During the teacher-parent conference, mention is probably made of possible dyslexia, or attention deficit disorder, or something like that, and the parent is surprised and troubled. This is followed by more tests, conducted in and perhaps out of school, and more conferences. Finally, in the best of cases, the child acquires a label that earns him nonstandard circumstances for all or part of the school day. He is taught in different ways, with the methods decided by the teacher, who was prepared for her job by college instructors who rarely, if ever, have had direct teaching experiences with this kind of child. In even worse cases, the child is simply labeled. The label becomes the reason for his school difficulties, and that is that.

In all cases, the child's school difficulties are *his* problems, not the school's. If he has an idiosyncratic brain, then he must pay the consequences. Indeed, even if special instructional circumstances are provided, the problem remains his and he is expected to overcome it in a reasonable length of time because schools cannot accommodate idiosyncratic needs forever. After all, "he has to become independent sometime," and "the sooner the better."

Do his teachers expect him to "get better"—to reach a point where he will learn the way "normal" children learn? Some may, but they are rare. Usually the label once attached remains attached, and with it acceptance of the "fact" that this child will endure his problem for life.

This is wrong both in principle and in fact. True, a good number of children enter school unready for the experience, and there is no reason to blame the schools for this. But neither is there reason to blame the child. He did not make the laws that condemned him to this fate, and he did not design the genetic, physiological, and experiential factors that made him what he is.

The job of the elementary school educational process is to teach children the information and skills they will need to perform satisfactorily in secondary school. Within this undertaking, the first major goal of the educational process is to teach the child how to be an accurate and fluent reader, speller, writer, and calculator (how to deal with information in symbolically coded form).

If that goal is achieved "on schedule"—typically, before the end of third grade—then the child has a good chance to go on successfully to intermediate and secondary education and, perhaps, beyond. If that goal is not achieved on schedule, then the child will be behind when he enters fourth grade, and the probabilities are that he will remain behind for the remainder of his school years. In fact, the gap between where he should be and where he is will widen, inevitably causing him frustration leading to anger toward the society that placed him in these circumstances, and toward himself and his failure.

The central theme of this book is that none of this need occur. *If* parents were aware of the importance of preschool development and how it influences early learning, and *if* schools were able and willing to identify and accommodate children who enter school not yet ready for standard conditions, then most of the children who bear the special education labels cited so often in the previous pages would never have been so labeled. They would have emerged from the primary grades appropriately fluent in the basic coding systems of the classroom and been able to move into the learning demands of the intermediate and secondary grades successfully.

My chief argument then is that there is no such thing as a permanent learning disability (as the term is currently defined). Rather, there are children with special instructional needs who become disabled (the way any individual may become disabled after experiencing some harmful event) because of society's failure to identify and treat them properly before they entered school, and because of their school's failure to recognize and serve their special (but not unreasonable) needs once they did enter.

A learning disability is not forever unless we allow it to be.

APPENDIX A
VISUAL PERCEPTUAL SKILLS

VISUAL PERCEPTUAL SKILLS—LEVEL 1

Equipment

1. Two 5-pin geoboards, 8 additional nuts and bolts, instructions for assembling a geoboard, and a supply of rubber bands
2. Geoboard patterns 1 through 48
3. Ten rubber washers (paper rings will do): four of one color, four of another color, and two of a third color. (For the activity descriptions below we have chosen four red, four yellow, and two black washers; however, you may use other colors when you perform these activities.)

Equipment Setup

Child sits beside adult, 5-pin geoboards placed side by side or one above the other.

Activities

1. Orient the child to the geoboard as follows: place a black washer over the center pin of one geoboard and say, "Make your board look just like mine. Put your black ring on the same pin on your board," that is, on the center one. If child responds correctly, place two washers of another color (e.g., yellow) over the pins on the right side of your board and ask the child to do the same. If child responds incorrectly, stop and instruct; illustrate the difference between top and bottom by positioning the two geoboards side by side; illustrate the difference between right and left by positioning the two geoboards one above the other. Do not use the words *right* and *left;* simply point and talk about "this side" or "this hand" and "that side" or "that hand." After the child reproduces what you have done, put the two remaining (red) washers on the left pins of your board and ask the child to do the

same. (If there is doubt about how well the child understands what he is to do, go through it a few times, changing the color arrangement each time.)

Goal: Child accurately reproduces 5-washer arrangement.

2. Remove colored washers. Construct pattern 1 with rubber bands on your geoboard; place it beside (or above) the child's geoboard and say, "Make your board look just like mine." (In constructing the patterns, use one rubber band for each of the lines, and if necessary, emphasize to the child that he must make his design step-by-step, in an organized, sequential manner.)

Goal: Child accurately copies geoboard pattern 1.

3. Repeat activity 2, using patterns 2 through 12.

Goal: Child accurately copies patterns 2 through 12.

4. Repeat activity 2, using patterns 13 through 20.

Goal: Child accurately copies patterns 13 through 20.

5. Add four more pins to each of the boards so that they make a 3 × 3 arrangement. Repeat activity 2, using patterns 21 through 48.

Special Instructions

If the child has significant difficulty with any pattern, go through it again by constructing the pattern, then rotating it a quarter or half turn. This will provide repeated experiences with patterns that are the same yet different.

VISUAL PERCEPTUAL SKILLS—LEVEL 2

Equipment

1. A 5-pin geoboard, instructions for assembling a geoboard, and a supply of rubber bands
2. Geoboard patterns 1 through 20
3. A 5-dot map, acetate cover, dark crayon, and facial tissue

Equipment Setup

Child sits beside adult.

Activities

1. Draw pattern 1 on acetate-covered 5-dot map. Place it before child, beside a 5-pin geoboard, and say, "Make your geoboard look like this. Use one rubber band for each of my lines." If child makes an error

that he does not recognize on his own, tell him, but do not show it to him. Have him search for it. If, ultimately, he does need more help and additional explanation, give it, stressing the strategies—reasoning process—he is to exercise rather than the mechanics of the activity. For example: "Where do you want to start?" "What comes next?" "How long is this line? How many pins or dots?"

Goal: Child accurately copies pattern 1 on his 5-pin geoboard.

2. Erase drawn pattern 1 with the tissue, rotate child's geoboard a quarter turn, give the child a blank, acetate-covered 5-dot map, and say, "Draw this design [point to geoboard] on your map the way it looks now."

Goal: Child accurately copies rotated design from 5-pin geoboard onto 5-dot map.

3. Repeat activities 1 and 2 with patterns 2 through 12.

Goal: Child accurately copies drawn patterns 2 through 12 on his 5-pin geoboard and draws them (rotated a quarter turn) on his 5-dot map.

4. Repeat activities 1 and 2 with patterns 13 through 20.

Goal: Child accurately copies drawn patterns 13 through 20 on his 5-pin geoboard and draws them (rotated a quarter turn) on his 5-dot map.

Special Instructions

If the child has significant difficulty with any of the patterns, go through those again, but this time rotate your drawing of the pattern a quarter or half turn before you ask the child to construct it on his geoboard, then rotate it another quarter or half turn when you give his construction back to him to be copied onto a 5-dot map. This will provide repeated experiences with patterns that are the same yet different.

VISUAL PERCEPTUAL SKILLS—LEVEL 3

Equipment

1. A 9-pin geoboard, instructions for assembling a geoboard, and a supply of rubber bands
2. Geoboard patterns 21 through 48
3. A 9-dot map, acetate cover, dark crayon, and facial tissue

Equipment Setup

Child sits beside adult.

Activities

1. Draw pattern 21 on acetate-covered 9-dot map. Place it before child beside a 9-pin geoboard and say, "Make your board look like this. Put one rubber band on your geoboard for each of my lines." If child makes an error that he does not recognize on his own, tell him, but do not show it to him. Have him search for it. If, ultimately, he does need help and additional explanation, give it, stressing the strategies—reasoning process—he is to exercise rather than the mechanics of the activity. For example: "Where do you want to start?" "What comes next?" "How long is this line? How many pins or dots?"
   Goal: Child accurately copies drawn pattern 21 on his 9-pin geoboard.
2. Erase drawn pattern 21 with the tissue, rotate child's geoboard a quarter turn, give child a blank, acetate-covered 9-dot map, and say, "Draw this design on your map, the way it looks now."
   Goal: Child accurately copies rotated design from 9-pin geoboard onto 9-dot map.
3. Repeat activities 1 and 2 with patterns 22 through 36.
   Goal: Child accurately copies drawn patterns 22 through 36 on his 9-pin geoboard and draws them (rotated a quarter turn) on his 9-dot map.
4. Repeat activities 1 and 2 with patterns 37 through 48.
   Goal: Child accurately copies drawn patterns 37 through 48 on his 9-pin geoboard and draws them (rotated a quarter turn) on his 9-dot map.

Special Instructions

If the child has significant difficulty with any of the patterns, go through those again, but this time rotate your drawing of the pattern a quarter or half turn before you ask the child to construct it on his geoboard, then rotate it another quarter turn when you give his construction back to him to be copied onto a 9-dot map. This will provide repeated experiences with patterns that are the same yet different.

VISUAL PERCEPTUAL SKILLS—LEVEL 4

Equipment

1. A 25-pin geoboard, instructions for assembling a geoboard, and a supply of rubber bands
2. Geoboard patterns 49 through 150
3. A 25-dot map, acetate cover, dark crayon, and facial tissue

Equipment Setup

Child sits beside adult.

Activities

1. Draw pattern 49 on acetate-covered 25-dot map, place it before child beside 25-pin geoboard and say, "Make your board look like this. Put one rubber band on your geoboard for each of my lines." If child makes an error that he does not recognize on his own, tell him, but do not show it to him. Have him search for it. If, ultimately, he does need more help and additional explanation, give it, stressing the strategies—reasoning process—he is to exercise rather than the mechanics of the activity. For example: "Where do you want to start?" "What comes next?" "How long is this line? How many pins or dots?"
   Goal: Child accurately copies drawn pattern 49 on his 25-pin geoboard.
2. Erase drawn pattern 49 with the tissue, rotate child's geoboard a quarter turn, give child a blank, acetate-covered 25-dot map, and say, "Draw this design on your map, the way it looks now."
   Goal: Child accurately copies rotated pattern 49 from 25-pin geoboard onto 25-dot map.
3. Repeat activities 1 and 2 with patterns 50 through 72.
   Goal: Child accurately copies drawn patterns 50 through 72 on his 25-pin geoboard and draws them (rotated a quarter turn) on his 25-dot map.
4. Repeat activities 1 and 2 with patterns 73 through 109.
   Goal: Child accurately copies drawn patterns 73 through 109 on his 25-pin geoboard and draws them (rotated a quarter turn) on his 25-dot map.
5. Repeat activities 1 and 2 with patterns 110 through 150.
   Goal: Child accurately copies drawn patterns 110 through 150 on his 25-pin geoboard and draws them (rotated a quarter turn) on his 25-dot map.

Special Instructions

If the child has significant difficulty with any of the patterns, go through them again, but this time rotate your drawing of the pattern a quarter or half turn before you ask the child to construct it on his geoboard, then rotate it another quarter turn when you give his construction back to him to be copied onto a 25-dot map. This will provide repeated experiences with patterns that are the same yet different. If child has no difficulty completing patterns of a given activity level, move on to the next. For example, if patterns 50 through 72 are not challenging, go on to patterns 73 through 109 (activity 4).

VISUAL PERCEPTUAL SKILLS—LEVEL 5

Equipment

1. Geoboard patterns 151 through 200
2. One 25-dot map, one 17-dot map, an acetate cover, a dark crayon, and facial tissue

Equipment Setup

Child sits beside adult.

Activities

1. Draw pattern 151 on acetate-covered 25-dot map, place it before the child beside acetate-covered 17-dot map and say, "Make your map look like mine. But notice that some of the dots are missing on your map. Don't draw in the missing dots; just pretend they are there, and draw the lines as though the dots were there." If child makes an error that he does not recognize on his own, tell him, but do not show it to him. Have him search for it. If, ultimately, he does need help and additional explanation, give it, stressing the strategies—reasoning process—he is to exercise rather than the mechanics of the activity. For example: "Where do you want to start?" "What comes next?" "How long is this line? How many pins or dots?"
   Goal: Child accurately copies drawn pattern 151 from a 25-dot map onto his 17-dot map.
2. Repeat activity 1 with patterns 152 through 178.
   Goal: Child accurately copies drawn patterns 152 through 178 from a 25-dot map onto his 17-dot map.
3. Repeat activity 1 with patterns 179 through 200.
   Goal: Child accurately copies drawn patterns 179 through 200 from a 25-dot map onto his 17-dot map.

Special Instructions

If the child has significant difficulty with any of the patterns, go through them again, but this time rotate your drawing of the pattern a quarter or half turn before you ask the child to draw it on his 17-dot map. This will provide repeated experiences with additional patterns that are the same yet different.

VISUAL PERCEPTUAL SKILLS—LEVEL 6

Equipment

1. Geoboard patterns 151 through 200
2. One 25-dot map, one 9-dot map, an acetate cover, a dark crayon, and facial tissue

Equipment Setup

Child sits beside adult.

Activities

1. Draw pattern 151 on acetate-covered 25-dot map, place it before the child beside acetate-covered 9-dot map and say, "Make your map look like mine. But notice that some of the dots are missing on your map. Don't draw in the missing dots; just pretend they are there, and draw the lines as though the dots were there." If child makes an error that he does not recognize on his own, tell him, but do not show it to him. Have him search for it. If, ultimately, he does need help and additional explanation, give it, stressing the strategies—reasoning process—he is to exercise rather than the mechanics of the activity. For example: "Where do you want to start?" "What comes next?" "How long is this line? How many pins or dots?"
   Goal: Child accurately copies drawn pattern 151 from a 25-dot map onto his 9-dot map.
2. Repeat activity 1 with patterns 152 through 178.
   Goal: Child accurately copies drawn patterns 152 through 178 from a 25-dot map onto his 9-dot map.
3. Repeat activity 1 with patterns 179 through 200.
   Goal: Child accurately copies drawn patterns 179 through 200 from a 25-dot map onto his 9-dot map.

Special Instructions

If the child has significant difficulty with any of the patterns, go through them again, but this time rotate your drawing of the pattern a quarter or half turn before you ask the child to draw it on his 9-dot map. This will provide repeated experiences with additional patterns that are the same yet different.

VISUAL PERCEPTUAL SKILLS—LEVEL 7

Equipment

1. Geoboard patterns 151 through 200
2. One 25-dot map, one 5-dot map, acetate cover, dark crayon, and facial tissue

Equipment Setup

Child sits beside adult.

Activities

1. Draw pattern 151 on acetate-covered 25-dot map, place it before the child beside acetate-covered 5-dot map and say, "Make your map look like mine. But notice that some of the dots are missing on your map. Don't draw in the missing dots; just pretend they are there, and draw the lines as though the dots were there." If child makes an error that he does not recognize on his own, tell him, but do not show it to him. Have him search for it. If, ultimately, he does need help and additional explanation, give it, stressing the strategies—reasoning process—he is to exercise rather than the mechanics of the activity. For example: "Where do you want to start?" "What comes next?" "How long is this line? How many pins or dots?"
   Goal: Child accurately copies drawn pattern 151 from a 25-dot map onto his 5-dot map.
2. Repeat activity 1 with patterns 152 through 178.
   Goal: Child accurately copies drawn patterns 152 through 178 from a 25-dot map onto his 5-dot map.
3. Repeat activity 1 with patterns 179 through 200.
   Goal: Child accurately copies drawn patterns 179 through 200 from a 25-dot map onto his 5-dot map.

Special Instructions

If the child has significant difficulty with any of the patterns, go through them again, but this time rotate your drawing of the pattern a quarter or half turn before you ask the child to draw it on his 5-dot map. This will provide repeated experiences with additional patterns that are the same yet different.

VISUAL PERCEPTUAL SKILLS—LEVEL 8

Equipment

1. Geoboard patterns 151 through 200
2. One 25-dot map, one 0-dot map, acetate cover, dark crayon, and facial tissue

Equipment Setup

Child sits beside adult.

Activities

1. Draw pattern 151 on acetate-covered 25-dot map, place it before the child beside acetate-covered 0-dot map and say, "Make your map look like mine. But notice that all of the dots are missing on your map. Don't draw in the missing dots; just pretend they are there, and draw the lines as though the dots were there." If child makes an error that he does not recognize on his own, tell him, but do not show it to him. Have him search for it. If, ultimately, he does need help and additional explanation, give it, stressing the strategies—reasoning process—he is to exercise rather than the mechanics of the activity. For example: "Where do you want to start?" "What comes next?" "How long is this line? How many pins or dots?"
   Goal: Child accurately copies drawn pattern 151 from a 25-dot map onto his 0-dot map.
2. Repeat activity 1 with patterns 152 through 178.
   Goal: Child accurately copies drawn patterns 152 through 178 from a 25-dot map onto his 0-dot map.
3. Repeat activity 1 with patterns 179 through 200.
   Goal: Child accurately copies drawn patterns 179 through 200 from a 25-dot map onto his 0-dot map.

Special Instructions

If the child has significant difficulty with any of the patterns, go through them again, but this time rotate your drawing of the pattern a quarter or half turn before you ask the child to draw it on his 0-dot map. This will provide repeated experiences with additional patterns that are the same yet different.

HOW TO MAKE A GEOBOARD

Although geoboards may be purchased, they are not difficult to construct. You will need a 9-by-9-inch square of perforated Masonite from your local lumber dealer for each geoboard you intend to make. This will yield a board that contains 81 holes, arranged in 9 rows of 9 holes each. You will also need 25 bolts, each approximately 1 inch long, and 25 nuts to secure the bolts to the board.

1. **To construct a 25-pin geoboard,** start at a corner hole on the board; insert a bolt in every other hole and secure it with a nut. When completed, the board will contain 25 bolts arranged in a 5-by-5 pattern.

2. **To construct a 9-pin geoboard,** simply do not insert the 16 bolts along the outside borders. This leaves only the 9 center bolts, arranged in a 3-by-3 pattern.

3. **To construct a 5-pin geoboard,** omit 4 more bolts—those positioned in the center of each of the remaining outside rows and lines. This leaves 4 bolts, arranged as the corners of a 3-inch square with one additional bolt in the center.

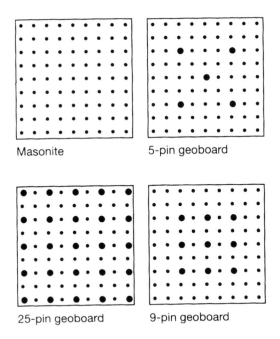

Masonite   5-pin geoboard

25-pin geoboard   9-pin geoboard

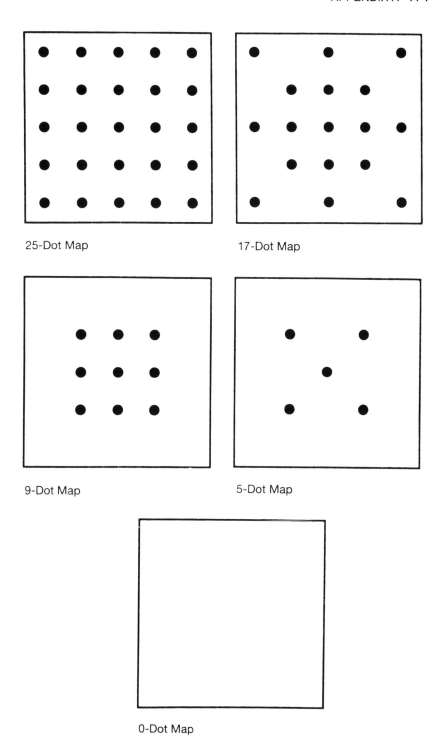

25-Dot Map

17-Dot Map

9-Dot Map

5-Dot Map

0-Dot Map

GEOBOARD PATTERNS

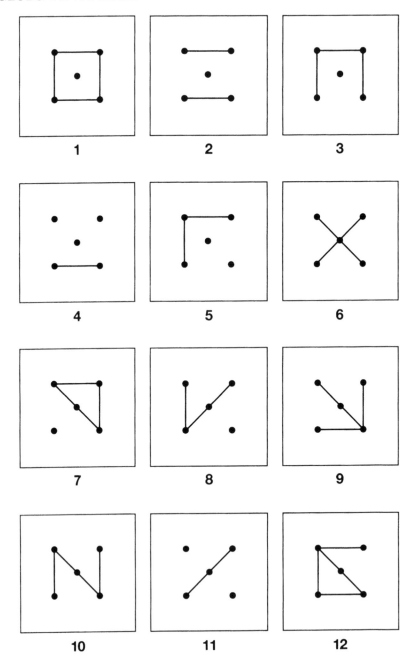

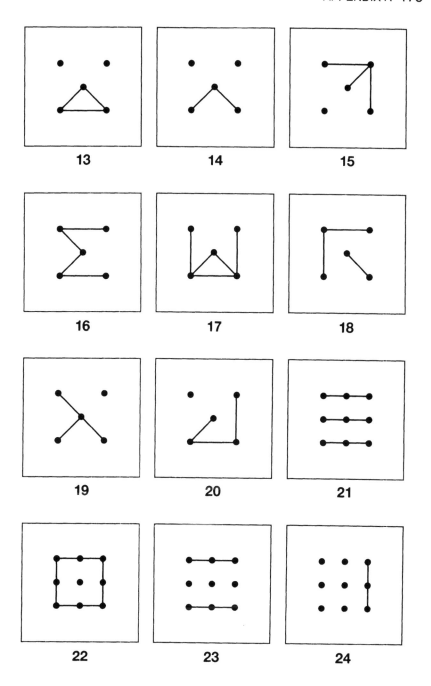

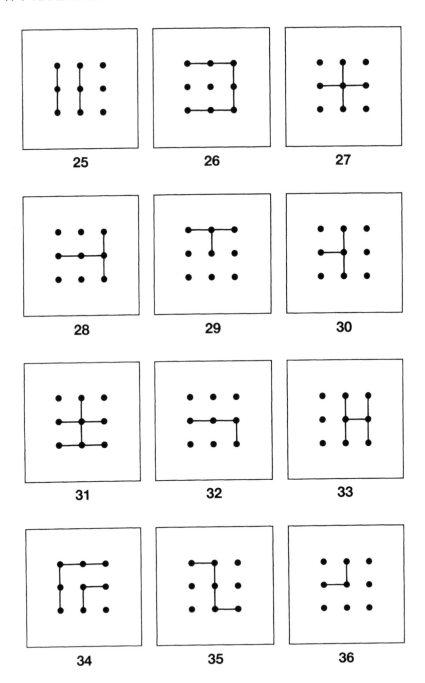

25   26   27

28   29   30

31   32   33

34   35   36

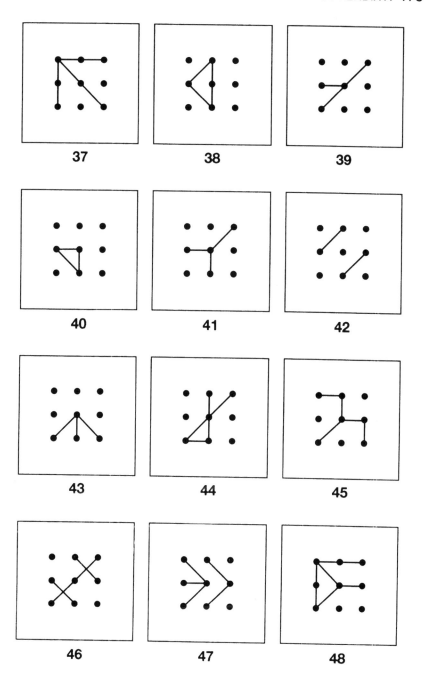

37

38

39

40

41

42

43

44

45

46

47

48

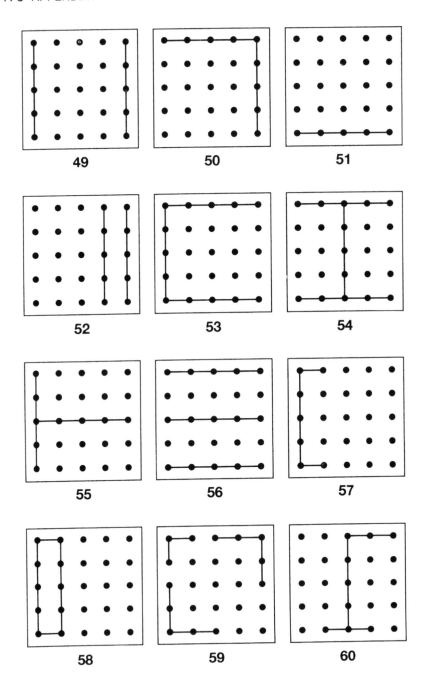

49

50

51

52

53

54

55

56

57

58

59

60

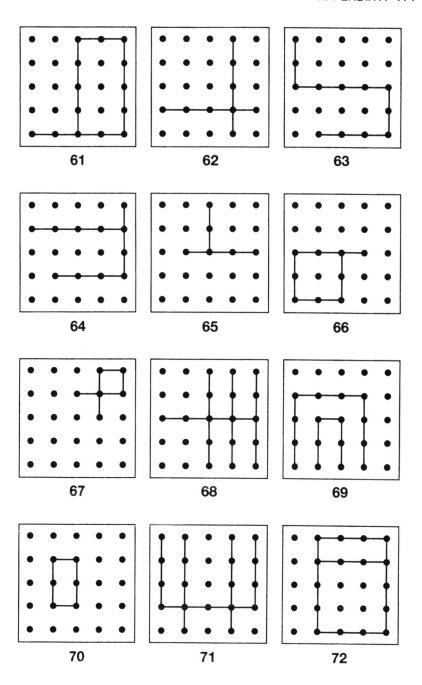

61

62

63

64

65

66

67

68

69

70

71

72

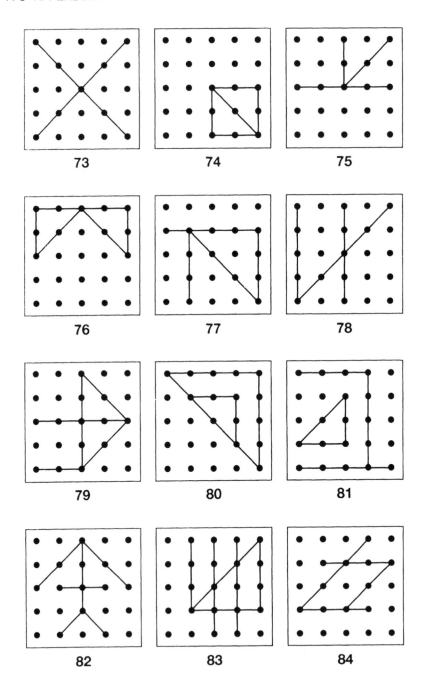

73

74

75

76

77

78

79

80

81

82

83

84

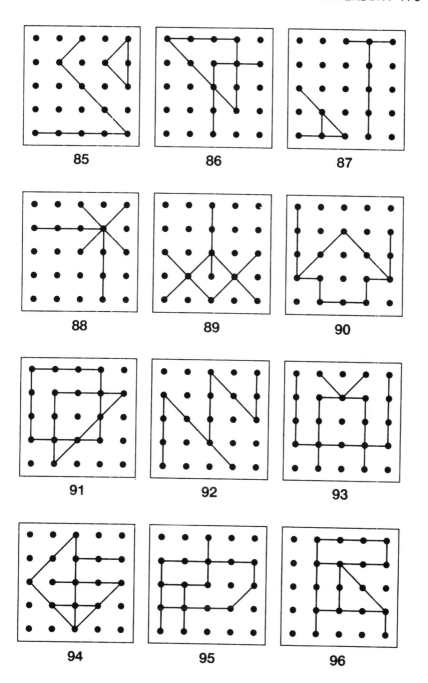

85

86

87

88

89

90

91

92

93

94

95

96

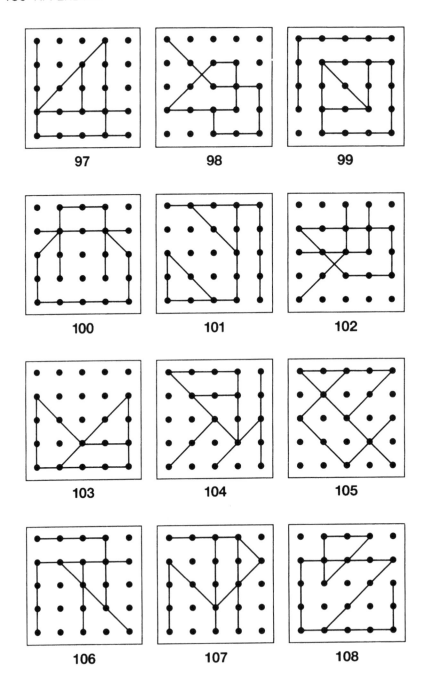

97

98

99

100

101

102

103

104

105

106

107

108

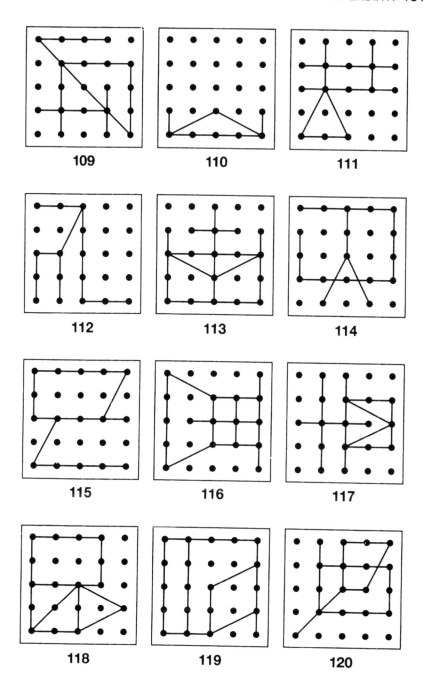

109

110

111

112

113

114

115

116

117

118

119

120

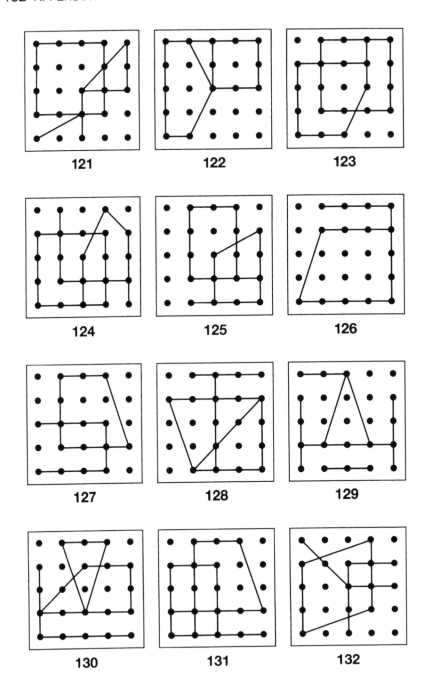

121

122

123

124

125

126

127

128

129

130

131

132

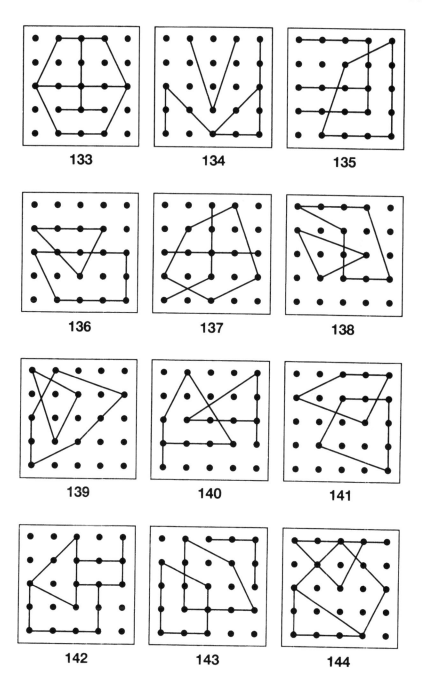

133

134

135

136

137

138

139

140

141

142

143

144

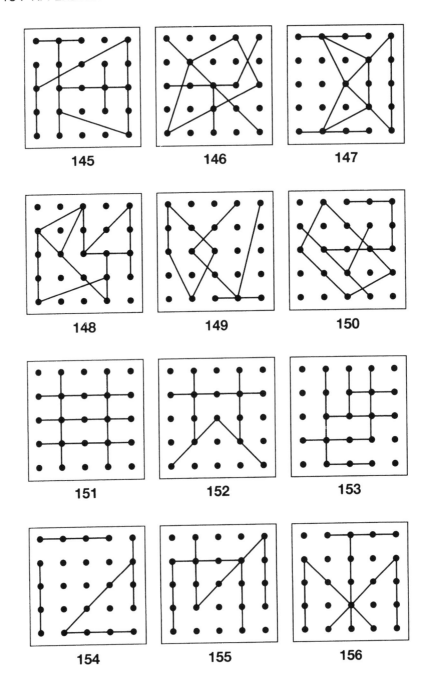

145

146

147

148

149

150

151

152

153

154

155

156

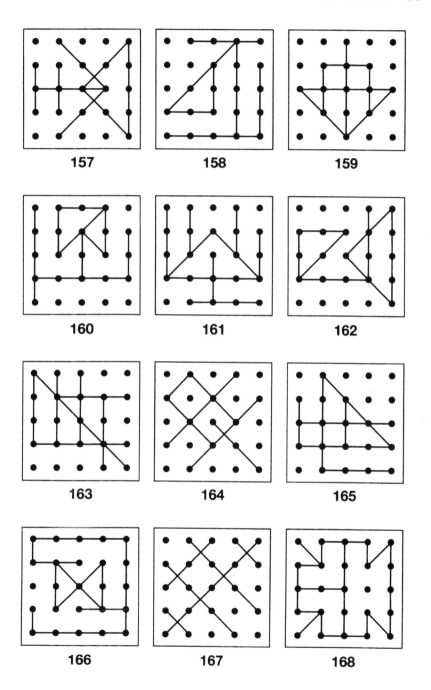

157   158   159

160   161   162

163   164   165

166   167   168

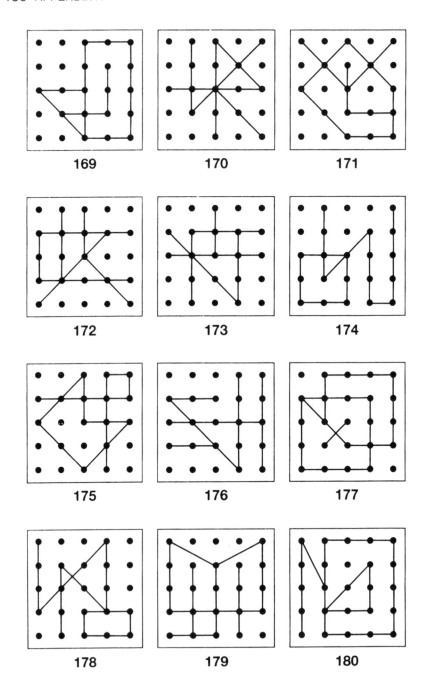

169   170   171

172   173   174

175   176   177

178   179   180

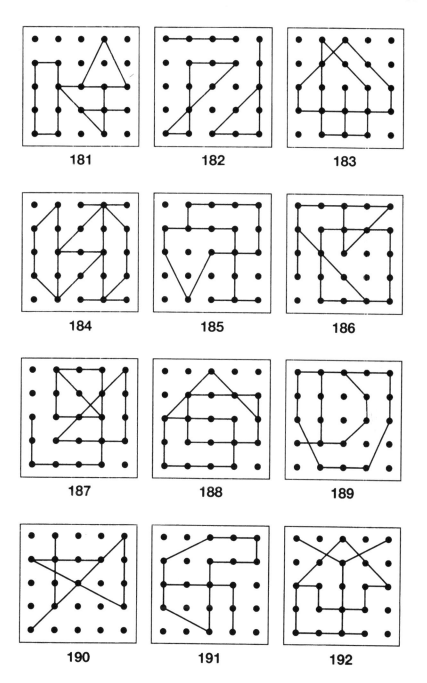

181

182

183

184

185

186

187

188

189

190

191

192

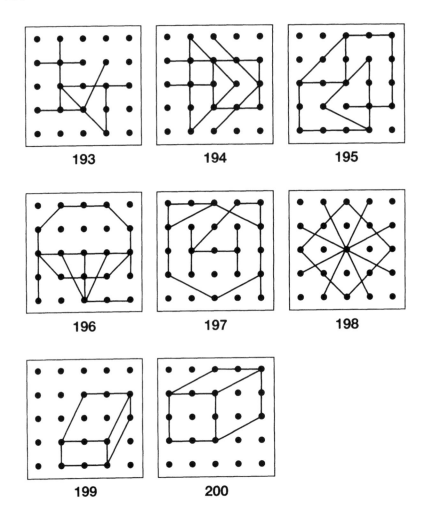

193

194

195

196

197

198

199

200

APPENDIX B
AUDITORY PERCEPTUAL SKILLS

AUDITORY PERCEPTUAL SKILLS—LEVEL 1

Equipment

Level 1 word lists

Activities

1. Teach the child to clap his hands in time to the syllables of a spoken two-syllable compound word from the list, saying the syllables as he claps them. "Say *base ball*." (Emphasize the two syllables.) "Now say it again, and clap your hands once for each part of the word; clap and say the parts at the same time."
   Goal: Child claps hands in accord with the number of syllables in at least four words from the appropriate level 1 word list.
2. Have the child draw a dash, from left to right, for each syllable in a two-syllable compound word from the list, saying them as he draws the dashes. "Say *base ball*." (Emphasize the two syllables.) "Now say it again and draw a dash for each part as you say it." Demonstrate to the child how the dashes are to be drawn—horizontally, from left to right—the first dash to be drawn as the first syllable is said, the second dash as the second syllable is said.
   Goal: Child draws dashes in accord with the number of syllables in at least four words from the appropriate level 1 word list.
3. Teach the child to "read" the dashes he has drawn, in any order you designate. For example, if he correctly drew two dashes for the word *baseball,* point to the left-hand dash and ask, "What does this one say?" (His response should be "base.") Then point to the right-hand dash and ask the same question. His response this time, "ball."
   Goal: Child "reads" the dashes correctly in at least four words from the appropriate level 1 word list.
4. Sensitize the child to embedded sounds; in this case, syllables. Ask

189

him to say *baseball*. Then, "Did you say *ball?*" "Is the word *ball* hidden in the word *baseball?*" "How about the word *doll?*" "Is the word *doll* hidden in the word *baseball?*" If this concept is too difficult for the child to grasp, incorporate the exercises of activity 3 and have the child draw and read dashes for the words he is being asked to work with, not just listen to. Then teach him to identify the embedded sounds without resorting to drawing or reading the dashes by pretending to draw or read them.

Goal: Child correctly identifies four embedded syllables and four nonembedded syllables from the appropriate level 1 word list without having to resort to drawing or reading dashes.

5. Using words from the level 1 word list, teach the child to "say the part that we left out." "Say the word *baseball*." "Now say *ball*." "What did we leave out that [second] time—what is missing?" Vary the pattern by sometimes leaving out a first syllable, sometimes the second. Here, too, the child may fall back on drawing or reading dashes as a way of helping him understand the task at hand. Ultimately, however, he is to be able to do the activity without drawing or reading the dashes.

Goal: Child responds correctly to at least five words from the appropriate level 1 word list.

6. Say the word after deleting a specified syllable. "Say *baseball*." "Now say it again, but don't say [leave out] *ball*." If the child displays confusion, illustrate the concepts by incorporating activities 1 through 4.

Goal: Child responds correctly to at least six words from the appropriate level 1 word list (i.e., "Say ＿＿＿＿＿ ＿＿＿＿＿." "Now say it again, but don't say ＿＿＿＿＿.").

7. Activity 6 is the end of level 1, although it is always advisable to review (practice) after the activity 6 goal is achieved. It is also useful to encourage the child to try to recognize words that would be appropriate for the level 1 word list, that is, compound, two-syllable words.

Level 1 Word List—Activities 1, 2, 3, 5, and 6

baseball	seesaw	motion
someplace	oatmeal	virtue
steamship	window	morbid
cowboy	recall	dispose
mister	paper	begin
cupcake	magic	defend
into	after	bashful
candy	dentist	cement
person	monkey	muffler

cartoon	sandwich	ocean
children	shoeshine	murky
sometime	napkin	concert
bookcase	daytime	vocal
forget	stingy	nasty
mountain	upset	native
doctor	bargain	precise
outside	surprise	measure
daddy	himself	ordeal
doorbell	mascot	selfish
fancy	cardboard	vibrant
funny	predict	indent
hunter	airplane	famous
party	eyelash	protest
business	demon	except
garden	hungry	obtain
barber	playmate	conceal
	ashtray	decay

Level 1 Word List—Activity 4

Say **more**	Is the word **more** hidden in the word	morning? farmer? mortgage? morbid?
Say **ball**	Is the word **ball** hidden in the word	ballgame? baseball? cowboy? bolt?
Say **bun**	Is the word **bun** hidden in the word	bunny? thunder? bundle? bunk?
Say **pay**	Is the word **pay** hidden in the word	repay? paper? daytime? pain?
Say **see**	Is the word **see** hidden in the word	seesaw? seaman? saddle? seed?

Say miss	Is the word miss hidden in the word	mistake? mister? master? mistletoe?
Say car	Is the word car hidden in the word	cargo? card? scar? star?
Say all	Is the word all hidden in the word	always? recall? illness? ball?
Say ant	Is the word ant hidden in the word	anthill? antelope? Andy? cant?
Say pick	Is the word pick hidden in the word	picnic? pickle? packet? picket?
Say ray	Is the word ray hidden in the word	Raymond? radio? rain? write?
Say won	Is the word won hidden in the word	wonder? once? window? wedding?
Say ban	Is the word ban hidden in the word	bandit? bank? Benny? banquet?

AUDITORY PERCEPTUAL SKILLS—LEVEL 2

Equipment
Level 2 word lists

Activities

1. Teach the child to clap his hands in time to the syllables of a spoken three-syllable compound word from the list, saying the syllables as he claps them. "Say *va-ca-tion.*" (Emphasize the three syllables.) "Now say it again, and clap your hands once for each part of the word; clap and say the parts at the same time."
   Goal: Child claps his hands in accord with the number of syllables in at least four words from the appropriate level 2 word list.
2. Have the child draw a dash, from left to right, for each syllable in a three-syllable compound word from the list, saying them as he draws the dashes. "Say *va-ca-tion.*" (Emphasize the three syllables.) "Now say it again and draw a dash for each part as you say it." Demonstrate to the child how the dashes are to be drawn—horizontally, from left to right—the first dash to be drawn as the first syllable is said, the third dash as the last syllable is said.
   Goal: Child draws dashes in accord with the number of syllables in at least four words from the appropriate level 2 word list.
3. Teach the child to "read" the dashes he has drawn, in any order you designate. For example, if he correctly drew three dashes for the word *vacation,* point to the first dash and ask, "What does this one say?" (His response should be "va.") Then point to the third dash and ask the same question. His response this time: "tion" (/shun/).
   Goal: Child "reads" the dashes correctly in at least four words from the appropriate level 2 word list.
4. Sensitize the child to embedded sounds; in this case, syllables. Ask him to say *vacation.* Then, "Did you say *va?*" "Is the word *va* hidden in the word *vacation?*" "How about the word *day?*" "Is the word *day* hidden in the word *vacation?*" If this concept is too difficult for the child to grasp, have the child return to the exercises of activity 3 and draw or read dashes for the words he is being asked to work with, not just listen to. Then teach him to identify the embedded sound without resorting to drawing or reading the dashes by pretending to draw or read them.
   Goal: Child correctly identifies four embedded syllables and four nonembedded syllables from the appropriate level 2 word list.
5. Using words from the level 2 word list, teach the child to "say the part that we left out." "Say the word *vacation.*" "Now say *cation.*"

"What did we leave out that [second] time—what is missing?" Vary the pattern by sometimes leaving out a first syllable, sometimes the second or third. Here, too, the child may fall back on drawing or reading dashes as a way of helping him understand the task at hand. Ultimately, however, he is to be able to do the activity without drawing or reading the dashes.

Goal: Child responds correctly to at least five words from the appropriate level 2 word list.

6. Say the word after deleting a specified syllable. "Say *vacation.*" "Now say it again, but don't say [leave out] *va.*" If the child displays confusion, illustrate the concepts by incorporating activities 1 through 5.

Goal: Child responds correctly to at least six words from the appropriate level 2 word list (i.e., "Say _____ _____." "Now say it again, but don't say _____").

7. Activity 6 is the end of level 2, although it is always advisable to review (practice) after the activity 6 goal is achieved. It is also useful to encourage the child to try to identify other words that would be appropriate for the level 2 word list, that is, compound words of three syllables or more.

Level 2 Word List—Activities 1, 2, 3, 5, and 6

cantaloupe	peppermint	silverware	emptiness
basketball	classical	decently	departure
trampoline	valentine	naturally	extravagant
important	buffalo	resonant	institute
defenseless	babydoll	ridiculous	important
memorize	refreshment	superlative	substitute
mistaken	emergency	pantaloon	impersonate
gorilla	peanut butter	favorite	performance
carelessly	destiny	fanciful	dedication
yesterday	peninsula	hardiness	devotion
cornerstone	introduce	laboratory	undertake
limousine	independent	abdicate	advantage
September	classification	diplomat	represent
understand	occupation	workmanlike	vivacious
remember	upside down	clumsiness	atmosphere
microphone	newspaper	excitement	indignant
forgotten	friendliness	evasive	enormous
gasoline			

Word List—Level 2, Activity 4

Say two	Is the word two	hidden in the word **tomorrow**?
toe	toe	
row	row	
mar	mar	

Say car	Is the word car	hidden in the word carpenter?
tar	tar	
curb	curb	
carp	carp	

Say man	Is the word man	hidden in the word **fisherman**?
fish	fish	
fast	fast	
dish	dish	

Say knee	Is the word knee	hidden in the word **honeymoon**?
noon	noon	
moon	moon	
honey	honey	

Say thunder	Is the word thunder	hidden in the word **understand**?
stand	stand	
under	under	
and	and	

Say permit	Is the word permit	hidden in the word **peppermint**?
mint	mint	
pep	pep	
pop	pop	

Say full	Is the word full	hidden in the word **wonderful**?
once	once	
one	one	
fun	fun	

Say milk	Is the word milk	hidden in the word **buttermilk**?
but	but	
bat	bat	
tire	tire	

Say ought	Is the word ought	hidden in the word **watermelon**?
melon	melon	
water	water	
tear	tear	

Say **pen**	Is the word **pen**	hidden in the word **independent**?
on	on	
dent	dent	
deeper	deeper	
Say **get**	Is the word **get**	hidden in the word **forgetful**?
full	full	
far	far	
for	for	
Say **cut**	Is the word **cut**	hidden in the word **caterpillar**?
pill	pill	
cat	cat	
pillow	pillow	
Say **fact**	Is the word **fact**	hidden in the word **manufacture**?
tear	tear	
man	man	
fit	fit	

AUDITORY PERCEPTUAL SKILLS—LEVEL 3

Equipment

Level 3 word lists

Activities

1. Using words from the level 3 word list, teach the concept of embedded sounds. Ask the child to "say *mat*." Then, "Does the word *mat* begin with a /m/ sound?" (Say the letter sound—"mmmm"—not the letter name.) Also, encourage the child to "think about how your mouth feels as you say and hear the word."
   Goal: Child responds correctly to at least six words that do or do not contain the embedded sound (words taken from the appropriate level 3 list).
2. Have the child say the sound that is missing: "Say *mat*." "Now say *at*." "What sound is missing in *at* that you heard in *mat*?" See level 3 word list for suitable words. Again at this level, it is often helpful for the child to think about how his mouth feels as he says and hears the words.
   Goal: Child responds correctly to at least six words taken from the appropriate level 3 word list.

3. Say the word without the beginning sound. "Say *mat*." "Now say it again, but don't say [leave out] the /m/ sound."
   Goal: Child responds correctly to at least six words taken from the appropriate level 3 word list.
4. Activity 3 is the end of this level, although it is always advisable to review (practice) after the activity 3 goal is achieved. It is also useful to encourage the child to try to recognize words that would be appropriate for the level 3 word list, that is, words that continue to have meaning after the beginning sound of each has been deleted.

Level 3 Word List—Activity 1

Does the word begin with a /**m**/ sound? (as in mother)

mix	Monday	money	fame
mate	time	make	time
neat	misty	came	monastery
comb	ram	many	name
fame	seam	melt	milkshake

Does the word begin with an /**a**/ sound? (as in apron)

aid	apple	ace	animal
ape	awful	August	afraid
open	acorn	ant	ate

Does the word begin with an /**e**/ sound? (as in eel)

Indian	evil	evict	team
eat	beef	ear	equal
even	every	sneeze	enemy

Does the word begin with an /**i**/ sound? (as in idea)

Indian	ice cream	find	grind
ant	item	icicle	ivy
ice	cry	pliers	bike

Does the word begin with an /**o**/ sound? (as in open)

under	opera	omen	blow
over	know	bone	open
on	ocean	ox	boat

Does the word begin with a /**u**/ sound? (as in useful)

use	grew	union	unity
yeoman	usual	yule	ukulele
blue	umbrella	group	under

Does the word begin with a /**b**/ sound? (as in big)

dig	boy	brown	breakfast
bag	drag	hag	slab
peg	basket	bicycle	crib

Does the word begin with a /**k**/ sound? (as in cup)

cat	scare	kite	across
skin	castle	cartoon	smash
bake	color	lock	cash

Does the word begin with a /**d**/ sound? (as in dog)

day	done	muddy	devil
sad	toad	door	blood
trip	drag	sled	danger

Does the word begin with a /**g**/ sound? (as in go)

juggle	green	glow	ghost
dig	ragged	drag	glove
gold	gate	bag	grain

Does the word begin with a /**h**/ sound? (as in hat)

home	hair	shove	show
omen	ahoy	him	history
hop	hang	they	hill

Does the word begin with a /**j**/ sound? (as in joke)

Jane	rage	badge	Jim
jump	joy	chew	chase
goat	gyp	jar	cash

Does the word begin with an /**l**/ sound? (as in lake)

lane	love	lend	lead
flood	pickle	glare	land
hill	log	flag	click

Does the word begin with a /**n**/ sound? (as in neck)

snip	no	anthill	knife
kneel	fan	in	instruct
onto	needless	nothing	needle

Does the word begin with a /**p**/ sound? (as in pick)

spell	paint	stop	part
pray	drag	open	pill
plunge	blond	spill	clap

Does the word begin with a /**r**/ sound? (as in ride)

real	bring	ride	far
dart	rag	drip	wrinkle
river	grieve	rent	truck

Does the word begin with a /**s**/ sound? (as in so)

sand	smack	misty	wrist
score	miss	spell	scold
zip	silly	whistle	stick

Does the word begin with a /v/ sound? (as in very)

vote	victory	Viking	win
wish	reef	love	vicious
vocal	vanish	fat	fish

Does the word begin with a /w/ sound? (as in win)

swell	hole	wit	twine
twinkle	warm	vote	wedding
wag	wiggle	swim	wine

Does the word begin with a /y/ sound? (as in yell)

yes	youth	hit	yard
win	twin	joke	beyond
hang	girl	yank	young

Does the word begin with a /z/ sound? (as in zip)

zoo	zone	snip	tease
sow	zeal	zenith	zigzag
is	zoom	rose	toes

Does the word begin with a /ch/ sound? (as in chew)

champ	ship	charge	jump
shoe	camp	general	chip
chunk	chuckle	show	school

Does the word begin with a /sh/ sound? (as in ship)

shallow	see	chair	rash
soup	shave	jar	shun
chew	shine	shell	shrug

Does the word begin with an /ĕ/ sound? (as in Eskimo)

end	edit	ever	except
Esther	apple	into	up
eagle	empty	olive	elephant

Does the word begin with an /ĭ/ sound? (as in igloo)

into	end	iodine	at
pet	illegal	if	ice
important	impact	up	tin

Does the word begin with an /ŏ/ sound? (as in octopus)

opera	rod	under	pot
open	odd	old	object
apple	modern	on	officer

Does the word begin with an /ŭ/ sound? (as in umbrella)

under	undermine	sun	urge
use	offer	hunter	bulge
unable	up	usual	ugly

Does the word begin with an /ă/ sound? (as in apple)

ant	pen	add	ladder
cat	ask	attic	aide
ape	enter	ate	astronaut

Level 3 Word List—Activity 2

mat–at	meeting–eating	hand–and	wax–ax
mice–ice	tangle–angle	sigh–I	turn–earn
tan–an	small–mall	tape–ape	supper–upper
pat–at	merge–urge	table–able	sink–ink
date–ate	moat–oat	sash–ash	mare–air
mace–ace	mangle–angle	fall–all	mend–end
ball–all	mate–ate	told–old	tax–ax
my–eye	tin–in	tar–are	bait–ate
part–art	four–or	totter–otter	door–oar
deal–eel	call–all	sit–it	gate–ate
mall–all	Sam–am	soften–often	toe–oh
faint–ain't	race–ace	tin–in	win–in
sour–our	mask–ask	tote–oat	send–end
gone–on	pink–ink	meager–eager	march–arch
many–any	mad–add	meal–eel	sand–and
hate–ate	neat–eat	time–I'm	surge–urge
seat–eat	maim–aim	pin–in	mart–art
jar–are	limp–imp	fan–an	mold–old
lend–end	sad–add	tall–all	tone–own
till–ill	page–age	nice–ice	motto–Otto
nor–or	sold–old	tale–ail	rise–eyes
sew–oh	came–aim	sill–ill	mink–ink
sought–ought	moan–own	socks–ox	marrow–arrow
tease–ease	fear–ear	sat–at	mow–owe
made–ade	tally–alley	will–ill	
tie–eye	tile–I'll	teach–each	
tear–air	soil–oil	make–ache	

Level 3 Word List–Activity 3

(n)or	(p)each	(w)oke	(p)itch	(m)ace
(b)urn	(b)ait	(p)ending	(n)ear	(m)ice
(h)eart	(h)arm	(r)ash	(f)ate	(s)our
(w)are	(d)oe	(w)onder	(b)eg	(l)ark
(p)ad	(j)oke	(d)are	(g)alley	(p)art

(r)oar	(g)ale	(h)ail	(b)all	(m)ake
(p)ink	(f)or	(r)each	(k)it	(f)all
(r)ant	(c)ash	(r)ally	(b)eat	(f)in
(c)all	(d)oubt	(w)ill	(h)aul	(m)at
(j)ar	(h)all	(h)ad	(l)ice	(f)an
(r)ail	(p)ouch	(p)air	(f)ern	(m)ill
(v)ery	(d)ate	(g)old	(h)am	(w)all
(p)ace	(b)oil	(d)ad	(h)and	(b)in
(b)at	(c)art	(b)ad	(h)eat	(r)an
(l)ake	(l)ark	(l)ace	(l)ad	(c)at
(l)it	(p)up	(g)oat	(k)eel	(p)ill
(f)ail	(d)art	(c)old	(n)ice	(s)in
(f)ace	(f)ox	(c)ame	(l)eave	(t)an
(f)oul	(c)an't	(h)as	(l)ax	(b)at
(l)ash	(j)am	(d)ear	(h)older	(s)ink
(g)ear	(l)ore	(d)ill	(w)age	(m)all
(l)earn	(b)and	(p)inch	(g)out	(s)eat
(v)an	(b)ake	(c)are	(w)itch	(t)each
(r)age	(r)amble	(b)ar	(v)owel	(b)each
(t)one	(w)eave	(w)ink	(p)arch	
(m)are	(t)ax	(s)old	(p)age	

AUDITORY PERCEPTUAL SKILLS—LEVEL 4

Equipment

Level 4 word lists

Activities

1. Using words from the level 4 word list, teach the concept of embedded sounds. Ask the child to "say *make*." Then, "Does the word *make* end with a /k/ sound?" (Say the letter sound, not the letter name.) Also encourage the child to "think about how your mouth feels as you say and hear the word."
   Goal: Child responds correctly to at least six words that do or do not contain the embedded sound (words taken from the appropriate level 4 word list).

2. Have the child say the sound that is missing. "Say *make*." "Now say *may*." "What sound is missing in *may* that you heard in *make*?" See level 4 word list for suitable words. Again at this level, it is often helpful for the child to think about how his mouth feels as he says and hears the words.

Goal: Child responds correctly to at least six words taken from the appropriate level 4 word list.
3. Say the word without the final sound. "Say *make*." "Now say it again, but don't say [leave out] the /k/ sound."
Goal: Child responds correctly to at least six words taken from the appropriate level 4 word list.
4. Activity 3 is the end of this level, although it is always advisable to review (practice) after the activity 3 goal is achieved. It is also useful to encourage the child to try to recognize words that would be appropriate for the level 4 word list, that is, words that continue to have meaning after the final sound of each has been deleted.

Level 4 Word List—Activity 1

Does the word end with a /**m**/ sound? (as in Sam)

bend	trim	mush	roam
limp	land	beam	bump
rhyme	steam	green	churn
stern	mean	dimple	mix
bump	came	come	time

Does the word end with a /**t**/ sound? (as in gate)

write	slot	hot	boat
hat	goat	mouth	toast
tame	fighter	had	sled

Does the word end with a /**k**/ sound? (as in make)

back	bag	slick	rack
rocker	lock	fig	crib
score	wrinkle	clap	rag

Does the word end with a /**b**/ sound? (as in gab)

big	bone	slab	bent
crab	dabble	bait	dent
dig	best	ribbon	web

Does the word end with a /**d**/ sound? (as in end)

dog	raid	rode	ladder
food	ditch	mouth	mustard
meet	sweet	loud	decide

Does the word end with a /**f**/ sound? (as in laugh)

love	with	live	growth
graph	stuff	cliff	sunfish
fame	fish	fancy	bluff

Does the word end with a /**g**/ sound? (as in pig)

bike	sling	lock	ghost
rag	haggle	fog	plug
grain	wag	page	stick

Does the word end with a /**j**/ sound? (as in edge)

lodge	bed	which	badge
generous	justice	magic	batch
wag	wage	wash	wish

Does the word end with an /**l**/ sound? (as in all)

long	hello	pail	silk
boil	star	pillow	steel
sill	a	listen	stolen

Does the word end with a /**n**/ sound? (as in in)

pin	grain	bend	team
stone	bandit	grim	gown
sandy	shine	nudge	something

Does the word end with a /**p**/ sound? (as in hop)

puzzle	ripple	tide	hopped
paper	trip	defend	heap
rope	raft	crib	feet

Does the word end with a /**r**/ sound? (as in or)

ball	sorry	park	race
fur	sir	tear	squirt
strip	read	furry	fire

Does the word end with an /**s**/ sound? (as in mess)

race	mist	base	toast
rash	sock	least	loose
rise	fasten	please	lose

Does the word end with a /**sh**/ sound? (as in push)

bush	mushy	squash	match
witch	latch	dash	wishing
rush	show	rubbish	lash

Does the word end with a /**z**/ sound? (as in eyes)

rise	froze	puzzle	choose
hose	loose	shoes	chosen
zoo	lose	splash	size

Level 4 Word List—Activity 2

make–may	loom–Lou	goat–go	grape–gray
beat–be	prime–pry	weight–way	bite–by

boil–boy	rhyme–rye	lime–lie	bait–bay
gate–gay	name–nay	like–lie	team–tea
made–may	same–say	mite–my	late–lay
rope–row	mean–me	base–bay	croak–crow
soap–so	safe–say	awake–away	freak–free
beam–be	rode–row	firm–fur	claim–clay
heat–he	soak–so	boat–bow	face–Fay
mate–may	toad–toe	loaf–low	feet–fee
home–hoe	ice–I	storm–store	grace–gray
lame–lay	pace–pay	time–tie	pike–pie
stake–stay	race–ray	type–tie	
boat–bow	dance–Dan	meat–me	

Level 4 Word List—Activity 3

wa(ke)	rai(l)	wa(ge)	ra(ke)	wea(l)
tri(te)	plea(t)	du(ke)	lea(p)	coo(p)
mea(l)	shi(ne)	ha(ze)	ho(ne)	li(fe)
lo(be)	loa(m)	see(p)	ma(te)	ma(de)
ja(de)	sta(ge)	la(me)	bea(d)	coi(n)
di(re)	tea(k)	mi(ne)	ri(de)	goe(s)
kee(p)	ra(ce)	sa(ke)	grow(n)	ra(ge)
wai(t)	trai(n)	mi(ght)	coo(l)	ho(se)
no(te)	no(se)	how(l)	mea(t)	hi(de)
bi(de)	coi(l)	loa(n)	ru(de)	tee(n)
fee(l)	lo(pe)	see(n)	mi(le)	ba(se)
gra(ce)	plea(d)	mee(k)	pri(ze)	sie(ge)
fu(se)	boa(t)	lea(gue)	li(ke)	gra(pe)
ti(le)	ty(ke)	grou(p)	ga(ze)	loa(d)
lea(se)	hai(l)	ho(pe)	hee(l)	soa(p)
bi(ke)	pla(gue)	see(k)	stai(n)	pi(le)
sa(ne)	sea(t)	ti(re)	law(n)	bea(m)
boi(l)	mo(de)	gai(l)	pa(ge)	pla(te)
rai(n)	frea(k)	mi(re)	si(de)	lea(n)
kee(n)	la(ce)	joi(n)	hea(t)	
new(t)	sea(l)	goa(t)	pa(ce)	

AUDITORY PERCEPTUAL SKILLS—LEVEL 5

Equipment

Level 5 word lists

Activities

1. Using words from the level 5 word list, have the child say the sound (part of a consonant blend) that is missing. "Say *slip*." "Now say *lip*." "What sound is missing in *lip* that you heard in *slip?*"
   Goal: Child responds correctly to at least six words taken from the appropriate level 5 word list.
2. Say the word without the sound that is part of a consonant blend. "Say *slip*." "Now say it again, but don't say [leave out] the /s/ sound."
   Goal: Child responds correctly to at least six words taken from the appropriate level 5 word list.
3. Activity 2 is the end of this level, although it is always advisable to review (practice) after the activity 2 goal is achieved. It is also useful to encourage the child to try to recognize words that would be appropriate for the level 5 word list, that is, words that continue to have meaning after one of the sounds contained in a consonant blend has been deleted.

Level 5 Word List—Activity 1

spider–cider	stack–sack	hand–had	scale–sale
slip–lip	spin–sin	cast–cat	bent–bet
stack–tack	store–sore	sent–set	beast–bet
spin–pin	black–lack	start–star	boast–boat
stare–tear	fist–fit	slag–sag	fern–fur
best–bet	best–Bess	spank–sank	bank–back
ghost–goat	snap–sap	bright–bite	blow–low
trap–rap	spoon–soon	crow–row	pest–pet
best–bet	stick–sick	lint–lit	snip–sip
trim–rim	slam–lamb	cram–ram	hulk–hull
stop–top	swell–well	built–bill	lend–led
cork–core	flip–lip	fast–fat	drown–down
snap–sap	snip–nip	triple–ripple	string–sting
rust–rut	mask–mack	fend–fed	black–back
skill–sill	store–tore	bent–Ben	just—jut
fork–for	sunk–sun	snap–nap	mark–mar
try–rye	stir–sir	stick–tick	chart–char
felt–fell	scoop–soup	slam–Sam	west–wet
skein–sane	stake–sake	store–tore	roast–rote
milk–mill	swing–wing	black–back	skip–sip
land–lad	bark–bar	vest–vet	stick–sick
fluster–flutter	bend–bed	wilt–will	sing–sing
drip–dip	clasp–clap	bunt–but	

blow–bow	cart–car	scold–sold
snap–sap	gland–glad	track–rack

Level 5 Word List—Activity 2

p(r)ay	(g)rub	fil(m)	c(l)aim	(c)lock
g(l)ow	hal(t)	fin(d)	c(l)amp	c(l)ock
(s)lip	ha(n)d	(f)lair	(c)lamp	(c)olt
f(r)og	ha(s)te	f(l)air	f(l)eet	c(l)ot
ca(m)p	he(l)d	(f)lake	(f)lier	c(l)ub
clas(p)	he(l)m	f(l)ake	f(l)ier	c(l)utter
e(n)d	he(m)p	(f)lame	(f)light	(c)raft
ha(s)te	hem(p)	f(l)ame	f(l)ight	(c)ramp
be(l)t	hi(l)t	(f)lash	(f)lit	c(r)amp
bel(t)	hum(p)	f(l)at	f(l)it	cra(m)p
be(n)t	li(l)t	(f)law	f(l)oor	cam(p)
ben(t)	(p)laid	(f)lee	f(l)orist	(c)rank
ben(ch)	p(l)aid	f(l)ee	(f)low	cra(n)k
(b)lack	(p)lain	(f)leece	f(r)ame	(c)rash
b(l)ack	(p)ray	p(l)ain	f(r)og	c(r)ash
(b)lank	(f)lap	p(l)aint	f(r)izzle	(c)reep
b(l)ank	s(l)ip	(p)lank	(f)lume	c(r)eep
(b)lare	(f)lake	plan(t)	f(r)ee	(g)low
b(l)are	clam(p)	(p)late	f(r)yer	g(l)ow
(b)leed	fi(s)t	p(l)aque	ga(s)p	(g)lue
b(l)eed	fin(d)	(p)ly	(g)lad	(g)race
(b)lend	p(l)y	p(l)y	(g)land	(g)rade
b(l)end	b(l)ond	(p)rank	(g)lade	(g)raft
ble(n)d	b(l)ood	(p)ray	(g)lare	(g)rail
(b)less	(b)loom	p(r)ay	(g)lass	g(r)ail
b(l)ess	b(l)oom	(p)ry	g(l)ass	(g)rain
(b)lest	(b)lot	pu(m)p	g(l)aze	g(r)ain
b(l)est	(b)low	ra(m)p	g(l)ide	(g)rasp
(b)light	b(l)ow	(g)loss	ran(k)	g(r)asp
b(l)ight	(b)race	(s)lap	ra(n)t	gras(p)
b(l)ind	(b)rag	(s)tick	ri(n)d	(g)rate
b(l)oat	b(r)ag	f(l)ake	ski(m)p	g(r)ate
(b)lock	(b)rain	cla(m)p	skim(p)	(g)rave
(c)rest	b(r)ain	bes(t)	s(l)ed	g(r)ave
cres(t)	(b)rake	fil(m)	(s)lid	(g)reed
(c)rib	(b)ranch	s(t)y	s(l)id	(g)ray
c(r)ook	bran(ch)	(b)rig	(s)lit	g(r)ay
(c)ruise	(b)rat	b(r)ig	(s)lide	(g)rill

(c)rush	b(r)at	(b)right	s(m)ell	g(r)ill
cu(l)t	(b)ray	b(r)ight	s(p)un	(g)rip
(d)raft	b(r)ay	(b)rim	(s)wing	(g)round
d(r)aft	(b)read	(b)ring	s(w)ing	(g)row
(d)rag	b(r)ead	(b)room	(g)low	s(l)ide
(d)rain	(b)reed	b(r)oom	s(l)ap	(t)rack
d(r)ain	b(r)eed	(b)rought	s(t)ick	t(r)ack
(d)raw	(b)rick	b(r)ought	buil(d)	(t)rap
(d)rank	(b)ride	(b)row	cla(s)p	t(r)ap
d(r)ank	d(r)ip	b(r)ow	be(s)t	(t)rim
d(r)awn	d(r)ive	(b)rush	fa(s)t	t(r)im
(d)read	(d)rove	bui(l)d	be(n)d	(t)ry
d(r)ead	d(r)ove	buil(d)	c(l)aim	t(r)y
(d)ream	(d)rug	bui(l)t	(c)lash	wi(l)t
d(r)eam	d(r)ug	buil(t)	c(l)ash	wil(t)
d(r)eary	(d)rum	ca(m)p	cla(s)p	s(l)it
(d)rill	d(r)um	cam(p)	(c)lass	(s)lim
d(r)ill	e(n)d	can(t)	(c)lean	(f)led
(d)rink	fe(n)d	ca(n)t	c(l)ean	
(d)rip	fen(d)	(c)laim	c(l)ing	

AUDITORY PERCEPTUAL SKILLS—LEVEL 6

Equipment

Level 6 word list

Activities

1. Using words from the level 6 word list, teach the concept of sound substitution. For example, ask the child to "Say *make*." Then, "Now say it again, but instead of /m/ say /t/." (Say the letter sound, not the letter name.) Also encourage the child to "think about how your mouth feels as you say these words and sounds."
   Goal: Child responds correctly to at least six words taken from the level 6 word list.

2. Activity 1 is the end of this level, although it is always advisable to review (practice) after the activity 1 goal is achieved. It is also useful to encourage the child to try to recognize words that would be appropriate for the level 6 word list, that is, words that continue to have meaning after one of the sounds has been replaced by another.

Level 6 Word List—Activity 1

Say **sad**	Now say it again, but instead of /**s**/ say /**m**/	**mad**
Say **kale**	Now say it again, but instead of /**k**/ say /**s**/	**sale**
Say **tan**	Now say it again, but instead of /**t**/ say /**m**/	**man**
Say **sat**	Now say it again, but instead of /**s**/ say /**k**/	**cat**
Say **table**	Now say it again, but instead of /**t**/ say /**k**/	**cable**
Say **my**	Now say it again, but instead of /**m**/ say /**s**/	**sigh**
Say **make**	Now say it again, but instead of /**m**/ say /**t**/	**take**
Say **kill**	Now say it again, but instead of /**k**/ say /**m**/	**mill**
Say **mare**	Now say it again, but instead of /**m**/ say /**k**/	**care**
Say **milk**	Now say it again, but instead of /**m**/ say /**s**/	**silk**
Say **call**	Now say it again, but instead of /**k**/ say /**t**/	**tall**
Say **sit**	Now say it again, but instead of /**s**/ say /**k**/	**kit**
Say **task**	Now say it again, but instead of /**t**/ say /**m**/	**mask**
Say **cage**	Now say it again, but instead of /**k**/ say /**s**/	**sage**
Say **more**	Now say it again, but instead of /**m**/ say /**t**/	**tore**
Say **main**	Now say it again, but instead of /**m**/ say /**k**/	**cane**
Say **take**	Now say it again, but instead of /**t**/ say /**s**/	**sake**
Say **mend**	Now say it again, but instead of /**m**/ say /**t**/	**tend**
Say **tin**	Now say it again, but instead of /**t**/ say /**k**/	**kin**
Say **seal**	Now say it again, but instead of /**s**/ say /**m**/	**meal**
Say **cash**	Now say it again, but instead of /**k**/ say /**s**/	**sash**
Say **tangle**	Now say it again, but instead of /**t**/ say /**m**/	**mangle**
Say **sell**	Now say it again, but instead of /**s**/ say /**t**/	**tell**
Say **moat**	Now say it again, but instead of /**m**/ say /**k**/	**coat**
Say **tend**	Now say it again, but instead of /**t**/ say /**s**/	**send**
Say **fill**	Now say it again, but instead of /**f**/ say /**h**/	**hill**
Say **heart**	Now say it again, but instead of /**h**/ say /**d**/	**dart**
Say **lace**	Now say it again, but instead of /**l**/ say /**p**/	**pace**
Say **dart**	Now say it again, but instead of /**d**/ say /**p**/	**part**
Say **goat**	Now say it again, but instead of /**g**/ say /**b**/	**boat**
Say **fame**	Now say it again, but instead of /**f**/ say /**g**/	**game**
Say **hall**	Now say it again, but instead of /**h**/ say /**w**/	**wall**
Say **toss**	Now say it again, but instead of /**s**/ say /**m**/	**tom**
Say **boss**	Now say it again, but instead of /**s**/ say /**t**/	**bought**
Say **bait**	Now say it again, but instead of /**t**/ say /**s**/	**base**
Say **beam**	Now say it again, but instead of /**m**/ say /**t**/	**beat**
Say **lace**	Now say it again, but instead of /**s**/ say /**t**/	**late**
Say **lame**	Now say it again, but instead of /**m**/ say /**s**/	**lace**
Say **rack**	Now say it again, but instead of /**k**/ say /**t**/	**rat**
Say **rack**	Now say it again, but instead of /**k**/ say /**m**/	**ram**
Say **gate**	Now say it again, but instead of /**t**/ say /**m**/	**game**
Say **mate**	Now say it again, but instead of /**t**/ say /**k**/	**make**

Say **mite**	Now say it again, but instead of /t/ say /s/	**mice**
Say **bake**	Now say it again, but instead of /k/ say /s/	**base**
Say **seat**	Now say it again, but instead of /t/ say /k/	**seek**
Say **prime**	Now say it again, but instead of /m/ say /s/	**price**
Say **late**	Now say it again, but instead of /t/ say /m/	**lame**
Say **bite**	Now say it again, but instead of /t/ say /k/	**bike**
Say **fake**	Now say it again, but instead of /k/ say /s/	**face**
Say **base**	Now say it again, but instead of /s/ say /k/	**bake**
Say **leak**	Now say it again, but instead of /k/ say /s/	**lease**
Say **flame**	Now say it again, but instead of /m/ say /k/	**flake**
Say **face**	Now say it again, but instead of /s/ say /t/	**fate**
Say **well**	Now say it again, but instead of /l/ say /t/	**wet**
Say **steel**	Now say it again, but instead of /l/ say /p/	**steep**
Say **cash**	Now say it again, but instead of /sh/ say /n/	**can**
Say **cuff**	Now say it again, but instead of /f/ say /b/	**cub**
Say **drug**	Now say it again, but instead of /g/ say /m/	**drum**
Say **bead**	Now say it again, but instead of /d/ say /n/	**bean**
Say **safe**	Now say it again, but instead of /f/ say /j/	**sage**
Say **league**	Now say it again, but instead of /g/ say /n/	**lean**
Say **page**	Now say it again, but instead of /j/ say /l/	**pale**
Say **loaf**	Now say it again, but instead of /f/ say /d/	**load**
Say **stage**	Now say it again, but instead of /j/ say /t/	**state**
Say **grade**	Now say it again, but instead of /d/ say /n/	**grain**
Say **hope**	Now say it again, but instead of /p/ say /z/	**hose**
Say **gain**	Now say it again, but instead of /n/ say /z/	**gaze**
Say **hide**	Now say it again, but instead of /d/ say /r/	**hire**
Say **pan**	Now say it again, but instead of /n/ say /s/	**pass**
Say **win**	Now say it again, but instead of /n/ say /g/	**wig**
Say **plead**	Now say it again, but instead of /d/ say /z/	**please**
Say **fair**	Now say it again, but instead of /r/ say /l/	**fail**
Say **mail**	Now say it again, but instead of /l/ say /d/	**maid**
Say **clock**	Now say it again, but instead of /ŏ/ say /ĭ/	**click**
Say **crash**	Now say it again, but instead of /ŏ/ say /ŭ/	**crush**
Say **crest**	Now say it again, but instead of /s/ say /p/	**crept**
Say **crash**	Now say it again, but instead of /r/ say /l/	**clash**
Say **draft**	Now say it again, but instead of /ă/ say /ĭ/	**drift**
Say **drink**	Now say it again, but instead of /ĭ/ say /ă/	**drank**
Say **drip**	Now say it again, but instead of /ĭ/ say /ŏ/	**drop**
Say **drive**	Now say it again, but instead of /ī/ say /ō/	**drove**
Say **flame**	Now say it again, but instead of /l/ say /r/	**frame**
Say **flash**	Now say it again, but instead of /ă/ say /ĕ/	**flesh**
Say **free**	Now say it again, but instead of /r/ say /l/	**flee**
Say **fryer**	Now say it again, but instead of /r/ say /l/	**flyer**
Say **gland**	Now say it again, but instead of /l/ say /r/	**grand**

Say **glass**	Now say it again, but instead of /l/ say /r/	**grass**
Say **glow**	Now say it again, but instead of /l/ say /r/	**grow**
Say **grain**	Now say it again, but instead of /ă/ say /ō/	**groan**
Say **grate**	Now say it again, but instead of /t/ say /n/	**grain**
Say **grip**	Now say it again, but instead of /ĭ/ say /ō/	**grope**
Say **lint**	Now say it again, but instead of /n/ say /s/	**list**
Say **plank**	Now say it again, but instead of /l/ say /r/	**prank**
Say **pray**	Now say it again, but instead of /r/ say /l/	**play**
Say **ramp**	Now say it again, but instead of /m/ say /s/	**rasp**
Say **sled**	Now say it again, but instead of /ĕ/ say /ĭ/	**slid**
Say **swing**	Now say it again, but instead of /w/ say /t/	**sting**
Say **track**	Now say it again, but instead of /ă/ say /ĭ/	**trick**
Say **trip**	Now say it again, but instead of /ĭ/ say /ă/	**trap**

APPENDIX C
TESTING AND TEACHING
DECODING ACTIVITIES

THE FOLLOWING SECTION delineates an activity that will make apparent to the child a system for memorizing reading words, that is, for building word recognition skills.

Shown on pages 223–70 are 108 sets of word lists. Each set is based upon a designated "decoding unit," or letter string. Each decoding unit set is organized into four levels (A–D) of increasing difficulty.

Notice that each of the words within a decoding unit set, regardless of level, contains that decoding unit (for example, *ag* or *ad*). To this extent, the words at each level within a set are similar. They differ, of course, in their length—or, said another way, in the context in which the decoding units appear.

The words in each Level A list are short—one syllable. The decoding unit occupies a major portion of the word; it is joined with a single consonant only. As such, when the child identifies the decoding unit, he has most of the word figured out. At Level B the words continue to be single syllable, but the decoding unit is joined with more than one consonant. Thus though the words are longer at this level than they are at Level A, the only vowels in them are the ones in the decoding unit. The additional length derives from additional consonants. Level C words are two syllables long, with the decoding unit appearing in one of the two syllables, the other syllable varying according to the word itself. Level D words are three or more syllables long; the decoding unit occurs in one of the syllables, with the other syllables, once more, varying from word to word in random fashion.

I will not dwell on the purposes for this organization other than to state what probably is already obvious to you: (a) it provides an orderly method for teaching the child to identify whole words by focusing on key portions of those words that are already familiar to him; (b) it leads the child into drill exercises with a number of different words of varying length—thereby increasing the chances of his becoming adept at reading them with a minimum of "sounding out" activity; (c) as such, it teaches the child one of the basic skills of reading—automatic recognition of printed words, a skill that is crucial to competent comprehension of printed language. All of this is consistent with my earlier statement that, though we use a variety of clues to help us remember words, the best clues are the phonic-based ones.

You will use these word lists for two purposes: to *test* the child and to *teach* the child. *To test the child.* The purpose of your tests will be to place the child, that is, determine his ability to recognize specific decoding units that, in turn, will help him recall, or figure out, whole words.

1. Start off by asking the child to read the Level D list of words in the first decoding unit set, the one based on *an*.* Keep a record of the words he can and cannot read.**
2. If he cannot read all, or just about all, of the Level D list, then move down to the Level C words in this set.
3. If he cannot read all, or just about all, of the Level C words, then move down to Level B.
4. If he cannot read all of these properly, then scale down to Level A.
5. Stop the testing within a decoding unit set at the level where the child can read just about all of the words adequately, that is, accurately and rapidly. Make the assumption that if he passes a particular level, he can read the lower-level words in the set and therefore need not be tested at those lower levels.
6. If the child can read the Level C or Level D words in this first decoding unit set, then go through the same testing steps (1–5) with Decoding Unit Set 2 *(ag)* and continue in this fashion until *(a)* you come to a set where the child cannot read the Level C words†; or *(b)* you have tested him with all of the sets.
7. Stop testing at this point.

What are you determining with this testing method? You are finding out: *(a)* whether the child can identify decoding units, made up of letter strings, when they occur in the context of meaningful words; and *(b)* the level of context complexity—word length—that he can deal with successfully.

8. Some children will not be able to read even the Level A list in a given

*Chances are that the child you are concerned about will not be able to read the words in the Level D list. If he can read the words in the Level D list of this and the other decoding unit sets, then he probably does not have a word recognition problem. Hence, the remainder of this section will not be pertinent to whatever difficulties he does have. Leave it and go to some of the other sections in this book that appear to be more relevant to his learning difficulties.

**To be considered adequate, the child's responses must be both accurate and instantaneous. Do *not* score his performance as acceptable if he reads the words slowly, albeit correctly, more or less sounding them out.

†For children in the second grade change this to read *Level B;* that is, continue testing until you come to a set where the child cannot read Level B words. For children in the first grade change this to read *Level A*.

decoding unit set. What are they showing? That they have not yet learned to perceive a part of a word—a letter string—as a decoding unit. In these instances you will have to find out if the child is able to read the decoding unit when it stands alone, out of word context.

9. That should be done now with those children who cannot read the Level A list adequately. To do this, show the child the decoding unit of that set and ask him to read it in this isolated, free-of-word-context state.

10. Suppose he cannot do even this very satisfactorily. What next? One final step will have to be taken eventually. You will have to determine if he knows that the separate letters of the decoding unit represent certain sounds. But there is no need to do this now. You will find that out when you start teaching him. Leave it until then.

11. You have completed the testing when you have done all that has been outlined in the preceding steps. You now have some idea of how well the child can identify decoding units, at least in the framework of this kind of test.

Once you have the test information, you can get started teaching the child how to do what the tests showed that he could not do.

To get started teaching the child to identify letter strings as decoding units:

1. Begin with the decoding unit set where the testing stopped.
2. Begin with the lowest level he failed.

The instructions that follow cover all possible test outcomes. They start with activities that are appropriate for the child who could not read even the decoding unit itself and go up from there.

Identify the entry level that is appropriate for your child and begin there. (But do not fret about the precise accuracy of your placement decision. If you find that he is overplaced or underplaced—and it will be immediately apparent—then simply move him up or down a level, as indicated. This will not be harmful, so long as you do not blame him for the misplacement.)

For the child who was not able to read the decoding unit of the set

1. Print on a chalkboard the decoding unit he was unable to read during testing. Let us assume, for illustration purposes, that this was the first decoding unit set. Hence the first decoding unit he should be taught is the an. (A chalkboard is best, but paper and soft pencil or felt-tip pen will do if a board is not available.)
2. Point to the an and say: "This says /ăn/."*

*When one or more letters are shown within a pair of slashes—such as /an/—it means that you are to say the letter sound(s), not the letter name(s).

3. Now ask: "What does the a-n say?"**
4. Once he responds correctly—that is, states that the a-n says /ăn/— then ask: "Which of these letters says /n/?"
5. If he does not respond correctly, tell him the answer ("The n says /n/."), then repeat your query and continue with this until he can accurately state, "The n says /n/."
6. When he is able to respond correctly, show him the decoding unit *an* and say: "The a-n says /ăn/. Which of these letters says /ă/?"
7. If he displays confusion, go back to step 2 and repeat the activities from that point.
8. When he can connect the /n/ (sound) and the /ă/ (sound) to the proper letters, then show him the full unit again—the *an*—and tell him: "Make it say /ă/; cover up (or erase) the part of the word that does not belong."
9. If he responds correctly (covers up the *n*), ask him: "Tell me what the letter *a* says." That is, you want to hear him tell you the /ă/ (sound).
10. When he can do this, then again show him the full unit—the *an*—and tell him: "Make it say /n/; cover up (or erase) that part of the word that does not belong."
11. When he has done this (covered up the *a*), then ask him: "Tell me what the letter *n* says." That is, you want to hear him tell you the /n/ (sound).
12. Once all of this has been accomplished correctly, show him the full decoding unit again—the *an*—and ask him: "Tell me what the a-n says."
13. When he shows that he knows the *an,* print this decoding unit on a 3″ × 5″ index card and store it in a file box, which you might want to call a Word Bank. These cards, as they accumulate, will be used for regular review.
14. It is now time to move up to a higher level (Level A) within this same decoding unit set.

For the child who was not able to read the Level A words accurately and rapidly but can read the decoding unit related to those words when it is shown in isolation

15. Print on a chalkboard one of the Level A words from the decoding unit set you are working on. If the child read any of the words correctly during the testing, use one of these for initial activities. If he did not read any of them correctly, then choose any word from the Level A list. For illustration purposes, let us assume that you are

---

**When letters are shown underlined and separated by a hyphen—such as the a-n—it means that you are to name the letters one at a time, as though spelling a word.

going to work with Decoding Unit 1—the *an*—and have decided to start off with the Level A word *tan*.

16. Point to the word *tan* and say: "This says /tăn/."
17. Now ask: "What does the t-a-n say?"
18. Once he responds correctly—that is, repeats what you told him—then ask: "Which letters say /ăn/?"
19. If he does not respond correctly, tell him the answer ("The a-n says /ăn/."), then repeat your query. If difficulty persists, consider dropping back to the lower-level activities (steps 1–14) described previously, where the focus is on teaching the child to read the decoding units. The assumption when working on this level is that the child *can* read the decoding units.
20. When he is able to respond correctly, ask: "Which of these letters says /t/?"
21. If he displays confusion here, go back to step 16 and repeat the activities from there on.
22. When he can connect /ăn/ and /t/ to the proper letters, show him the full word again—*tan*—and tell him: "Make it say /ăn/; cover up (or erase) that part of the word that does not belong."
23. When he responds correctly (covers up the *t*), ask him: "Tell me what the a-n says."
24. When he can do this, then again show him the full word—*tan*—and tell him: "Make it say /t/; cover up (or erase) that part of the word that does not belong."
25. When he has done this (covered up the *an*), then ask him: "Tell me what the *t* says."
26. Once all of this has been accomplished correctly, show him the full word again—*tan*—and ask him: "Tell me what t-a-n says."
27. When he shows that he knows *tan*—can read it accurately and without delay—print it on a 3″ × 5″ index card and store it in his Word Bank.
28. Now choose another word from the Level A list (decoding unit *an*)—*ban*, for example—and go through these same steps (15–27).
29. When you are satisfied that the child can correctly read these two words and, further, can relate the /ăn/ (sound) to the letter string a-n, the /t/ (sound) to the letter *t*, and the /b/ (sound) to the letter *b*, then print one of the two words on the chalkboard and ask him to read it to you.
30. Start with *tan*, for example. He should be able to respond correctly, of course. Once he does, ask him to: "Make it say /băn/; change it so that it says /băn/ instead of /tăn/."
31. Work your way through all of the Level A words in this decoding unit set (1) this way—steps 15–30—stopping finally when the child can change any one of them to any other one on request, as illustrated in

step 30. For example, when he can change /tăn/ to /făn/ to /păn/ and so on.

Where to next? You have two options. You might work up into the next level (Level B) within this same decoding unit set, or you might move on, at the same level (Level A) to the next decoding unit (Decoding Unit Set 2, for example). As a general rule, if the child is in the second grade or above, do the former—move up to Level B within the same decoding unit set. If he is in the first grade, move on to a new decoding unit set, remaining at the same level.

If you take this latter route, then your instructions remain the same as already covered here. Return to step 15 and start over with the Level A words from this new set. If, instead, you are now ready to move up to Level B within the same decoding unit set, then proceed with the steps described in the following.

For the child who was not able to read the Level B words accurately and rapidly but can read the Level A words from the same decoding unit set

32. Print on a chalkboard one of the Level B words from the decoding unit set you are working on. If the child read any of the words correctly during the testing, use one of these for initial activities. If he did not read any of them correctly, then choose any word from the Level B list. For illustration purposes, let us assume that you are working with the decoding unit *an* and have decided to start off with the word *ranch*.

33. Point to the word *ranch* and say: "This says /ranch/. The r̲ says /r/, the a̲-n̲ says /ăn/, and the c̲-h̲ says /ch/."

34. Now ask: "What does r̲-a̲-n̲-c̲-h̲ say?"

35. Once he responds correctly—that is, repeats what you told him— then ask: "Which letters say /ăn/?"

36. If he does not respond correctly, consider dropping back to a lower-level activity. The assumption, when working on this level, is that the child can read these decoding units out of context and is now ready to use them in context.

37. When he responds correctly, ask: "Which of these letters says /r/? Which say /ch/?"

38. If he displays confusion here, go back to step 33 and repeat the activities from there on.

39. When he can correctly connect the /r/ to r̲, the /ăn/ to a̲-n̲, and the /ch/ to the c̲-h̲, show him the full word again—*ranch*—and tell him: "Make it say /răn/; cover up (or erase) that part of the word that does not belong."

40. When he responds correctly (covers up the c-h), ask him: "Tell me what the r-a-n says."

41. Once all of this has been accomplished correctly, show him the full word again—*ranch*—and tell him: "Make it say /ănch/; cover up (or erase) that part of the word that does not belong."

42. When he has done this (covered up the *r*), then ask him: "Tell me what the a-n-c-h says."

43. Once he has done this correctly, show him the full word again—*ranch*—and tell him: "Make it say /ăn/; cover up (or erase) those parts of the word that do not belong."

44. When he responds correctly (covers up the r and the c-h, then show him the full word again—*ranch*—and ask him: "Tell me what r-a-n-c-h says."

45. When he shows that he knows *ranch*—can read it accurately and without delay—print it on a 3" × 5" index card and store it in his Word Bank.

46. Now choose another word from the Level B list of this decoding unit set—*scan*, for example—and go through these same steps (32–45) again.

47. When you are satisfied that the child can correctly read the first two words you worked on from this Level B list and, further, can relate the various single letters and decoding units to their appropriate sounds, then print one of the two words on the chalkboard and ask him to read it to you.

48. For example, let us assume that you started with *ranch*. He should be able to respond correctly, of course. Once he does, tell him: "Make it say /scăn/; change it so that it says /scăn/ instead of /rănch/."

49. Work your way through all of the Level B words in this decoding unit set this way—steps 32–48—stopping finally when the child can change any one of them to any other one on request, as illustrated in step 48. For example, when he can change /ranch/ to /scan/ to /bland/ to /pant/ and so on.

Where to next? You have two options. You might work up to the next level (Level C) within this same decoding unit set, or you might choose to move on to another decoding unit, beginning in that unit at the highest level possible for the child, as indicated by testing.

As a general rule, if the child is in the third grade or above, do the former—move on to Level C within the same decoding unit set. If he is in the first or second grade, move to a new decoding unit set, using the test procedures to determine his starting level.

If you take this latter route, then your instructions remain the same as already covered here. If, instead, you opt to move up to Level C within this same decoding unit set, then proceed with the steps described in the following.

For the child who was not able to read the Level C words accurately and rapidly but can read the Level B words from the same decoding unit set

50. Print on a chalkboard one of the Level C words from the decoding unit set you are working on. If the child read any of the words correctly during the testing, use one of these for the initial activities. If he did not read any of them correctly, then choose any word from the Level C list. For illustration purposes, let us assume that you are going to work with the decoding unit *an,* starting off with the Level C word *began.*
51. Point to the word *began* and say: "This says /began/. The b-e says /bē/, and the g-a-n says /găn/."
52. Now ask: "What does b-e-g-a-n say?"
53. Once he responds correctly—that is, repeats what you told him—then ask: "Which letters say /găn/?"
54. If he does not respond correctly, consider dropping back to a lower-level activity. The assumption, when working on this level, is that the child can read the syllables that contain the decoding unit and is now ready to learn to read the unit in the context of polysyllabic words.
55. When he responds correctly, ask: "Which of these letters say /bē/?"
56. If he displays confusion here, go back to step 51 and repeat the activities from there on.
57. When he can correctly connect the b-e) to /bē/ and the g-a-n to /găn/, show him the full word again—*began*—and tell him: "Make it say /găn/; cover up (or erase) that part of the word that does not belong."
58. When he responds correctly (covers up the b-e), ask him: "Tell me what the g-a-n says."
59. Once all of this has been accomplished, show him the full word again—*began*—and ask him to "Make it say /bē/; cover up (or erase) that part of the word that does not belong."
60. When he has done this (covered up the g-a-n), then ask him: "Tell me what the b-e says."
61. When he shows that he knows *began*—can read it accurately and without delay—print it on a 3″ × 5″ index card and store it in his Word Bank.
62. Now choose another word from the Level C list of this decoding unit set—*manner,* for example—and go through these same steps (50–61) again.
63. When you are satisfied that the child can correctly read the first two

words you worked on from this Level C list and, further, can relate the various syllables to their appropriate sounds, then print one of the two words on the chalkboard and ask him to read it to you.

64. For example, let us assume that you started with the word *began*. He should be able to respond correctly, of course. Once he does, tell him: "Make it say /manner/; change it so that it says /manner/ instead of /began/."

65. Work your way through all of the Level C words in this decoding unit set this way—steps 50–64—stopping finally when the child can change any one of the words to any other in the list on request, as illustrated in step 64. For example, when he can change /began/ to /manner/ to /cannot/ to /candle/ and so on.

Where to next? You have two options. You might work up to the next level (Level D) within this same decoding unit set, or you might choose to move over to another decoding unit, beginning in that set at the highest level possible for the child, as indicated by the testing.

As a general rule, if the child is in the fourth grade or above, do the former—move up to Level D within the same decoding unit set. If he is in the third grade or below, move to a new decoding unit set, using the test procedures to determine his starting level.

If you take this latter route, then your instructions remain the same as already covered here. If, instead, you opt to move up to Level D within this same decoding unit set, then simply repeat the activities you carried out at the preceding level (steps 50–65), substituting the Level D words for those of Level C.

By now you have had a chance to go through the instructions, and you should have a fairly good idea of what is involved. It probably strikes you as a massive task. It is not. It requires some self-discipline and self-scheduling, but it can be worked through with a very reasonable amount of effort.

The following suggestions are pertinent to administering the activities and should serve as general guidelines for teaching the child to identify decoding units as aids in memorizing reading words:

1. Devote about ten to fifteen minutes *each day* to the activities spelled out on the previous pages. Start off each new day at approximately the place you stopped the day before. Ten to fifteen minutes each day may not sound like enough time to accomplish what has to be accomplished, but the cumulative effects will please you—and the child.

2. Spend about two to three additional minutes each day reviewing the words in his Word Bank. The goal here is instant recognition of the

words. (It will also be helpful if you take time during this activity to define those words that the child is uncertain about.)

3. At the completion of each day's session write down a few sentences that contain the words that the child has been working on. Better yet, have him assist you in constructing these sentences. Then have him read the sentences at a pace that approximates fluent reading, no sounding out permitted. If, the first time through them, he stumbles and/or reads too slowly, have him reread the sentences often enough to acquire a fluent pace.

4. One word of caution, particularly relevant to the words contained in the Level C and Level D lists. In one sense the activities are designed to help the child memorize these specific words. But, more important, the activities are designed to help the child learn to use a *system* for learning new words in general, not these words specifically.

With this in mind, I want to caution you that it is not critical for the child to learn every word on every list. I have used these activities often enough—and measured the effects on a child's reading abilities—to assure you that one more memorized word is not the key factor. What counts here is that the child catches on to the fact that there is a *system* available—a strategy that involves hunting out decoding units larger than single letters—that can help him remember his reading words. This, combined with a growing knowledge of the spoken language and the subject matter being addressed in the text, *plus steady reading practice,** will change a stumbling reader, even someone who is almost a nonreader, into a fairly competent one who will continue to improve with continued exercising of proper reading habits.** And in essence that is what you are after with these activities: the establishment of proper reading habits.

---

*See pages 131–32 for specific suggestions.
**Please do not interpret this phrase to mean that all that the child needs is motivation, that if he practiced, he would not have a reading problem. That is not the case. Sure, practice helps, but only if you practice the proper things. First you have to show him *what* to practice; then it will be helpful to motivate him to do so.

List of 108 Common Decoding Units

Decoding Unit Set #	Decoding Unit	Decoding Unit Set #	Decoding Unit
1	*an*	40	*ut*
2	*ag*	41	*ud*
3	*ad*	42	*ub*
4	*at*	43	*um*
5	*ap*	44	*uck*
6	*as*	45	*ash*
7	*ab*	46	*ast*
8	*am*	47	*act*
9	*and*	48	*ank*
10	*ack*	49	*ang*
11	*it*	50	*iff*
12	*ip*	51	*ing*
13	*in*	52	*ink*
14	*id*	53	*ish*
15	*ig*	54	*ay*
16	*im*	55	*ace*
17	*ib*	56	*ade*
18	*ill*	57	*ape*
19	*ick*	58	*ate*
20	*op*	59	*ane*
21	*od*	60	*ake*
22	*og*	61	*ame*
23	*ot*	62	*ale*
24	*ong*	63	*age*
25	*om*	64	*are*
26	*ob*	65	*ide*
27	*en*	66	*ind*
28	*ed*	67	*ite*
29	*ess*	68	*old*
30	*ell*	69	*one*
31	*et*	70	*oke*
32	*em*	71	*eat*
33	*eck*	72	*eam*
34	*eb*	73	*ar*
35	*est*	74	*all*
36	*ent*	75	*aw*
37	*up*	76	*ice*
38	*ug*	77	*ock*
39	*un*	78	*uff*

Decoding Unit Set #	Decoding Unit	Decoding Unit Set #	Decoding Unit
79			
80	ush	94	ee
81	able	95	alk
82	ight	96	ev
83	oll	97	er
84	on	98	ew
85	ook	99	ir
86	or	100	ire
87	ore	101	oa
88	(s)ow	102	oi
89	(c)ow	103	(b)oo(t)
90	(b)ull	104	ou
91	(d)ull	105	eve
92	us	106	ue
93	ai	107	ure
94	are	108	tion

SET 1

Decoding unit	A	B	C	D
an	ban	ranch	began	Santa Claus
	can	scan	manner	fantasy
	Dan	bland	demand	fantastic
	fan	pant	cannot	understand
	Jan	hand	handle	Canada
	man	chant	candle	outlandish
	Nan	stand	banner	ancestor
	pan	span	spaniel	animal
	ran	strand	Spanish	anniversary
	tan	land	standard	grandstand
	van	brand	dandy	antelope
		plant	landing	bandanna
			lantern	advantage
			mantle	manufacture
			vanish	manager
			vandal	chimpanzee
			scandal	reprimand

SET 2

Decoding unit	A	B	C	D
ag	bag	drag	haggle	magazine
	hag	slag	swagger	aggravate
	jag	snag	braggart	magnify
	lag	stag	dragon	magnetize
	nag	shag	jagged	vagabond
	rag	brag	sagging	antagonize
	sag	crag	bagpipe	magnolia
	tag	flag	magnet	stagnation
	wag		stagger	agnostic
	gag		fragment	fragmentary
			flagship	
			flagstone	
			lagoon	
			saga	
			stagnant	
			straggle	
			wagon	

SET 3

Decoding unit	A	B	C	D
ad	bad	clad	bladder	readmit
	cad	glad	badger	radical
	dad	badge	daddy	advisor
	fad	add	paddle	admiral
	gad	shad	saddle	adventure
	had	brad	shadow	administer
	lad		admit	gladiator
	mad		caddy	admiration
	pad		padding	graduate
	sad		padlock	advertise
	tad		address	badminton
			adore	disadvantage
			adult	
			gladly	
			haddock	
			raddish	
			tadpole	

SET 4

Decoding unit	A	B	C	D
at	bat	chat	matter	satisfy
	cat	flat	chatter	attitude
	fat	hatch	clatter	habitat
	gat	slat	matching	latitude
	hat	spat	rattle	automatic
	mat	that	satin	smattering
	Nat	match	battle	tattered
	pat	scratch	splatter	gratitude
	rat	brat	batman	catapult
	sat	batch	attic	caterpillar
	vat	catch	attract	Saturday
			catcher	
			batter	

SET 5

Decoding unit	A	B	C	D
ap	cap	clap	happen	Japanese
	gap	slap	apple	apparatus
	lap	flap	happy	aptitude
	map	strap	napkin	appetite
	nap	wrap	wrapper	capitol
	sap	trap	rapid	happiness
	tap	scrap	napping	captivate
	zap	lapse	dapper	collapsible
	pap	chapped	captain	
	rap		captive	
	yap		trapper	
			mishap	
			madcap	

SET 6

Decoding unit	A	B	C	D
as(s)	bass	glass	passing	classification
	lass	brass	classy	exasperate
	mass	flask	cascade	fascinate
	pass	last	sassy	dastardly
	sass	blast	basket	gasoline
	gas	vast	nasty	
		crass	asset	
		grass	tassel	
		class	hassle	
		fast	morass	
		hasp	impass	
		task		
		clasp		

SET 7

Decoding unit	A	B	C	D
ab	cab	slab	shabby	fabulous
	dab	blab	blabber	habitual
	gab	drab	prefab	habitat
	jab	crab	cabin	laboratory
	lab	grab	Abner	tabulate
	nab	flab	habit	absolute
	tab	scab	rabbit	cabinet
		stab	rabid	metabolism
			absent	abdomen
			Sabbath	abdicate
			fabric	prefabricate
			abduct	
			absorb	
			baboon	
			cabbage	
			jabber	

SET 8

Decoding unit	A	B	C	D
am	cam	damp	camel	camera
	dam	champ	hamlet	lamplighter
	gam	lamp	lamplight	examination
	ham	ramp	stampede	ambition
	jam	tamp	sample	ambulance
	ram	stamp	pamper	family
	Sam	gram	rampant	enamel
	tam	lamb	exam	example
	yam	slam	ambush	stamina
		tramp	scamper	anagram
		vamp	bamboo	
		sham	gamble	
			campus	
			damage	
			glamour	
			vampire	
			Amtrak	

SET 9

Decoding unit	A	B	C	D
and	band	bland	handy	standardize
	land	grand	sandbox	candidate
	hand	brand	random	bandwagon
	sand	strand	candy	bandanna
		stand	expand	dandelion
		gland	command	understand
			standard	grandmother
			scandal	chandelier
			forehand	sandpaper
			handle	scandalous
			landscape	slanderous
			bandage	reprimand
			dandy	ampersand
			demand	incandescent
			grandstand	misunderstanding

SET 10

Decoding unit	A	B	C	D
ack	back	black	attack	mackerel
	hack	crack	blacken	packaging
	Jack	flack	hacksaw	racketeer
	lack	slack	cracker	lumberjack
	pack	stack	slacker	lackluster
	rack	shack	lacking	lackadaisical
	sack	track	tackle	
	tack	smack	racket	
		knack	package	
			blackboard	
			background	
			bracket	
			backpack	
			ack-ack	
			smokestack	

SET 11

Decoding unit	A	B	C	D
it	bit	mitt	armpit	visitor
	fit	knit	bitter	Italy
	hit	itch	rabbit	situation
	kit	twitch	pitcher	critical
	lit	switch	kitchen	literature
	pit	flit	visit	pitiful
	sit	spit	city	titillate
	wit	slit	little	handwritten
		grit	witness	
		quit	fitness	
			unfit	
			spittoon	

SET 12

Decoding unit	A	B	C	D
ip	dip	whip	catnip	hippopotamus
	hip	chip	chipmunk	Mississippi
	lip	trip	zipper	slippery
	nip	strip	slipper	equipment
	pip	flip	clipper	whippersnapper
	rip	drip	shipmate	stipulate
	sip	slip	zipcode	citizenship
	tip	blip	turnip	battleship
	zip	skip	parsnip	

SET 13

Decoding unit	A	B	C	D
in	bin	spin	inside	cabinet
	din	shin	winter	winterize
	fin	skin	ginger	independent
	pin	print	splinter	kindergarten
	sin	sprint	napkin	vicinity
	tin	grin	winsome	integrate
	win	inch	dinner	origin
	kin	wind	finish	cinema
		since	muffin	kinescope
			urchin	topspin
			muslin	
			kinfolk	

SET 14

Decoding unit	A	B	C	D
id	bid	slid	fiddle	midwestern
	did	ridge	middle	candidate
	hid	bridge	hidden	rapidly
	kid	skid	widow	vividly
	lid	quid	candid	consider
	mid	squid	kidney	kidnapper
	rid		midway	avidly
			midwest	forbidden
			rancid	humidity
			solid	videotape
			acid	
			arid	
			rapid	
			midnight	
			giddy	
			stupid	
			hybrid	

SET 15

Decoding unit	A	B	C	D
ig	big	twig	piglet	astigmatism
	dig	swig	bigger	ignorance
	fig	brig	jigsaw	dignity
	jig	prig	wiggle	dignify
	pig	sprig	spigot	thingamajig
	rig		wigwam	whirligig
	wig		trigger	iguana
	zig		ignore	significant
			igloo	
			bigot	
			giggle	
			zigzag	

SET 16

Decoding unit	A	B	C	D
im	dim	limb	limit	simplify
	him	trim	timid	immaterial
	rim	limp	himself	important
	vim	slim	chimney	immortal
	imp	brim	whimper	interim
		prim	improve	superimpose
		blimp	thimble	imposition
		whim	shimmer	
		skim	dimly	

SET 17

Decoding unit	A	B	C	D
ib	bib	crib	tribute	biblical
	fib	glib	quibble	bibliography
	jib	squib	ribbon	liberty
	nib		sibling	gibberish
	rib		scribble	attribute
			giblet	tributary
			dribble	contribute

SET 18

Decoding unit	A	B	C	D
ill	dill	chill	silly	illiterate
	fill	skill	pillow	silliness
	gill	spill	willow	willowy
	hill	still	until	illusion
	mill	drill	billboard	oscillate
	pill	thrill	sawmill	dillydally
	sill	trill	spillage	pillory
	till	frill	filly	pillowcase
	will	grill	shilling	
	kill	quill	pillar	
			instill	
			willful	
			fulfill	

SET 19

Decoding unit	A	B	C	D
ick	hick	stick	sticker	bricklayer
	lick	slick	wicked	hickory
	pick	trick	tricky	maverick
	sick	click	sickly	limerick
	tick	chick	sickness	rickety
	wick	quick	bicker	
	kick	brick	flicker	
		crick	picket	
			ticklish	
			stricken	
			icky	
			cowlick	
			sticky	
			cricket	
			wicket	
			sidekick	

SET 20

Decoding unit	A	B	C	D
op	cop	chop	sloppy	property
	hop	slop	stopper	opera
	mop	stop	chopping	lopsided
	pop	crop	popcorn	opportunity
	top	prop	hopscotch	operator
	fop	drop	copper	popular
	lop	flop	option	popover
	sop	shop	shopper	soporific
	opt	strop	atop	optical
			poplar	
			poplin	
			topple	
			shortstop	

SET 21

Decoding unit	A	B	C	D
od	cod	shod	shoddy	bodyguard
	hod	plod	codfish	godfather
	Tod	trod	body	somebody
	sod	clod	fodder	oddity
	rod	prod	sodden	moderate
	pod	dodge	modern	Ichabod
	nod	lodge	coddle	bodily
	mod		lodger	
	odd		tripod	
			slipshod	
			bodkin	
			peapod	

SET 22

Decoding unit	A	B	C	D
og	bog	smog	groggy	dogmatic
	cog	grog	dogged	togglebolt
	dog	flog	logger	logarithm
	fog	frog	jogging	loggerhead
	hog	togs	fogbound	epilogue
	log	clog	hogwash	toboggan
	jog		frogman	underdog
			soggy	
			boggle	
			prologue	
			eggnog	

SET 23

Decoding unit	A	B	C	D
ot	cot	scot	cannot	pottery
	dot	slot	blotter	lottery
	got	shot	plotting	Ottawa
	hot	plot	hotdog	cottonwood
	jot	trot	otter	botany
	lot	spot	cotton	tommyrot
	not	blotch	totter	polyglot
	pot	blot	robot	
	rot	clot		
	sot	botch		
	tot			

SET 24

Decoding unit	A	B	C	D
ong	bong	wrong	belong	belonging
	gong	prong	Ping-Pong	congregate
	long	strong	prolong	wrongfully
	pong	throng	Congo	Mongolia
	song	tongs	longterm	evensong
		thong	mongrel	
			stronghold	
			King Kong	
			headstrong	
			along	
			singsong	

SET 25

Decoding unit	A	B	C	D
om	Tom	stomp	bombard	combatant
	Dom	romp	Bombay	combination
	mom	pomp	common	commentator
		bomb	combat	communist
		clomp	combine	competent
			complex	dominate
			pompous	pomegranate
			somber	ominous
			pompon	

SET 26

Decoding unit	A	B	C	D
ob	Bob	slob	hobble	obstruction
	cob	blob	jobless	observatory
	fob	glob	lobster	lobbyist
	gob	knob	clobber	hobgoblin
	job	throb	obstruct	cobblestone
	lob		observe	obsolete
	mob		lobby	
	nob		hobby	
	rob		goblin	
	sob		goblet	
			cobbler	
			corncob	
			doorknob	

SET 27

Decoding unit	A	B	C	D
en	Ben	when	Jenny	opening
	den	wren	pencil	sensitive
	hen	send	open	sensational
	Jen	went	dentist	ventilate
	Ken	rent	mentor	tenderly
	men	sense	rental	enjoyment
	pen	blend	entrance	energy
	ten	trench	tender	seventeen
	fen	bench	encounter	entertain
	wen	then	penny	potential
	yen	bent	attend	gentlemen
	end	fence	amend	century
		mend	avenge	venison
		trend	seven	stupendous
			splendid	dimension
			central	encounter
			fender	
			vendor	

SET 28

Decoding unit	A	B	C	D
ed	bed	sled	meddle	federal
	led	sped	bedding	comedy
	Ned	fled	acted	editorial
	red	shred	wedding	meditate
	Ted	shed	pedal	sedative
	wed	bled	edit	sedition
	fed	bred	reddish	remedy
			redhead	medical
			cheddar	pedestal
			biped	quadruped
			worsted	pedigree
				underfed

SET 29

Decoding unit	A	B	C	D
ess	Bess	stress	confess	penniless
	less	press	homeless	messenger
	mess	chess	blackness	successful
	Tess	tress	message	possessive
	Jess	bless	lesson	merciless
		guess	unless	
			dresser	
			mistress	

SET 30

Decoding unit	A	B	C	D
ell	bell	swell	mellow	mellowing
	dell	smell	bellow	bellower
	fell	shell	fellow	rebellion
	hell	quell	befell	intelligent
	jell		Jello	excellence
	pell		yellow	cellular
	sell		hello	
	tell		belly	
	well			
	yell			
	cell			

SET 31

Decoding unit	A	B	C	D
et	bet	fret	forget	settlement
	get	etch	kettle	detonate
	jet	stretch	upset	lettering
	let	fetch	metal	letterhead
	met	ketch	network	metallic
	net	wretch	lettuce	petrify
	pet		letter	veteran
	set		metric	etcetera
	vet		petty	
	wet			
	yet			

SET 32

Decoding unit	A	B	C	D
em	gem	stem	temper	democratic
	hem	them	empty	feminine
	Lem	hemp	lemon	remedy
		tempt	member	memory
			embrace	membership
			temple	themselves
			hemlock	empathy
			remnant	demonstrate
			tremor	lemonade
			emblem	membrane
			blemish	seminar
			contempt	temporary
				eminent
				contemplate

SET 33

Decoding unit	A	B	C	D
eck	beck	fleck	beckon	reckoning
	deck	wreck	reckless	checkerboard
	heck	check	freckle	woodpecker
	neck	speck	feckless	
	peck		bedeck	
			heckler	
			checkers	
			necklace	
			shipwreck	

SET 34

Decoding unit	A	B	C	D
eb	deb	webs	Debbie	February
	reb		rebel	nebulous
	web		debris	Nebraska
	ebb		debut	debutante
	Jeb		pebble	nebula
			treble	rebellion
			debit	ebony

SET 35

Decoding unit	A	B	C	D
est	best	wrest	invest	yesterday
	jest	crest	hardest	interest
	lest	quest	bequest	restfulness
	nest	guest	biggest	destination
	pest	blest	restful	estimate
	test		festive	ancestor
	vest		arrest	estuary
	west		suggest	indigestion
	rest		question	easiest
			digest	protester
				restaurant
				crestfallen

SET 36

Decoding unit	A	B	C	D
ent	bent	spent	present	gentlemen
	dent	scent	convent	tentative
	gent		sentence	ventilation
	lent		entry	apartment
	pent		center	enterprise
	sent		repent	different
	tent		penthouse	centerpiece
	went		rental	centimeter
	vent		dentist	century
	cent		venture	entrance
	rent		event	portent
			enter	ventriloquist
			gentle	
			mentor	
			plenty	

SET 37

Decoding unit	A	B	C	D
up	cup		upset	buttercup
	pup		supper	supporting
	sup		uproot	abruptly
			support	corruption
			abrupt	interrupt
			erupt	upstanding
			pickup	upholster
			upper	
			upon	
			stirrup	
			puppy	
			rupture	

SET 38

Decoding unit	A	B	C	D
ug	bug	shrug	struggle	bugaboo
	dug	slug	ugly	ugliness
	hug	plug	buggy	pugnacious
	jug	smug	drugstore	ladybug
	lug	chug	humbug	repugnant
	mug	snug	dugout	
	pug	drug	nugget	
	rug	thug	luggage	
	tug		druggist	
			smuggler	

SET 39

Decoding unit	A	B	C	D
un	bun	bunt	bunting	understand
	fun	spun	bunches	bungalow
	gun	stun	under	undecided
	nun	bunk	funny	fundamental
	pun	munch	punish	punishment
	run	lunch	hunger	asunder
	sun	bunch	sunshine	unhappiness
		crunch	thunder	moribund
		trunk	rotund	
		runt	refund	
		grunt		
		shun		

SET 40

Decoding unit	A	B	C	D
ut	but	shut	butter	utterly
	cut	hutch	cutting	buttercup
	gut	crutch	cutlet	butterfly
	hut	strut	gutter	buttonhole
	nut	Dutch	nutmeg	shutterbug
	jut	smut	sputter	uppercut
	rut	glut	butler	guttersnipe
		putt	button	peanutbutter
			cutworm	
			stutter	
			utmost	
			haircut	
			peanut	

SET 41

Decoding unit	A	B	C	D
ud	bud	stud	budget	suddenly
	cud	thud	cuddle	suddenness
	dud	spud	sudden	ombudsman
	mud	fudge	huddle	
		suds	rudder	
		budge	buddy	
			udder	
			rosebud	
			shudder	
			puddle	
			muddy	

SET 42

Decoding unit	A	B	C	D
ub	cub	drub	rubber	publication
	dub	scrub	bubble	publicity
	hub	snub	blubber	submarine
	pub	stub	chubby	subtraction
	rub	club	hubbub	substitute
	sub	shrub	publish	subdivide
	tub		public	shrubbery
	nub		grubby	
			rubbish	
			subtract	
			subway	
			subdue	
			bathtub	

SET 43

Decoding unit	A	B	C	D
um	bum	dumb	slumber	umbrella
	gum	thumb	pumpkin	summertime
	hum	numb	album	summarize
	rum	slum	plumber	minimum
	sum	chum	umpire	modicum
	mum	dump	grumpy	cucumber
	yum	lump	thumbnail	
		stump	bumper	
		jump	dumpling	
		plum	summon	
		clump	summer	
		bump	umbrage	
		glum	mummy	
			talcum	
			rummage	

SET 44

Decoding unit	A	B	C	D
uck	buck	struck	bucket	chuckwagon
	duck	truck	duckling	puckering
	luck	shuck	woodchuck	buckeroo
	puck	chuck	buckskin	
	suck	stuck	huckster	
	tuck	cluck	buckle	
	muck		truckle	
			plucky	
			sawbuck	
			rucksack	

SET 45

Decoding unit	A	B	C	D
ash	bash	clash	fashion	bashfulness
	cash	crash	cashier	fashionable
	dash	brash	bashful	balderdash
	hash	flash	dashing	eyelashes
	gash	slash	flashes	
	lash	splash	ashtray	
	mash	thrash	flashlight	
	rash	trash	dashboard	
	sash	stash	ashen	
			rashness	
			thrasher	
			rehash	
			sashay	

SET 46

Decoding unit	A	B	C	D
ast	cast	blast	plaster	castaway
	fast	caste	master	fantastic
	last		chastise	asteroid
	mast		aster	castanet
	past		casting	masterful
	vast		vastly	astronomer
			drastic	astonish
			repast	gastronomic
			caster	masterpiece
			aghast	newscaster
			nasty	broadcasting
			miscast	pastoral
			forecast	astronaut
				pasteurized

SET 47

Decoding unit	A	B	C	D
act	fact	tract	actor	bacteria
	pact		fracture	factory
	tact		actress	tactfully
			active	practical
			tactic	practically
			tactful	factual
			protract	activate
			react	intractable
			action	counteract
			impact	cataract
			enact	attractive
				interaction

SET 48

Decoding unit	A	B	C	D
ank	bank	crank	hanker	thankfully
	dank	flank	thankful	bankruptcy
	rank	spank	lanky	frankfurter
	sank	stank	banker	mountebank
	tank	thank	blanket	lankiness
	yank	clank	anklet	cantankerous
		shank	ankle	
		plank	cranky	
			Yankee	
			plankton	

SET 49

Decoding unit	A	B	C	D
ang	bang	clang	mango	manganese
	fang	sprang	banging	angrily
	gang	swang	jangle	angular
	hang		strangle	triangle
	pang		angry	untangle
	rang		angle	stranglehold
	sang		bangle	boomerang
			angler	
			hangman	
			gangplank	
			hanger	
			mangle	
			tangle	
			gangster	
			mustang	
			tango	

SET 50

Decoding unit	A	B	C	D
if(f)	tiff	whiff	differ	difference
	miff	stiff	fifty	difficult
		shift	stiffen	stiffening
		cliff	nifty	whiffenpoof
		skiff	jiffy	chiffonier
		sniff	sheriff	terrific
		drift	bailiff	
		thrift	riffle	
			riffraff	
			chiffon	
			tariff	

SET 51

Decoding unit	A	B	C	D
ing	ding	bring	finger	opening
	ping	sling	jingle	dingaling
	ring	sting	nothing	atingle
	sing	fling	kingly	anything
	wing	cling	wringer	
	king	string	singer	
		swing	singing	
		thing	gringo	
			tingling	

SET 52

Decoding unit	A	B	C	D
ink	fink	clink	tinker	tinkerer
	kink	drink	slinky	brinkmanship
	link	slink	kinky	shrinkproof
	mink	blink	inkling	rinkydink
	pink	shrink	twinkling	unthinkable
	sink	stink	trinket	
	wink	brink	twinkle	
	rink	think	sprinkler	

SET 53

Decoding unit	A	B	C	D
ish	dish	swish	Spanish	fisherman
	fish	squish	dishes	accomplish
	wish		fishing	abolish
			vanquish	wishywashy
			publish	polisher
			mishmash	punishment
			selfish	publisher

SET 54

Decoding unit	A	B	C	D
ay	bay	tray	payment	repayment
	day	play	mayor	displaying
	gay	sway	rayon	bayonet
	hay	clay	replay	mayflower
	jay	slay	daytime	mayonnaise
	lay	stay	daylight	payable
	may	pray	repay	holiday
	nay	bray	dismay	popinjay
	pay	fray	playmate	stowaway
	say		saying	
	ray		essay	
	way		away	
			jaywalk	
			assay	

SET 55

Decoding unit	A	B	C	D
ace	face	space	misplace	replacement
	lace	trace	retrace	disgraceful
	mace	grace	spaceship	gracefully
	pace	place	deface	embraceable
	race	brace	pacer	populace
			placement	outerspace
			embrace	
			bracelet	
			apace	

SET 56

Decoding unit	A	B	C	D
ade	fade	spade	degrade	renegade
	jade	grade	faded	lemonade
	made	trade	parade	barricade
	wade	blade	invade	colonnade
	lade	slade	evade	invader
		shade	tirade	cavalcade
			cadence	motorcade
				balustrade

SET 57

Decoding unit	A	B	C	D
ape	cape	grape	escape	videotape
	nape	scrape	taper	drapery
	tape	shape	paper	jackanapes
	aped	apes	scraper	
	gape	drape	grapefruit	
	jape		seascape	
			scapegoat	
			tapeworm	
			caper	
			landscape	

SET 58

Decoding unit	A	B	C	D
ate	date	grate	rebate	detonate
	fate	slate	inflate	invigorate
	gate	plate	relate	renovate
	hate	spate	debate	operator
	late	crate	grateful	arbitrate
	mate	state	statement	investigate
	rate	skate	berate	abdicate
	sate		crated	exterminate
			create	celebrate
				communicate
				innovate
				caterer
				hatemonger
				refrigerator
				dislocate
				irrigate

SET 59

Decoding unit	A	B	C	D
ane	bane	crane	airplane	windowpane
	cane	plane	insane	cellophane
	dane	thane	inane	sugarcane
	lane		humane	weathervane
	mane		mundane	counterpane
	pane		arcane	hydroplane
	sane			
	vane			
	wane			

SET 60

Decoding unit	A	B	C	D
ake	bake	stake	baker	bakery
	cake	flake	maker	undertaker
	fake	shake	earthquake	mistaken
	lake	spake	mistake	forsaken
	make	brake	snowflake	fakery
	quake	drake	retake	johnnycake
	rake	slake	snakepit	
	sake	snake	milkshake	
	take	quake	rattlesnake	
	wake		makeshift	
	hake			

SET 61

Decoding unit	A	B	C	D
ame	dame	shame	nameless	shamefully
	fame	blame	rename	shamelessly
	game	flame	lamely	
	lame	frame	nickname	
	name		became	
	same		inflame	
	tame		selfsame	
	came		gamely	
			blameless	

SET 62

Decoding unit	A	B	C	D
ale	bale	stale	resale	balefully
	dale	scale	female	stalemated
	gale	shale	baleful	haybaler
	male	whale	alewife	nightingale
	pale		impaled	
	sale		inhale	
	tale		alehouse	
	vale			
	hale			
	kale			

SET 63

Decoding unit	A	B	C	D
age	cage	stage	engage	engagement
	gage	aged	enrage	outrageous
	page		sagebrush	
	rage		outrage	
	sage		ageless	
	wage		stagecoach	
			wager	
			teenage	
			agent	
			presage	
			cagey	

SET 64

Decoding unit	A	B	C	D
ave	cave	knave	pavement	slavery
	gave	brave	enslave	bravery
	pave	stave	concave	enslavement
	rave	shave	forgave	slavetrader
	save	slave	repave	misbehave
	wave	crave	enclave	
	nave	grave	behave	
	lave		deprave	
			engrave	
			navel	
			quaver	
			haven	

SET 65

Decoding unit	A	B	C	D
ide	bide	pride	bridegroom	tidewater
	hide	bride	aside	hideaway
	ride	slide	abide	homicide
	side	chide	glider	cyanide
	tide	stride	reside	idealism
	wide	glide	inside	countrywide
	ides		outside	override
			divide	
			provide	
			confide	
			astride	
			ideal	
			rider	
			strident	

SET 66

Decoding unit	A	B	C	D
ind	bind	grind	remind	reminder
	find	blind	kindness	unwinding
	hind		unwind	kindliness
	kind		blinders	womankind
	mind		mankind	mastermind
	rind		mindful	hindsight
	wind		behind	
			binder	
			grinder	

SET 67

Decoding unit	A	B	C	D
ite	bite	white	invite	dynamite
	mite	smite	polite	appetite
	site	spite	ignite	satellite
	kite	sprite	despite	stalagmite
	cite	write	item	recondite
		quite	campsite	incitement
		trite	recite	plebiscite
			lignite	exciting

SET 68

Decoding unit	A	B	C	D
old	bold	scold	resold	unfolding
	cold		soldier	goldenrod
	fold		golden	old fashioned
	gold		colder	refolded
	mold		molding	manifold
	hold		goldfish	smoldering
	sold		older	
	told		folder	
			stronghold	

SET 69

Decoding unit	A	B	C	D
one	bone	phone	postpone	telephone
	hone	stone	alone	saxophone
	lone	drone	ozone	tonelessly
	tone	shone	trombone	onerous
	zone	prone	toneless	cortisone
	cone	throne	condone	monotone
		crone	hailstone	baloney
		clone	lonely	microphone
			backbone	

SET 70

Decoding unit	A	B	C	D
oke	joke	bloke	joker	provoker
	poke	spoke	awoke	artichoke
	yoke	smoke	invoke	pokeberry
	woke	choke	provoke	pawnbroker
		broke	poker	
		stroke	hokey	
		stoke	token	
			yokel	
			broker	

SET 71

Decoding unit	A	B	C	D
eat	beat	cheat	repeat	eggbeater
	feat	eats	retreat	defeated
	heat	wheat	meatball	eatery
	meat	treat	treaty	repeater
	neat	cleat	neatness	
	seat	bleat	defeat	
	peat	pleat	meatloaf	
			heater	
			cheater	
			entreat	

SET 72

Decoding unit	A	B	C	D
eam	beam	scream	dreamer	streamliner
	ream	stream	dreaming	steam fitter
	seam	cream	steamboat	mainstreaming
	team	dream	daydream	
		steam	upstream	
		gleam	streamers	
			teamwork	
			moonbeam	
			squeamish	

SET 73

Decoding unit	A	B	C	D
ar	far	spar	afar	carpenter
	bar	star	darling	armory
	car	part	darkness	argument
	jar	scar	market	arbitrate
	par	dart	carpet	regardless
	tar	shark	farther	partnership
	gar	dark	ajar	motorcar
	mar	start	cigar	remarkable
	par	hard	startle	
		bard	army	
		card	harvest	
		smart	argue	
		lard	regard	
			partner	
			crowbar	

SET 74

Decoding unit	A	B	C	D
all	ball	stall	baseball	installer
	call	small	football	wallpaper
	fall	squall	nightfall	gallbladder
	hall		recall	waterfall
	tall		install	
	wall		taller	
	gall		appall	
	mall		enthrall	
			hallway	

SET 75

Decoding unit	A	B	C	D
aw	jaw	straw	outlaw	withdrawing
	haw	flaw	awful	strawberry
	law	claw	drawing	jawbreaker
	raw	thaw	lawyer	
	saw	gnaw	sawmill	
	caw	draw	mawkish	
	paw	bawl	southpaw	
	yaw	squaw		
		yawl		
		lawn		
		craw		
		crawl		

SET 76

Decoding unit	A	B	C	D
ice	dice	twice	device	sacrifice
	lice	splice	nicer	viceroy
	mice	slice	nicest	niceties
	nice	price	allspice	enticement
	rice	trice	iceberg	
	vice	spice	suffice	
		thrice		

SET 77

Decoding unit	A	B	C	D
ock	dock	clock	jockey	poppycock
	lock	knock	rocket	rockingchair
	mock	stock	pocket	pocketbook
	rock	flock	tick-tock	hammerlock
	sock	smock	hockey	landlocked
	cock	shock	unlock	crockery
	hock	block	peacock	mockery
	pock	crock	shocking	
		frock	stocking	
			blockhead	

SET 78

Decoding unit	A	B	C	D
uff	cuff	bluff	cufflink	suffering
	huff	fluff	puffy	ruffian
	muff	stuff	suffer	
	puff	gruff	handcuff	
	buff	snuff	puffing	
	luff	scuff	fluffy	
	ruff		buffer	
	guff		shuttle	
			scuffle	
			dandruff	
			muffin	
			creampuff	

SET 79

Decoding unit	A	B	C	D
ush	hush	flush	mushy	mushrooming
	lush	crush	brushing	hushabye
	mush	thrush	blushes	
	rush	brush	mushroom	
	gush	blush	gusher	
		slush	toothbrush	
		shush	usher	

SET 80

Decoding unit	A	B	C	D
able	cable	stable	unable	miserable
	fable	tabled	disable	
	gable		enable	
	sable		cablecar	
	table		unstable	

SET 81

Decoding unit	A	B	C	D
ight	fight	fright	fighter	frightening
	light	bright	frightful	oversight
	might	slight	uptight	nightingale
	night	knight	mighty	unsightly
	right	blight	rightful	fortnightly
	sight	height	upright	righteous
	tight	sleight	insight	foresighted
	bight		tightrope	lightning

SET 82

Decoding unit	A	B	C	D
oll	doll		holly	hollering
	moll		golly	jolliest
	loll		collar	collector
			dollar	collegiate
			trolley	volleyball
			volley	follicle
			jolly	follower
			folly	rollicking
			follow	
			college	

SET 83

Decoding unit	A	B	C	D
on	Don	fond	convict	vagabond
	con	font	convent	continent
	non	bond	bonfire	convention
	don	blonde	fondly	correspond
	Von	pond	nonsense	ponderous
	yon	frond	ponder	gondola
			tonsil	nonagenarian
			bonbon	
			icon	
			upon	
			ponder	
			sonnet	
			yonder	
			beyond	
			abscond	

SET 84

Decoding unit	A	B	C	D
ook	book	crook	foresook	bookkeeper
	cook	brook	bookshelf	
	hook	shook	rooky	
	look		cookie	
	nook		bookcase	
	rook		cookout	
	took		crooked	
			cookbook	
			mistook	
			lookout	
			outlook	

SET 85

Decoding unit	A	B	C	D
or	for	morn	dormant	forgetful
	nor	north	forget	organize
	tor	tore	morning	tornado
	ore	short	organ	toreador
		bore	resort	torpedo
		snort	shopworn	tormented
		sort	order	
		worn	border	
		lore	morbid	
		more	torpor	
		score	boring	
		yore	dormouse	
		fort		
		sport		

SET 86

Decoding unit	A	B	C	D
ore	bore	chore	restore	explorer
	core	store	deplore	furthermore
	fore	shore	storage	pinafore
	gore	swore	foreground	applecore
	lore	score	explore	
	more	snore	ignore	
	pore	spore	adore	
	tore		ashore	
	wore		scoreboard	
	ores		seashore	
			foreswore	
			folklore	
			boredom	
			furore	

SET 87

Decoding unit	A	B	C	D
ow	low	slow	bowstring	lawnmower
	bow	snow	mower	overflow
	mow	throw	towboat	overthrow
	row	stow	slowly	stowaway
	tow	glow	elbow	furbelow
		grow	window	wheelbarrow
		blow	shadow	
		crow	below	
		flow	rainbow	
		grown	scarecrow	
		show	bellow	
			bowtie	
			snowbound	
			borrow	

SET 88

Decoding unit	A	B	C	D
ow	cow	brow	towel	allowance
	bow	chow	trowel	cowardly
	how	brown	allow	anyhow
	now	plow	somehow	powderpuff
	vow	dhow	rowdy	allowance
	wow	scow	coward	dowager
	sow	frown	chowder	
		crown	renown	
		town	downtown	
		crowd	countdown	
		down		

SET 89

Decoding unit	A	B	C	D
ul(l)	bull		pulley	beautiful
	full		spoonful	powerfully
	pull		bully	wonderfully
			bullet	plentiful
			awful	
			fully	

SET 90

Decoding unit	A	B	C	D
ul(l)	dull	skull	seagull	skulduggery
	cull	scull	insult	repulsive
	gull	mulch	duller	lullabye
	hull	gulf	mullet	scullery
	null	bulk	annull	nullify
	lull	cult	dullard	mulligatawny
	mull	hulk	impulse	difficult
			adult	
			result	
			consult	

SET 91

Decoding unit	A	B	C	D
us	bus	must	mustard	disgusted
	Gus	dust	mustang	discussion
	pus	fuss	musty	justify
		just	dusty	custody
		lust	gusty	sustenance
		rust	hustle	omnibus
		trust	discuss	justified
		plus	fluster	suspicion
		cuss	lustre	
		crust	cluster	
		thus	fussy	
		muss		

SET 92

Decoding unit	A	B	C	D
ai	air	bait	repaid	retainer
	aid	wait	waiter	faithfully
	ail	raid	failure	derailment
	aim	braid	sailboat	tailormade
		maid	tailor	curtailment
		paid	strainer	raillery
		waif	faithful	trailblazer
		bail	reclaim	
		fail	maiden	
		hail	detail	
		jail		
		mail		
		nail		
		pail		
		snail		
		rail		
		trail		
		rain		
		train		
		brain		
		strain		
		hair		
		claim		

SET 93

Decoding unit	A	B	C	D
are	bare	stare	prepare	unprepared
	care	scare	rarely	unaware
	dare	share	hardware	barefooted
	fare	snare	compare	faretheewell
	hare	flare	ensnare	daredevil
	mare	square	scarecrow	carefully
	rare	blare	nightmare	
	ware	spare	declare	
	pare		fanfare	
			farewell	

SET 94

Decoding unit	A	B	C	D
ee	bee	beef	sixteen	unforeseen
	see	feel	unseen	seventeen
	fee	knee	sweetheart	teenager
	tee	seen	meeting	greenery
	gee	seed	seeker	
	lee	seek	beseech	
	wee	reed	between	
		reef	seedling	
		reek	careen	
		steel		
		keen		
		feet		
		sheet		
		fleet		
		sleet		
		street		
		screech		
		creed		
		geese		

SET 95

Decoding unit	A	B	C	D
alk	talk	chalk	talking	talkative
	walk	stalk	walker	walkaway
	balk		chalkboard	
			chalkmark	
			sidewalk	

SET 96

Decoding unit	A	B	C	D
ev	rev		ever	everyone
			never	revolution
			seven	however
			clever	reverend
			devil	forever
			sever	inevitable
			lever	severance
			bevel	brevity
				several
				levity

SET 97

Decoding unit	A	B	C	D
er	her	herd	hermit	permanent
	per	perk	vermin	international
		germ	hunter	conference
		term	refer	concerted
		fern	permit	underrated
		pert	answer	concertina
		tern	lawyer	conservation
		jerk	barber	interview
		perch	burner	
		berth	termite	
		stern	kernel	
		serve	certain	
		terse		
		verse		

SET 98

Decoding unit	A	B	C	D
ew	dew	stew	jewel	jewelry
	few	flew	renew	renewable
	new	blew	dewdrops	brewery
	hew	chew	fewer	chewable
	yew	view	steward	newspaper
	mew	brew	mildew	
		crew		
		drew		
		slew		

SET 99

Decoding unit	A	B	C	D
ir	fir	first	circus	confirmation
	sir	stir	firmly	thirstily
		shirt	stirrup	infirmary
		bird	chirping	virtuous
		firm	thirsty	flirtation
		third	birthday	circumference
		chirp	circle	circular
		squirt	confirm	circumnavigation
		thirst	virtue	
		shirk	stirrup	
		birth	circuit	
		birch	dirty	
		girl		
		gird		
		flirt		
		dirge		

SET 100

Decoding unit	A	B	C	D
ire	dire	spire	admire	
	fire	squire	retire	
	hire		transpire	
	mire		expire	
	sire		require	
	tire		umpire	
	wire		aspire	
			direct	
			fireman	
			hireling	
			desire	
			wireless	
			tireless	

SET 101

Decoding unit	A	B	C	D
oa	oat	boat	toaster	overcoat
	oaf	foam	uproar	
	oar	loam	lifeboat	
	oak	roam	loafer	
		soap	seacoast	
		roar	steamboat	
		soar	uproar	
		hoax	oatmeal	
		toast		
		roast		
		loan		
		moan		
		groan		
		goat		
		throat		
		oath		
		loaf		
		toad		

SET 102

Decoding unit	A	B	C	D
oi	oil	foil	tinfoil	rejoicing
		soil	jointly	poisonous
		toil	poison	avoidance
		join	Detroit	joinery
		void	moisture	toiletries
		coil	pointy	
		roil	ointment	
		coin	avoid	
		choice	doily	
		moist	toiler	
		noise	toilet	
		joint	devoid	

SET 103

Decoding unit	A	B	C	D
oo	boo	boom	raccoon	uprooted
	coo	boon	hootowl	paratrooper
	moo	boost	looter	proofreader
	too	boot	rooted	bandicoot
	goo	cool	trooper	
	woo	coon	booster	
	zoo	food	loosely	
		shoot	caboose	
		loot	moonstruck	
		root	papoose	
		proof	moonshot	
		roof	balloon	
		spoon	yoohoo	
		troop	reproof	
		boost		
		booth		
		choose		
		goose		
		spoof		
		school		
		spool		

SET 104

Decoding unit	A	B	C	D
ou	out	bout	around	boundary
	our	rout	bounty	bountiful
		loud	cloudy	cloudiness
		pout	proudly	roundabout
		oust	aground	tantamount
		tout	profound	
		bound	downspout	
		round	outright	
		clout	doubtful	
		shout		
		doubt		
		flour		
		hound		
		trout		
		stout		
		ground		
		drought		
		proud		
		found		
		pound		
		spouse		
		scout		

SET 105

Decoding unit	A	B	C	D
ove	dove	shove	shovel	governor
	love	glove	cover	recover
			grovel	discover
			hover	coveralls
			plover	
			oven	
			above	
			lover	
			hovel	

SET 106

Decoding unit	A	B	C	D
ue	cue	flue	Tuesday	discontinue
	due	glue	imbue	avenue
	rue	blue	pursue	residue
	hue	clue	subdue	ruefully
	sue	true	bluebird	misconstrue
		fuel	value	overdue
		gruel	duet	
		duel	argue	

SET 107

Decoding unit	A	B	C	D
ure	lure		endure	furniture
	pure		culture	reassure
	sure		obscure	manicure
	cure		vulture	immature
			impure	premature
			mature	literature
			unsure	expenditure
			inure	temperature
				surety

SET 108

Decoding unit	A	B	C	D
tion			nation	sensation
			ration	inflation
			station	devotion
			notion	commotion
			lotion	liberation
			potion	taxation
			caution	examination

Encourage the child to use sensory channels in addition to his eyes and ears to examine the concrete aspects of a task.

This will force his attention to more of the pertinent details and further facilitate his ability to recall what he has experienced.

This means, simply, that you should have the child write and say what he sees and hears. It acknowledges the fact that you have to look at and/or listen to more of the details in a pattern of sensations (visual or acoustical) in order to reproduce something than you do to merely identify it.

Representative activities

When you are conducting a lesson in identifying decoding units, stress to the child the importance of thinking about "how his mouth feels" when he repeats a decoding unit or a word and what his hand is doing when he writes these on the chalkboard.

If the child tends to lose his place on the page, and/or read certain words in reverse, such as *was* for *saw,* instruct him to use his index finger as a pointer. Insist that he always use the same hand—the one he prints with. Teach him to synchronize the movement of that finger with his eyes and his voice; in other words, the finger is to be pointing directly at the word he is looking at and reading, nowhere else. His finger is a source of support and will direct his eyes—show them where to look.

Provide enough repeated experiences to establish the information securely in the child's long-term memory.

The key concern here—once the *what* has been established and the system for helping him remember it, the *how,* has been taught—is that the child spend enough time in various drill activities so that he can perform virtually automatically, with a minimum of conscious effort.

In other words, the child should become so familiar with the *what* that he no longer has to use the system you taught him—the *how*—to figure it out: He simply knows it; he has the information at his fingertips. This does not come about without extended practice sessions—especially with children who are hard to teach.

In general these activities are task related. Hence I will not attempt to spell them out here. Just follow the basic rule of thumb that says it is not enough to know *how.* The child must practice to the point that he no longer has to resort to the *how* strategy.

For example, it is not enough to be able to sound out the words in a sentence. The child should practice reading those sentences over and over again, to the point where he reads them fluently, the way a reader should read. This is critical. Without fluency there is no comprehension;

without comprehension there is no reason to read; without a reason the child will not read; and if he does not read, he can hardly be expected to become adept at it, fluent.

Stress practice, but do take care to make certain that what the child practices is worth the effort. Identifying that *what* is what this book is all about.

BIBLIOGRAPHY

Baker, E. L. Beyond objectives: domain referenced tests for evaluation and instructional improvement. *Educational Technology,* 1974; 14:6, 10–16.

Bateman, B. D. Educational implications of minimal brain dysfunction. *In* F. de la Cruz, B. Fox, R. Roberts (eds.), *Minimal Brain Dysfunction.* New York: Annals of the New York Academy of Sciences, 1973.

————. The efficacy of an auditory and a visual method of first grade reading instruction with auditory and visual learners. *College of Education Curriculum Bulletin,* 1967; 23: 278, Eugene, OR: University of Oregon, 6–14 (a).

Beck, I. L., and Mitroff, D. D. *Rationale and Design of a Primary Grades Reading System for an Individualized Classroom.* Pittsburgh: Learning Research and Development Center, 1972 (LRDC Publication 1972/4).

Bender, L. A. *A Visual Motor Gestalt Test and Its Clinical Use.* New York: American Orthopsychiatric Association, 1938 (Research Monograph No. 3).

Bereiter, C., and Engelmann, S. *Teaching Disadvantaged Children in the Preschool.* Englewood Cliffs, NJ: Prentice-Hall, 1966.

Birch, H. Dyslexia and maturation of visual function. *In* J. Money (ed.), *Reading Disability. Progress and Research Needs in Dyslexia.* Baltimore: Johns Hopkins Press, 1962.

Bond, Guy L., Tinker, Miles A. *Reading Difficulties: Their Diagnosis and Correction.* Second Edition. New York: Appleton-Century-Crofts, Inc., 1967.

Bradley, L., and Bryant, P. E. Categorizing sounds and learning to read: A causal connection. *Nature,* 1973; 301: 419–21.

Bruce, D. J. The analysis of word sounds by young children. *British Journal of Educational Psychology,* 1964; 34:158–70.

Bruner, I. S. *Studies in Cognitive Growth.* New York: Wiley, 1967.

Bryant, P. *Perception and Understanding in Young Children: An Experimental Approach.* New York: Basic Books, 1974.

Carter, D. B. Vision and learning disorders. *In* Carter, D. B. (Ed.), *Approaches to Learning Disorders*. Philadelphia: Chilton Books, 1970.

Chalfont, J. C., Scheffelin, M. A. *Central Processing Dysfunctions in Children: A Review of the Research*. Washington, DC: U.S. Department of Health, Education, and Welfare, 1969 (NINDS Monograph No. 9).

Chall, J. *Learning to Read: The Great Debate*. New York: McGraw-Hill Book Company, Inc., 1967.

Clements, S. D. *Minimal Brain Dysfunction, Terminology and Identification*. Washington, DC: U.S. Department of Health, Education, and Welfare, 1966 (NINDB Monograph No. 3, Public Health Service Bulletin No. 1415).

———. *Minimal Brain Dysfunction in Children*. Washington, DC: U.S. Department of Health, Education, and Welfare, 1969 (N&SDCP Monograph, Public Health Service Bulletin No. 201S).

Coleman, B. The relationship between auditory and visual perceptual skills and first grade reading achievement under an initial structural linguistics reading approach. Unpublished doctoral dissertation, University of Pittsburgh, 1974.

Deutsch, M. The role of social class in language development and cognition. *American Journal of Orthopsychiatry*, 1965; 2S: 78–88.

Dong, D. Relationships among copy form tests. Unpublished thesis. School of Optometry, University of California, Berkeley, 1978.

Duffy, F. H., and Geschwind, N. (eds). *Dyslexia: A Neuroscientific Approach to Clinical Evaluation*. Boston: Little, Brown and Co., 1985.

Espenschade, A. S. and Eckert, H. M. *Motor Development*. Columbus, OH: Charles E. Merrill, Inc., 1967.

Fernald, G. *Remedial Techniques in the Basic School Subjects*. New York: McGraw-Hill Book Co., 1956.

Flesch, R. *Why Johnny Can't Read and What You Can Do About It*. Harper & Brothers: NY, 1955.

Foorman, B. R. Non-alphabetic codes in learning to read: The case of the Japanese. *In* Foorman, B.R., and A. W. Siegel (eds.), *Acquisition of Reading Skills: Cultural Constraints and Cognitive Universals*. Hillsdale, NJ: Lawrence Erlbaum Associates, 1986.

Frierson, E. C., and Barbe, B. B. *Educating Children With Learning Disabilities: Selected Readings*. New York: Appleton-Century-Crofts, 1967.

Frostig, M. *Frostig Program for the Development of Visual Perception*. Chicago: Follett Publishing Co., 1964.

Frankenburg, W. K., Goldstein, A. D., and Camp, B. W. The revised

Denver Developmental Screening Test: Its accuracy as a screening test. *Journal of Pediatrics,* 1971; 79(6): 988–95.

Gagne, R. M. Contributions of learning to human development. *Psychological Review,* 1968; 75:177–91.

——. *The Conditions of Learning* (Rev. ed.). New York: Holt, 1970.

Gagne, R. M., and Rohwer, W. D. Instructional psychology. *In* P. H. Mussen and M. R. Rosenzweig (eds.), *Annual Review of Psychology.* Vol. 20. Palo Alto, CA: Annual Review, 1969, 381–418.

Gattegno, Caleb. *Words in Color.* Chicago: Encyclopaedia Britannica Inc., 1964.

Gesell, A. *Infant Development.* New York: Harper & Brothers, 1952.

Gesell, A., Ilg, F., and Bullis, G. *Vision: Its Development in Infant and Child.* New York: Paul B. Hoeber, Inc., 1949.

Gesell, A., et al. *The First Five Years of Life: A Guide to the Study of the Preschool Child.* New York: Harper & Row, 1940.

Glaser, R. Adaptive Education. Paper presented at the Conference on University Teaching and Learning, McGill University, Montreal, Canada, October 20–23, 1971.

——. Educational psychology and education. *American Psychologist,* 1973; 28:7.

Haring, N. G., and Batemen, B. *Teaching the Learning Disabled Child.* Englewood Cliffs, NJ: Prentice-Hall, 1977.

Hein, A., and Jeannerod, M. (eds.). *Spatially Oriented Behavior.* New York: Springer-Verlag, 1983.

Helveston, E., Ellis, F. D., Weber, J. C., Helveston, B. H., and Miller, K. Performance test to accompany ophthalmic examination in the young school age child: The "draw a bicycle" test. *Journal of Pediatric Ophthalmology,* 1985; 22:17–19.

Held, R., Hein, A. Movement-produced stimulation in the development of visually guided behavior. *Journal of Comparative Psychology,* 1963; 56: 872–76.

Hively, W. Domain-referenced testing. *Educational Technology,* 1974; 14: 5–10.

Howard, I. P., Templeton, W. B. *Human Spatial Orientation.* New York: Wiley, 1966.

Ilg, F., and Ames, L. *School Readiness.* New York: Harper & Row, 1964.

Kaluger, G., Kolson, C. *Reading and Learning Disabilities.* Columbus, OH: Charles E. Merrill, Inc., 1969.

Kephart, N. C. *The Slow Learner in the Classroom.* Columbus, OH: Charles E. Merrill, Inc., 1960.

Klein, S. D. *Psychological Testing of Children. A Consumer's Report.* Boston: The Exceptional Parent Press, 1977.

Laurendeau, M., Pinard, A. *The Development of the Concept of Space in the Child.* New York: International University, 1970.

Lenneberg, E. H. *Biological Foundations of Language.* New York: Wiley, 1967.

Levine, M. D., Brooks, R., Shonkoff, J. P. (eds). *A Pediatric Approach to Learning Disorders.* New York: John Wiley & Sons, 1980.

Liberman, I. Y., Shankweiler, D., Liberman, A. M., Fouler, C., Fischer, F. W. Phonetic segmentation and recoding in the beginning reader. In Reber, A. S., and L. D. Scarborough (eds). *Toward a Psychology of Reading.* Hillsdale, NJ: Lawrence Erlbaum Associates, 1980.

Luria, A. R. *Higher Cortical Functions in Man.* New York: Basic Books, Inc., 1966.

Maccoby, E. E. Some speculations concerning the lag between perceiving and performing. *Child Development,* 1965; 36: 367–78.

Mauser, A. J. *Assessing the Learning Disabled.* Novato, CA: Academic Therapy Publications, 1981.

McCarthy, I. J., McCarthy, J. F. *Learning Disabilities.* Boston: Allyn and Bacon, 1969.

McInnis, P. *McInnis/Hammondsport Plan.* New York: Walker Educational Book Corporation, 1977.

Miller, R. E. The effects of a physical education program on perceptual development and reading readiness in kindergarten children. Unpublished doctoral dissertation, University of Pittsburgh, 1973.

Miles, T. R. *Dyslexia, the Pattern of Difficulties.* New York: Granada, 1983.

Money, J., and Schiffman, G. (eds). *The Disabled Reader: Education of the Dyslexic Child.* Baltimore: Johns Hopkins Press, 1966.

Pavlides, G. T., and Miles, T. R. *Dyslexia Research and Its Application to Education.* New York: John Wiley & Sons, 1981.

Phelps, D. A modified association method for use with learning disabled children. *Academic Therapy,* 1978; 14(i): 35–8.

Piaget, J. *Psychology of Intelligence.* Paterson, NJ: Littleton, Adams & Co., 1960.

Resnick, L. B. *Design of an Early Learning Curriculum.* Pittsburgh: Learning Research and Development Center, 1967 (Working Paper 16).

Rosner, J. Adapting primary grade reading instruction to individual differences in perceptual skills. *Reading World,* 1975; 14(4): 293–307.

———. Application of the IPI Model to a perceptual development curriculum. In J. I. Arena (ed.), *Meeting Total Needs of Learning Disabled Children: A Forward Look.* Proceedings of the Seventh Annual International Conference of the Association for Children with Learning Disabilities. San Rafael, CA: Academic Therapy Publications, 1971, 95107 (also, LRDC Publication 1971/12).

———. Auditory analysis training with prereaders. *The Reading Teacher,* 1974; 27(4): 379–384 (also, LRDC Publication 1974/1).

———. Changes in first grade achievement and predictive validity of I.Q. scores, as a function of an adaptive instructional environment. *Educational Technology,* 1974; 14(1): 32–36 (LRDC publication 1973/5). Originally presented at the annual meeting of the American Educational Research Assn., New Orleans, 1973.

———. The Development and Validation of an Individualized Perceptual Skills Curriculum. Pittsburgh: Learning Research and Development Center, University of Pittsburgh, 1972 (Publication 1972/7).

———. Individualization of instruction. In F. D. Connor, J. R. Wald, and M. J. Cohen (eds.), *Professional Preparation for Educators of Crippled Children.* New York: Teachers College, Columbia University, 1970.

———. Language arts and arithmetic achievement, and specifically related perceptual skills. Paper presented at the annual meeting of the International Reading Association, Detroit, MI, 1972 (also, *American Educational Research Journal,* 1973; 10(1): 59–68, and LRDC Publication 1973/2).

———. *The Perceptual Skills Curriculum.* New York: Walker Educational Book Corporation, 1973.

———. Testing for teaching in an adaptive educational environment. In Hively, W., and M. C. Reynolds (eds.), *Domain-Referenced Testing in Special Education.* Reston, VA: Council for Exceptional Children, 1975.

———. Visual analysis training with preschool children, *American Optometric Association Journal,* 1974; 45(5): 584–591.

———. Richman, V., and Scott, R. H. The Identification of Children With Perceptual-Motor Dysfunction. Pittsburgh: Learning Research and Development Center, University of Pittsburgh, 1969 (Working Paper 47).

———. *Helping Children Overcome Learning Difficulties.* 2d ed. New York: Walker Publishing Co., 1979.

———. Phonological skills and learning to read and write: reactions and implications. In Foorman, B., and A. Siegel (eds.), *Acquisition of Reading Skills: Cultural Constraints and Cognitive Universals.* Hillsdale, NJ: Lawrence Erlbaum Associates, 1986.

Rosner, J., & Gruber, J. Differences in the perceptual skills development of young myopes and hyperopes. *American Journal of Optometry and Physiological Optometry,* 1985; 62:501–504.

Rosner, J. and Rosner, J. Management of perceptual skills disorders in a primary care practice. *Journal of the American Ophthalmological Association,* 1986; 57: 56–59.

Rosner, J., and Simon, D. The Auditory Analysis Test: an initial report. *Journal of Learning Disabilities,* 1971; 4(7): 38–392 (also, LRDC Publication 1971/3).

Simon, H. *The Sciences of the Artificial.* Cambridge, MA: The MIT Press, 1969.

Slingerland, B. *Screening Test for Identifying Children with Specific Language Disabilities.* Cambridge, MA: Educators Publishing Service, 1962.

Starr, A. *The Rutgers Drawing Test,* New Brunswick, NJ: Author, 1961.

Traub, Nina. *Recipe for Reading.* 2nd ed. Cambridge, MA: Educators Publishing Service, Inc., 1975.

Weaver, P., and Rosner, J. Relationships between visual and auditory perceptual skill and comprehension independent of decoding. *Journal of Learning Disabilities* 1979;12(9):617–621.

Wechsler, D. *The Wechsler Preschool and Primary Scale of Intelligence.* New York: The Psychological Corporation, 1967.

Weigers, R. M. An Investigation of an Individualized Visual-Motor Curriculum on a Piagetian Test of Space Perception and the Visual-Motor Placement Test. Unpublished doctoral dissertation, University of Pittsburgh, 1973.

White, B. L. Experience and the development of motor mechanisms in infancy. In K. J. Connolly (ed.), *Mechanisms of Motor Skill Development.* New York: Academic Press, 1970, 95–136.

Witkin, H. A., Dyk, R. B., Faterson, H. F., Goodenough, D. R., and Karp, S. A. *Psychological Differentiation.* New York: Wiley, 1962.

INDEX

279

6138708R0

Made in the USA
Lexington, KY
04 August 2010